Funny Frames

Funny Frames
The Filmic Concepts of Michael Haneke

Oliver C. Speck

NEW YORK • LONDON

2010
The Continuum International Publishing Group Inc
80 Maiden Lane, New York, NY 10038

The Continuum International Publishing Group Ltd
The Tower Building, 11 York Road, London SE1 7NX

www.continuumbooks.com

Copyright © 2010 by Oliver C. Speck

All rights reserved. No part of this book may be reproduced, stored in a retrieval system, or transmitted, in any form or by any means, electronic, mechanical, photocopying, recording, or otherwise, without the written permission of the publishers.

ISBN: 978-1-4411-8124-4 (hardcover)
       978-1-4411-9285-1 (paperback)

Library of Congress Cataloging-in-Publication Data
Speck, Oliver C.
  Funny frames : the filmic concepts of Michael Haneke / by Oliver C. Speck.
    p. cm.
  Includes bibliographical references and index.
  ISBN-13: 978-1-4411-8124-4 (hardcover : alk. paper)
  ISBN-10: 1-4411-8124-5 (hardcover : alk. paper)
  ISBN-13: 978-1-4411-9285-1 (pbk. : alk. paper)
  ISBN-10: 1-4411-9285-9 (pbk. : alk. paper) 1. Haneke, Michael, 1942–Criticism and interpretation. I. Title.

PN1998.3.H36S64 2010
791.43023'3092–dc22

2009048870

Typeset by Newgen Imaging Systems Pvt Ltd, Chennai, India

CONTENTS

Acknowledgments	vii
Photo Credits	viii

INTRODUCTION: FRAMING HANEKE   1

Frame I   THE CONCEPTUAL FRAME OF REFERENCE   28
    Shifting Frames   28
    The Frames of Narratology   33
    The Truth of the Perspective   38
    Anti-cinema and the Viewer   44
    A Cinema of Cruelty   52

Frame II   A MOVEMENT THROUGH HANEKE'S OEUVRE   58
    Films for Television   63
    Fraulein—ein deutsches Melodram/Fraulein   74
    Der siebente Kontinent/ The Seventh Continent   76
    Benny's Video   82
    71 Fragmente einer Chronologie des Zufalls/71 Fragments of
       a Chronology of Chance   83
    Funny Games and Funny Games U.S.   85
    La Pianiste/The Piano Teacher   87
    Le temps du loup/The Time of the Wolf   90
    Code inconnu: Récit incomplet de divers voyages/
       Code Unknown   92
    Caché   93
    Das weiße Band: Eine deutsche Kindergeschichte/
       The White Ribbon   99

Frame III   A MARRIAGE OF PAST AND PRESENT—
       THE OVERCOMING OF FASSBINDER   103
    Genre and Self-Reflexivity: Dialogue with Past Images   107
    Framing and Re-Framing   110
    Quoting from Collective Memory   116
    Virtual Decisions   123

Contents

Frame IV	THINKING THE EVENT—THE VIRTUAL IN MICHAEL HANEKE	129
Frame V	A NEW ORDER: THE METHOD OF MADNESS	146
Frame VI	SELF/AGGRESSION: VIOLENCE IN FILMS BY MICHAEL HANEKE	160

    Suicide and Politics   161
    A State of Exception   164
    Auto-Aggression   169
    The Paradox of the Witness   172

Frame VII	THE MORAL OF THE LONG TAKE	178
Frame VIII	THE FUNNY FRAME	190
Frame IX	PLOT REVIEWS	197

    Drei Wege zum See/Three Paths to the Lake   197
    Lemminge, Teil 1 Arkadien/Lemmings, Part 1 Arcadia and
      Lemminge, Teil 2 Verletzungen/Lemmings, Part 2 Injuries   199
    Variation   201
    Wer war Edgar Allan?/Who was Edgar Allan?   202
    Fraulein: Ein deutsches Melodram/Fraulein   202
    Der siebente Kontinent/The Seventh Continent   204
    Benny's Video   207
    Die Rebellion/Rebellion   208
    71 Fragmente einer Chronologie des Zufalls/71 Fragments of a Chronology of Chance   210
    Funny Games and *Funny Games U.S.*   211
    Lumière et compagnie/Lumière and Company   213
    Das Schloß nach Franz Kafka/The Castle   213
    Code inconnu: Récit incomplet de divers voyages/Code Unknown   215
    La Pianiste/The Piano Teacher   218
    Le temps du loup/The Time of the Wolf   219
    Caché/Hidden   221
    Das weiße Band: Eine deutsche Kindergeschichte/The White Ribbon   223

Notes   226
Bibliography   241
Index   255

ACKNOWLEDGMENTS

I would like to express my sincere gratitude to all the people to whom I am indebted, especially Margaret Ozierski, who proofread my manuscript and provided essential insights and to whom I dedicate this book. I would also like to thank the editors and anonymous reviewers who provided valuable feedback on the chapters that appeared elsewhere and who allowed me to use and rework them for this book. A shorter version of Chapter II will appear in *Michael Haneke and his Films*, ed. Stefanie Knauß and Alexander D. Ornella (Eugene, OR: Wipf and Stock, 2010). A version of Chapter III was published in *The Cinema of Michael Haneke*, ed. Ben McCann and David Sorfa (London: Wallflower Press, 2010). Chapter IV appeared as "The New Order: Madness in the Cinema of Michael Haneke," in *Crime and Madness in Modern Austria: Myth, Metaphor and Cultural Realities*, ed. Rebecca Thomas (Newcastle upon Tyne: Cambridge Scholars Press, 2008) and was extended for this book. Chapter V was originally written for a special issue of Modern Austrian Literature, edited by Robert von Dassanowsky. David Barker, editor at Continuum Press, New York, helped me to get the manuscript into shape. I also received valuable advice from the anonymous readers of my manuscript and I would like to thank them as well. I am especially grateful to Robert von Dassanowsky who provided invaluable advice on the manuscript.

Special thanks go to Agathe Valentin and Lise Zipci at Les Films du Losange, Paris, who graciously allowed me to see *Das weiße Band* before its release date and in time to complete the text of my book. I would also like to express my gratitude to Karin Oehlenschläger from the Goethe Institut Boston who gave me access to *Fraulein* and other TV-films by Michael Haneke and whose organizational talent and hard work made it possible for Haneke's TV-films to be shown in the US.

PHOTO CREDITS

My heartfelt thanks to the following companies who graciously allowed me to use screenshots from Michael Haneke's films for this book:

Cover: detail from *Das weisse Band* used by friendly permission of Les Films Du Losange, Paris. Screenshots on p. 101 from *Das weisse Band* (© Copyright film: X FILME CREATIVE POOL, LES FILMS DU LOSANGE, WEGA FILM, LUCKY RED), on pp. 29 and 142 from *Caché* (© Copyright film: LES FILMS DU LOSANGE, WEGA FILM, BAVARIA FILM ET BIM DISTRIBUZIONE), on pp. 91 and 155 from *Temps du loup* (© Copyright film: BAVARIA FILM / CANAL+ / CENTRE NATIONAL DE LA CINÉMATOGRAPHIE (CNC) / EURIMAGES / FRANCE 3 CINÉMA / LES FILMS DU LOSANGE / WEGA FILM / ARTE FRANCE CINÉMA) courtesy of Les Films Du Losange, Paris, France.

Screenshots on p. 2 from *Code Inconnue* (© Copyright film: 2000 MK2 PRODUCTIONS/CINEMANUEL/FRANCE 2 CINÉMA/ARTE FRANCE CINÉMA/LES FILMS ALAIN SARDE / BAVARIA FILMS) and p. 89 from *La Pianiste/The Piano Player* (p.) (© Copyright film: 2001 WEGA FILM / MK2 SA / ARTE FRANCE CINÉMA / LES FILMS ALAIN SARDE) courtesy of MK2, Paris, France.

Screenshot on p. 64 from *Drei Wege zum See* courtesy of SÜDWESTRUNDFUNK, SWR MEDIA SERVICES GMBH, Stuttgart, Germany.

Still on p. 67 from *Wer war Edgar Allen* and p. 72 from *Rebellion* courtesy of ÖSTERREICHISCHER RUNDFUNK (ORF), Vienna, Austria.

The screenshots from *Fraulein* (pp. 113 and 114) licensed by SAARLÄNDISCHER RUNDFUNK, Saarbrücken, Germany.

Due to a regrettable difference of opinion concerning the title of this book, I was not allowed to use shots from the "glaciation of feelings-trilogy" produced by Wega Films, Vienna. I paid for the use of the stills from *Benny's Video* (© WEGA FILM / BERNARD LANG AG / THE KOBAL COLLECTION) on pp. 80, 81, 134 and *Der siebente Kontinent* (© WEGA FILM / THE KOBAL COLLECTION) on p. 85.

INTRODUCTION: FRAMING HANEKE

A short scene from *Code Inconnu* (2005) can serve as a typical example of the exercise that Michael Haneke expects from his viewer. The scene—about two-thirds into the movie—opens with a shot from a medium height position, roughly 2 feet from the ground, showing a person who is in the middle of delivering a brief eulogy about a "little Françoise," a person whom we haven't met. Then, one by one, people throw sand onto the coffin. Only after the seventh person do we recognize Anne, the main character, who was not visible behind the other mourners and who is standing with her head bowed. The camera—in a continuous take—follows Anne when she steps away to shake hands with the deceased girl's family and then when she silently walks with the old woman who lives on the same floor of her apartment building. Anne shows no emotions, while her neighbor has a grotesque teardrop hanging from her nose. In the almost three and a half minutes of this sequence shot, the viewer has to process visual and aural information and remember the neighbor whose face was shown only very briefly in a scene before to finally come to the conclusion that this was the girl whose screams Anne heard earlier, and that she probably died from abuse. This knowledge comes as a shock, a revelation. Here, with simple means, Haneke strengthens the emotional impact of information by linking our recognition to a process of deduction that is more a looking for traces, a hermeneutic labor. Haneke refuses any explanations or clues, for example, a close-up of the neighbor's face to facilitate recognition or a line of dialogue expressing guilt about the failure to alarm the authorities. Instead, the film is constructed such that it forces us to actively search for clues until it dawns on us what probably happened. Haneke's skilful use of timing in the economy of narration is, I think, unsurpassed. After all, we mourn the passing of a character whom we had not even seen.

FIGURE 1 Funeral for Françoise

This scene is crucial not only for the film, but as a way of opening my discussion of Haneke, since it provides a clear example of the shifting frame of reference that is the stated topic of this book. Watching a film by Haneke, the viewer must permanently adjust his or her interpretation of what is being shown on the screen. Even if we disregard the major role marketing plays to shape audience expectations, films that are released commercially always follow a generic framework that allows the audience to understand what is going on. To put it bluntly, should we walk into the wrong film in the local multiplex, cues such as music, film-style, acting, etc., will quickly alert us to what kind of movie we can expect and will help us to understand what is happening on the screen by providing a frame. Sometimes, however, particularly in hybrid genres of postmodernity, we might encounter a mix of genres that we didn't expect—a film that begins with a spaceship but ends with a monster-slaying. In this case, the frame needs to be adjusted. It is this method of a hermeneutic construction that I attempt to grasp in this analysis, calling it the image of a shift. Indeed, the shift is taking place on two levels in films by Haneke: first, the film is shifting the major part of the process of making meaning on to the viewer, who is thus forced to perform a task that is normally done for the audience in mainstream cinema, that is, providing connections and explanations. Then, on a metatextual level, the film forces us not only to reflect on these shifts and our involvement in the process, but, indeed, reflect on the process *as* what is represented. With the latter shift, I want to articulate the process of representation as being this shifting of frames of reference and to make the stronger claim that this process is indissociable from what is known as the "content" of the film, a content typically considered separate from the process of representation. Furthermore, the scene that I chose as a curtain-raiser here touches on violence, cruelty, and other themes that are equally important for this book. In short, it is the shifting of frames of reference by the film and the viewer that I consider throughout this book in all its aspects and meanings, including considerations of genre. It is not the intention of this study to apply contemporary theories of film, spectatorship, and visual construction to Haneke's art, but indeed to examine Haneke as theoretician and philosopher in his own right and in his own medium.

What I referred to above as revelation is in itself a relatively simple device: the spectatorial position interpolating the viewer into the film withholds information from him or her, reserving or withholding selected bits of it for a deferred understanding of the plot. Especially in Haneke's two fragmented films, *71 Fragmente einer Chronologie des Zufalls* and *Code Inconnu*, but also in his other films, scenes often become understandable only after the fact. In one short fragment in *Code Inconnu*, to stay with the example from above, Georges, Anne's fiancé, seems to look at a pretty girl who sits across from him on the Paris métro. Later, without explanation, black and white pictures are shown of people who seem to be unaware of being photographed. A viewer has to process the puzzling information, remember a short scene where Georges strapped a camera around his neck, as well as the scene with Georges opposite the pretty girl, then deduce that Georges was actually taking pictures on his métro-ride with a hidden camera. It is this adjustment of a frame of reference that will always be new in Haneke's films. Haneke, instead of establishing the spectator as an all-seeing subject, demands that the viewer provide additional information, thereby not just negating, but indeed reversing the much-lampooned "Hollywood rule of three," according to which information vital to the plot has to be explained three times, once for the smart person, once for the average viewer, and once for the "Slow Joe in the Back Row" (Bordwell and Thompson 1985: 31). By restricting and limiting the spectatorial position, Haneke indeed forces the viewer to remember moments and even to actively rewind the film and look for clues.

One way that Haneke restricts the viewing position is through open inclusion of the extratextual, the real world so to speak, and it should be stressed that a strong pedagogical impetus lies behind this.[1]

To educate the viewer, Haneke often provides not just clues but deliberately false clues, framing his films at first as a relationship drama, period picture, or thriller, only to disappoint audience expectations over the course of the film. It is important to note that the point here is not the simple switching from one frame to another, that is, moving gratuitously from one genre to another, but the process of the transition itself through which the shifting of the frame of reference can also—simultaneously if not seamlessly—take place on the narrative level. This paradoxical movement through narrative space could be seen as a migration between positions that are strictly separate in an average film but whose overlapping is programmatic in nature in Haneke. The famous beginning of *Caché* (2005) features a shot that looks like a neutral establishing shot but is suddenly revealed to be the point of view of somebody else who is watching a recording of this shot. At the end of the same film, a shot appears that is "un-framed," a shot that might be either another person's point of view or a just a neutral shot, signaling an unresolved question with far-reaching consequences for the meaning of the entire film. In any case, the transition between these levels, or frames, does not happen between one shot and the next, but by adding a frame of reference in the form of a voice-over that comments on the shot in the former example and by refusing such a frame in the latter.

These limitations put on the viewer, the unexpected shifts in frame of reference and also the self-reflexive elements—the so-called "breaking of the fourth wall," for example, by addressing the spectator directly or by using the same actors and the same names—demand an active participation from him or her. This viewer, by virtue of countless movies and TV-shows and news, is used to a long-established form/content divide. Even a film with a challenging topic or one that occasionally breaks the fourth wall still provides an omniscient perspective and fuses or "sutures"—if we want to use this concept of psychoanalytic film theory—the viewer with the text. Haneke here actively re-creates the rift between the viewer and the filmic text. Throughout this book, I therefore maintain a distinction between the position of the spectator in Haneke—which I define as a purely structural position in the filmic text—and the viewer implied by the filmic text who is made aware of the spectatorial perspectives that the filmic text provides, that is, the structures that the viewer normally unconsciously accepts. In other words, Haneke brings out exactly what a commercial film suppresses in order for its ideology to work.

We should avoid the hasty conclusion that Haneke is opposed to genre as such, insofar as such a conclusion would confuse the teller with the tale. The basic quality of the generic frame of reference, as well as of the shift itself as a movement between one frame of reference and another, has to be taken into account. For the generic frame is essential to the text. In this context, Jacques Derrida provocatively states that "there is no genreless text" (Derrida 1980: 212). A text inevitably belongs to a genre because there is always a marker, a code at the margins of the text that signals the recipient to which genre a text supposedly belongs.[2] This marker that thereby frames the text can be misleading or false or even mark by its own absence, but it nevertheless puts the text into perspective. What we encounter here, and what Derrida implies, is the basic paradox of hermeneutics, namely, that to understand the whole, there must already be a pre-understanding, a prejudice (*Vorurteil*) as Gadamer following Heidegger puts it, of the parts, which, in turn, determines the whole. We can therefore state that the sudden shifting of a frame of reference touches on understanding as the existential condition of being via the hermeneutic circle of (textual) understanding. As all of Haneke's films seem to toy with the generic frame, this issue will be addressed throughout this book.

"The cinema of," the genre to which this book belongs, provides a proven frame, even a formula, through which a body of films by a given director can be seen. However, Michael Haneke's oeuvre seems to resist such a classic approach, as if the impossibility were built into his cinematic machine. This is why I have adopted a different approach involving conceptual frames that resemble the very functioning of frames—shifts and all—in a Haneke film. But first, let us follow a brief excursus into attempts to provide a "big picture," so as to better understand why such an approach does not work, and look at characteristics of Haneke's cinema and of Haneke criticism that might warrant taking such an approach.

The most obvious trait is that Michael Haneke's films bear the marks of creation by a classic *auteur*: the recurring use of names (Georges and Anne), of stories (the breaking down of the basic family unit), of plot devices (real or imagined traumas, an open ending), motifs (the droning noise of television, sudden violence without justification or explanation); there are also obvious signature shots, such as the extreme close-up on objects of ritualized actions (preparing breakfast) and on objects of exchange (the often equally-ritualized actions of shopping or buying drugs), and, of course, the long take from a stationary camera. Writing a book on Michael Haneke, it is tempting to trace the occurrence of these distinctive aesthetic markers in a given body of texts. However, such a taxonomy introduces the illusion of a continuous body of work, whereas Haneke's oeuvre appears to clearly break into three distinct periods: his films for German and Austrian television, beginning with *Liverpool* (1974) and ending with *Fraulein* (1986), his four German language feature films—the "glaciation of feelings trilogy,"[3] *Der siebente Kontinent/ The Seventh Continent* (1989), *Benny's Video* (1992), *71 Fragmente einer Chronologie des Zufalls/ 71 Fragments of a Chronology of Chance* (1994) plus *Funny Games* (1997)—and the four films he shot in France with international art-house stars Isabelle Huppert, Juliette Binoche, and Daniel Auteuil: *Code inconnu: Récit incomplet de divers voyages/ Code Unknown* (2000), *La Pianiste/ The Piano Teacher* (2001), *Le temps du loup/ The Time of the Wolf* (2003), and *Caché/ Hidden* (2005), critically and commercially his most successful film so far. His most recent film, the award-winning *Das weiße Band/ The White Ribbon* (2009), is his first period picture since the adaptation of the Joseph Roth novella, *Die Rebellion/ The Rebellion*, for Austrian television in 1993, his second period picture after *Fraulein*, and seems to signal a return to German-language cinema, as well as a new direction.

Concentrating on periods of Haneke's oeuvre thus broken up would suppress his foray into the American market, the controversial shot-by-shot remake of his own film as *Funny Games US* (2007). It would also ignore the two films Haneke made for television, the above-mentioned *Die Rebellion* (1993) and *Das Schloß/ The Castle* (1997), while his reputation as art-house director was already steadily growing. As both these TV-films are adaptations from a literary source, it would seem that a differentiation between Haneke's adaptations and his original screenplays should be a central point of an investigation of Haneke's oeuvre. For example, a comparison between the adaptation of a short story by Ingeborg Bachmann, *Drei Wege zum See/ Three Paths to the Lake* (1976, TV) and *La Pianiste/ The Piano Teacher*, based on the novel by Elfriede Jelinek, both notoriously difficult writers, could trace the transformations from page to screen, looking at the challenges of translating a feminine *écriture* into film. As already stated, the central focus of this study is not translation from medium to medium, but the wider conceptual context in which such a translation can take place for very specific reasons and in specific ways.

All these possible approaches underestimate the scope and ambition, indeed, the decisive conceptual quality of Haneke's project. As this book will demonstrate, Michael Haneke is an *auteur* who is not primarily interested in telling a story but, rather, in solving problems. To be precise, Haneke thinks *in* images to solve a given problem. Since the medium in which Haneke works is film, the problems mentioned here are, first and foremost, problems of representation. It is in frustrating the viewer with false clues and in adding shifting frames of reference that Haneke poses questions that, when thought through carefully, allow a specific aesthetic problem to come into focus. These problems, it needs to be stated again, are problems of representation that do not concern a simple "how." To return to an example from above, Haneke is not interested in translating a feminine *écriture* from book to screen, but rather, in posing questions: "what problem does feminine *écriture* attempt to solve?" and "can this problem be solved with and in another medium?"

This study concentrates on those elements in Haneke's films where the solving of a given problem can be observed best and therefore does not necessarily follow a chronological order. In the third chapter, for example, I will argue that one major aesthetic breakthrough for Haneke—the solving of a representational problem—can be observed in the last film he made for German television, the period picture *Fraulein*, a film that is a complex overcoming of Rainer Werner Fassbinder and a bitter indictment of post-war Germany. And Chapter II (or Frame II, as I call it), a survey of Haneke's films and the reviews and scholarship they inspired, looks at Haneke's adaptations of literary texts as strategies for solving problems with filmic means that he finds in the source material. Because the following chapters do not follow the classic "one film-one chapter" approach (and do not necessarily need to be read in order), I do not review the plot every time I discuss a film. Instead, Frame IX at the end of this book lists in chronological order all films that are discussed here and briefly presents a plot review. Because Haneke typically does not provide crucial information until mid-sequence or, as in the extremely fragmented "tales" of *72 Fragmente* and *Code Inconnu*, inserts puzzling shots that can only be understood in retrospect, as I already pointed out, the plot reviews at the end of this book (Frame IX) provide the reader with a necessary tool for a better understanding of Haneke's films. Frame IX also contains information pertaining to the technical aspects of the films, as well as information about the cinematography and the actors.

Throughout this book, I return to mainstream films in order to illustrate how exactly Haneke differs from other filmmakers. And while the different theoretical concepts I use to analyze the cinema of Michael Haneke are not new and have been discussed at length elsewhere, I understand them to be conceived already as flexible concepts—concepts in movement and moving—that can and must change when seen through the lens of Haneke's cinema. I will therefore introduce those concepts briefly in the first chapter and then discuss the concepts in depth in relation to Haneke's films in the chapters that follow.

One characteristic that links Haneke's cinema to mainstream films is violence. It merits mentioning here at length because it opens the way to understanding other important characteristics of Haneke's cinema—namely, authorial gesture and the modernist question of form/content—while considering critical takes on Haneke. Keeping in mind that Haneke's films play with well-established generic frames, it is crucial to understand that the films under discussion here are not violent in the way that films that receive a PG-13 rating in the US are,[4] but rather are critical reflections on these representations. That is, the films under discussion do not decry the occurrence of violence in our culture, as many critics erroneously claim, but instead look at the *representation* of violence, something that Haneke himself stresses. Three of the many recent films openly referencing the so-called "war on terror" in their political subtext, all rated PG-13, can serve to clarify my point: Using hand-held cameras at eye-level, War of the Worlds (Steven Spielberg 2005) deliberately copies the aesthetic of eye-witness videos and news reports from the 9/11 terrorist attacks and the immediate aftermath. The film features a scene where human captives are ground up by aliens and the bloody pulp sprayed in order to fertilize the soil. To take another example, the character of The Joker in *The Dark Knight* (Christopher Nolan 2008) is called a terrorist on several occasions. He rams a pencil into a gangster's brain and also burns a corrupt banker alive. In *Taken* (Pierre Morel 2008), an enraged father and Ex-CIA operative tortures a kidnapper to death while mentioning his experience in torturing suspected terrorists. Even though these sadistic acts are not shown directly on-screen—thus warranting the lower rating—the violence, arguably, does not happen off-screen, but, rather, in what could be called "in-between screens," that is, in the "timeless" fraction between two shots. The film shows the set-up, for example, The Joker arranging a pointed pencil on the table, then a gangster approaching him, followed by a shot of the Joker forcing his victim down, then the immediate reaction—the shocked observers and the body falling out of sight.

The political commentary intended by these films is too obvious to merit pointing out here. However, the comparison to Haneke's cinema—often-called "anti-psychological"—is interesting. Notably, all post-9/11 films eschew any psychological motivation on the side of "the aliens" who are living in our midst. The alien invaders in *War of the Worlds*—who literally break out of the ground in the middle of a busy intersection in one memorable scene—want to take over our planet's resources. In the other examples mentioned here, the evil Joker is in it "for fun," while the Eastern European immigrants are just after the money. The male heroes of these films, in turn, are motivated by revenge and the need to save a woman in their care. All three films evoke the strong emotions of helpless fear and frustrated rage that certainly many Americans felt after 9/11 in order to bring the viewer closer to the hero and to provide him or her with the cathartic fantasy of eliminating the alien threat once and for all. Not surprisingly, violence in these films is always justified and presented as a means to an end. More importantly, it is a clean violence that is hidden by a quick cut and therefore exists only implicitly. This excuses violence, and denies it, in one move. The point is that a more explicit version is always possible (and in some cases is indeed released as the "unrated director's cut" on DVD), which suggests a clear separation of form and content. That is, films like those mentioned here skillfully use the representations of a real event and the strong negative affects these medial-representations effected to represent a story in the most realistic way possible without qualitative changes to the form being occasioned by different versions of the film.

Comparing violence in these mainstream films, for which countless other examples can be found without difficulty, to the violence in such films as *Benny's Video* (1992) and *Funny Games* (1997 and 2007), one notices immediately that the gruesome acts of violence that are at those films' core—a girl is slowly slaughtered with a bolt gun, a young boy is killed by a shotgun blast in front of his parents—though not shown are explicitly present. Indeed, in contrast to the "in-between" violence, these acts happen truly in the "off," an *hors champ* that is explicitly there, out of the camera's view, and are always simultaneously present via the sound of gunshots and the victims' cries. In contrast to mainstream films, the form/content divide in Haneke is sublated into the actions of a narrative authority who openly dictates what the viewer is allowed to see, and who also openly withholds a cathartic punishment of the perpetrators. In Haneke, the decision to forego in-between, hidden violence in favor of violence just off-screen has serious consequences for the film and the viewer watching. As concerns the film, the form is wedded to the content, which is effected such that there is no going back to another version—not without violence to the medium itself, as illustrated by the infamous rewinding of the film in *Funny Games* that truly violates the film. As concerns the viewer, there is no way to pretend, in bad faith, that the film he or she is viewing is not really so violent after all, that he or she is in it for the entertaining plot and the heroic redemption. This authorial and authoritative gesture that is experienced as a form of coercion is certainly a point of contention with many critics. However, as I argue in this book, there is a pedagogical impetus in Haneke to open up a critical space between shots, thereby putting into relief the in-between violence of commercial cinema while pointing out its implicit ideological machinations. Tellingly, Haneke's own post-9/11 film, *Le temps du loup* (2003),[5] only shows the aftermath of an unknown violent event that might have been an ecological catastrophe or a terrorist attack, contrasting the ethical state of nature of children with the immoral actions of adults.

The question of violence is raised not only on the extradiegetic level of authorial instance, but also as a theme on the diegetic level of the films. In both films, *Benny's Video* and *Funny Games*, characters openly ask the question of how violence could be realistically represented in a movie. These self-referential questions show that Haneke is certainly aware of the paradox inherent in a representation of representation as there is no external and superior position that could guarantee the truth of the observation. This might appear obvious, but—as discussed in more detail in the second chapter—many critics characterize Haneke's films simply as dealing critically with phenomena of cultural decline and conclude that Haneke is therefore implicitly asking for a return to values. In the first chapter, or "frame," I consider this question, reframing it in terms of cruelty, rather than violence per se. Furthermore, as opposed to the violence that is done to others, scenes of violence against one's own body are shown directly in Haneke's cinema. Most notable here is Majid's suicide in *Caché*. I discuss this important difference in detail in Frame VI, where I look at violence and self-aggression in Haneke. It cannot be overstressed that, rather than constituting a return to lost values, Haneke's cinema calls for a "thinking through" of representations of violence and of our relationship to them, thus also putting the burden of ethical reflection directly on the viewer, who already performs an ethical duty when he or she adeptly adjusts frames of reference. In other words, the viewer is responsibilized by the film to perform shifts of frame of reference him or herself, thus acquiring the status of ethical viewer rather than the ethically questionable position of nostalgic mourner of a waning culture with its disappearing values.

In considering the unique opportunity to perform ethics that Haneke holds out and to which the viewer gives his consent by his or her active reading of the film, it is important to be precise about Haneke's methods and strategies, beginning with self-referentiality. While his films draw attention to their textual status, they are not simply critical of certain cultural trends. *Natural Born Killers* (1994) by Oliver Stone would be a perfect example of a film that criticizes the representation of violence in media by showing grotesque forms of violence purportedly caused by "too much TV," as the film points out. Self-referentiality in itself, however, does not prevent the representation of violence as something natural in the first place, as the exacerbated effect of a cause. Nowadays, of course, most Hollywood blockbusters contain playful self-referential elements without being aesthetically and politically daring. In contrast, Haneke's films are truly political in the sense that they attempt to open up a new thinking by taking ideology head on. As Louis Althusser has famously shown, ideology is not a false consciousness that could just be explained away. Ideology has indeed a material existence that manifests itself in its practices and that effectively constitutes the subject that misrecognizes itself as the cause and origin of ideology (see here Althusser 1972: 166 and 170–171). In other words, a film like *Schindler's List* (1993) by Steven Spielberg that was certainly created with the best intentions and that even makes it a point to distinguish between fiction and reality by pairing the actors with the survivors they portray in the last scene of the film, interpellates, to borrow Althusser's term, the spectator as a full subject to which a historical occurrence is truthfully represented. As Yosefa Loshitzky shows in her analysis, *Schindler's List* is a pastiche of different film styles from past genres (for example, German expressionism, *film noir*), using in addition a black and white documentary style that suggests a barely mediated access to reality (1997: 109–10). And Robert von Dassanowsky astutely observes that

> Spielberg's close-up shots of the Ghetto Jews calling out their names to be added to Schindler's factory detail is a clear quote from Scene 5 of *Triumph*: close-ups of the workers of the Reich Labor Service calling out the various regions of Germany [. . .]. Whereas the men of *Triumph* identify themselves by region, ritualistically supporting Nazi concepts of race, geopolitics, and the anonymous mass, Spielberg's version enforces the importance of, and battle for, the individual in a genocidal order. (1995: 129/FN 84)

Even though Spielberg attempts to subvert the content of Riefenstahl's message by emulating only her style, *Schindler's List* still falls into the trap of ideology by interpellating a full subject, one who has no real ethical stakes in viewing the film because he is a recipient of truth, of a truthful filmic representation. In other words, the moment the viewer is in such a quasi-religious position—that of the recipient of God's truth, for only the omniscient God's eye view sees Truth—the viewer is absolved of responsibility vis-à-vis what he or she has seen. Further, a film that supposedly educates us about resistance represents the Holocaust (the term is in itself a representation) as an abstract event of a confrontation of good and evil, as well as something that is safely sealed away in the past. Haneke does away with both the petrified, absolved viewer and the demonic, godlike author, favoring the authorial instance that, again, responsibilizes the viewer as an ethical being and as his peer.

Seeing Haneke's strategy vis-à-vis ideology, we should take care not to misunderstand the difference between a critical film, such as *Schindler's List*, and a truly political film, such as the typical Haneke film, as a problem of representation being "not realistic enough," or "never realistic enough." Nor should we misunderstand Haneke as furnishing a paradoxical proof of Adorno's famous dictum about the impossibility of poetry after Auschwitz, that is, as a veritable aniconism. What draws the ire of filmmakers that work against the mainstream, like Haneke or Jean-Luc Godard, to take another prominent example, is the handling of an aesthetic problem, and not the fact of making a film that is set during the time of the Holocaust.

Before any treatment of the role of representation of violence in our culture can be undertaken, a meta-reflection has to take place that examines the condition of the representation itself, keeping in mind, again, that this reflection has neither a firm ground, nor a fixed, pre-determined, and privileged subject to receive it. Such a subject is, indeed, the subject of ideology that misrecognizes itself as a cause or—what is more pertinent here—a plenitude where there are only conjectures and absences to be encountered. Thus, the basic "Haneke problem" could be summed up as moving beyond simple self-referentiality to the more complex problem of self-reflexive representation: "How can I represent the politics of representation?"

It is crucial to differentiate between Haneke's diagnostic abilities and his aesthetic-political thinking. The power of Haneke's gaze—it has been compared to a surgical instrument[6]—directed at the postmodern malaise has received most, if not all, critical attention so far, to the point of eclipsing a different approach to Haneke that accounts for the real "movements" going on in his films, for example, the shifts in frame of reference that perform a different relation between *auteur* and viewer. What is truly new about Haneke's cinema is a construction of movement, of becoming. If we failed to understand this—and I consider this point to be my main disagreement with the current discussion of Haneke's oeuvre—Haneke would indeed be just another *auteur* who skillfully ups the ante, only claiming to criticize violence while actually aestheticizing it in new ways. In this regard, the negative tenor in many reviews, especially coming from Haneke's American critics, is not surprising as audiences might be less and less used to texts that address issues of representation other than openly, that is, allegorically. Challenging the way images are normally consumed must appear, then, as pedantic admonishments by a kill-joy, high-brow *auteur* from Europe, a position which especially film critics tend to take. For example, the *New York Times* critic A. O. Scott, normally a fan of *auteur*-cinema, offers the following accusation: "Americans—to a European intellectual this almost goes without saying—are especially deserving of the kind of moral correction Mr. Haneke takes it upon himself to mete out. [. . .] The 'Hostel' pictures and their ilk revel in the pornography of blood and pain, which Mr. Haneke addresses with mandarin distaste, even as he feeds the appetite for it" (2008). And the *Village Voice* entitles its negative review "One-Trick Phony" and claims that "Haneke is pretty much a humorless pedant" (Hoberman 2008). That Haneke, a prolific interpreter of his own texts, untiringly emphasizes in his many interviews the perils of gratuitous violence in the media, only contributes to, rather than alleviates, this perception.[7]

Most critics have misunderstood or have proved entirely blind to the strategy Haneke employs to undo this paradoxical problem of representing representation, which is, not surprisingly, in itself highly self-reflexive and—we might credit this to his study of philosophy—highly conceptual. It can only be formulated as an *aporia*: since the problem is one of representation, the unrepresentable politics and conditions of possibility of that representation have to be represented as well. As I hope to show in this book, Haneke's cinema shares a strong affinity with Gilles Deleuze's concepts of the virtual and the related concept of the time image, insofar as the solution to Haneke's problem is movement. Not the movement of something in front of the camera, or of the camera, but pure movement in a Deleuzian sense. Indeed, as I argue, especially in Frame IV, Haneke is a Deleuzian filmmaker insofar as he subverts representational images. He goes beyond what Deleuze calls the "movement-image" in order to bring up a "time image," a virtual image that has to be created. Thinking the virtual is always a political thinking that eschews deeply-engrained practices of representation and allows the creation of new perspectives.

The creation of a virtual time image must be understood as aesthetic elements rallied in resistance to the already-mentioned form/content divide, a practice that constitutes the political component in Deleuze and Haneke.

Considering the role misinformation plays in his films, it is futile to wonder whether Haneke is serious in his interviews or not. Sam Peckinpah, to invoke another director who has the reputation of criticizing violence with violent means, certainly played the part of the barely articulate brute in public interviews, whereas there is clear evidence that he carefully analyzed films by other directors.[8] Indeed, especially film directors are known to play a role in their public appearances, creating an image which might or might not coincide with their persona on the set or even at home. Unless directly quoted, "Haneke" will therefore generally not refer to the real, photogenic, and erudite Austrian director, born in 1942, who might or might not primarily target the bourgeois intelligentsia to which he and his audience belong for reasons rooted in his unconscious, but to the *auteur* who makes the aesthetic decisions concerning the *mise-en-scène*. To cite the well-known definition by Wayne Booth: "The 'implied author' chooses, consciously or unconsciously, what we read, we infer him as an ideal, literary, created version of the real man; he is the sum of his own choices" (Booth 1983: 74/75). The hidden ending of *Caché* would then reveal the positions of the implied author, who chose not to direct the spectator's attention to the conversation with a close-up, as well as the position of a narrative instance in the text, the surveillance camera. However, Haneke's public image as "Minister of Fear" (Wray 2007) and "Bearded Prophet" (Foundas 2002) is, of course, something that influences the reception of his films, vying for attention with the implied author. I will return to this topic in the next chapter.

In the tradition of the French, post-Nietzschean thought to which Haneke shows a great affinity, and which does not put much value on what an author, the real-life person, has to say about his own works, listening instead to what the works say for themselves, I consider Michael Haneke's sometimes-controversial statements only as an artist's public comments on his own work. To give an example, Michael Haneke is quoted in several interviews that both versions of *Funny Games* were made in order to shake an American audience out of its complacency.[9] However, the remake of his own 1997 film into *Funny Games U.S.*, released in 2008, was certainly not seen by many in the United States, especially not the typical consumers of violent films. A look at boxofficemojo.com, a website that tracks the gross income of films released in the US, shows that *Funny Games U.S.* made only 16.7% (=$1,294,919) of the total income domestically and 83.3% in foreign markets ($6,467,795 of a worldwide total of $7,762,714). At the same time, a film like *The Strangers* (2008) by Bryan Bertino, released just a few weeks later and a take on the horror/slasher subgenre of the "home invasion thriller" that was compared favorably to *Funny Games U.S.* in some reviews,[10] made $52,597,610 domestically and $29,036,785 abroad (64.4% and 35.6%, respectively, of its total gross of $81,634,395). Tellingly, *Funny Games U.S.* was only released in 288 theaters, while *The Strangers* was shown in 2,477 theaters. The question seems to be whether the director Michael Haneke really expected to attract an audience that normally seeks the thrills of bloody vigilante justice in a multi-screen cinema, or if he just toyed with the critics and his audience, which is mostly European and not likely to watch violent blockbusters.

Only one point can be objectively argued: although they strictly avoid psychology, all of Haneke's films, including his early films for TV, invite identification from the audience with the main characters via a specific class consciousness. Unlike, for example, Rainer Werner Fassbinder, whose films run the gamut of social class—from the sub-proletarian milieu of prostitutes, gangsters, and fairground workers, to the working class, to the *grande bourgeoisie*—Haneke's films always focus on characters that are situated in the middle class. The markers for class are subtle at times but always allow a reading of the characters by their choice of clothes, their furniture, their diction, even their food, etc. This insistence on class, something that is mostly repressed in films geared towards entertainment, is a clear indicator of a political thinking in Haneke. Indeed, Haneke seems to be one of the most class-conscious filmmakers especially because the class he depicts is relatively homogenous. This milieu of self-described liberals—store owners, engineers, journalists, teachers, in short, educated citizens—is quite specific to Central Europe and is known in Germany and Austria as *Bildungsbürgertum* ("educated bourgeoisie") or, in a derogatory term, as *Spießbürger* (an American equivalent would be the figure of "Babbitt"). Looking at the core values, an equivalent in the United States would be what the economist and social scientist Richard Florida (2002) calls the "Creative Class," an urban, well-educated, and affluent class with white-collar jobs that actively engages in creative jobs in media, science, and education and that in its spare time is also drawn to more intellectual pastimes such as visiting museums and galleries. In the Anglo-Saxon context, the moniker "the chattering classes" has also been used. It should be pointed out, though, that the socio-economic status is somewhat different in the case of Europe, where art generally receives generous subsidies and where the so-called "cultural capital" might count more towards the social standing than actual income, especially when the two are not commensurate. In *La Pianiste*, Haneke stresses the point that the piano teacher's status as *Kulturschaffende* (a generic term for people who work in fields connected to the arts) gives her access to Vienna's upper class.

To create the conditions for a middle-class viewer's identification with the portrayed characters, Haneke takes pains to highlight not only the provenance, but the anxieties of the *Bildungsbürger*. Significantly, all families in Haneke's films come from a traditional background in the countryside (*Der siebente Kontinent, Benny's Video, Code Inconnu, Caché*) or a small town, as, for example, in the two-part TV-film *Lemminge/ Lemmings* (1979) or in *Drei Wege zum See/ Three Paths to the Lake* (1976), the Ingeborg Bachmann adaptation that Haneke himself considers his first real film (Grissemann and Omasta 1991: 195). In all of those early works, as is typical for the post-war generation, the often first-time college attendees quickly rise in social status, taking white-collar jobs with a high social standing. To return to an example from above, the double-income family in *Benny's Video* is prototypical for this *Bildungsbürgertum*, including the humble roots from which they, as they would probably see it, freed themselves—a fact proudly displayed as a sign of a well-deserved new status. In the video that Benny shoots and that begins the film, we see his father jovially playing the gentleman farmer as he watches how a pig is killed. And, as the reaction of the father to the news that his son has killed a girl shows, a loss of status and not the murder per se is perceived as catastrophic.

In *La Pianiste*, the mother seems to be most devastated by what she perceives as her family's low social standing, while neither her husband's mental illness nor her daughter's obvious problems seem to bother her. And *Caché*'s Georges, the farmer's son who became the host of a literary show on TV, does not care about literature as much as he cares about the right "look." Whereas the extreme anxiety of losing this hard-earned social status fits into the image of this class, the family's decision in *Der siebente Kontinent* to destroy themselves, along with their worldly possessions for which they worked so hard, is even more shocking, especially as the parents were clearly living the same core values, diligently working to raise their status. While Haneke certainly does not give any explanations for the family's actions, he clearly points out that the parents are still bound by their petit bourgeois milieu.

The family's last meal before the suicidal potlatch does not consist of a lavish feast of caviar and expensive champagne, but of an assortment of cold cuts that were bought at a local delicatessen instead of the supermarket where the family normally shops to economize. Under the gaze of Haneke's camera, the platter arranged in a traditional, "festive" manner—carefully shrink-wrapped and stored in the fridge for the next day—becomes emblematic for the limited mind-set of this milieu.

Finally, the family in *Funny Games*, especially in the original version that provides more clues to the European viewer, is certainly what all the other families aspire to be: Not just affluent, but part of a class of highly successful and cultured people. Here, Haneke pays special attention to the consumerist attitude towards culture that marks the members of this self-perceived meritocracy. Culture here becomes a pawn in a game, a piece of a larger picture that signals the membership in an exclusive community. The guessing game at the beginning of the film is part of this community's self-image as much as the clothes, the brand names, and the talk that the killers know how to emulate so well. Tellingly, when the father in *Benny's Video* takes it upon himself to carve up the body of the girl his son just slaughtered, he does not just book a trip to Mallorca or a similar popular destination, but sends his wife and his son on a holiday of "cultural tourism" to Egypt.

Regardless of the fine differences that the middle class and its various milieus display within Europe or North America, it is clear that it comprises Haneke's core audience.[11] The casting of art house stars Isabelle Huppert, Juliette Binoche, and Daniel Auteuil in his French films—all of whom are prominently featured in the advertisements[12]— was certainly one of the main reasons for his success. It could be said, then, that all of Haneke's films directly target educated, liberal, middle class viewers who accept an ethos of hard work, incorporating into their attitude towards art the conviction that it requires an effort in order to receive a rewarding aesthetic experience. Indeed, it seems that Haneke is more than willing to oblige his audience, demanding a masochistic exertion from them, and it might be tempting to look for a psychological explanation in an author who was born into a well-connected family of German and Austrian artists. John Wray (2007) gives a short biographical sketch of Michael Haneke:

> Haneke was born on March 23, 1942, in Munich, to a genteel theatrical family—his father, Fritz Haneke, was a respected actor and director, and his mother, Beatrix von Degenschild, was an actress in her own right and a daughter of the

local aristocracy. [...] As soon as he graduated from high school, Haneke lost no time in moving to the capital, where he studied psychology, philosophy and—naturally enough—theater at the University of Vienna. [...] After attending the University of Vienna, he returned to Germany in 1967, where he spent the next four years working for Bavaria's equivalent of the BBC as a producer before becoming a freelance screenwriter and director. His first theatrical feature film, "The Seventh Continent," made at the age of 47, was released on the big screen only after having been rejected by a German television station.

From other sources, we learn that his father was German, that Haneke grew up with his aunt, that he once considered becoming a pianist, and that he is married and has four children.[13] Following this biographical path, however, we would quickly run into a critical impasse, as the Freudian implications of a German-born Austrian filmmaker with an absent Austrian mother could only lead to wild speculations. Of course, the point could be made that Haneke was born into a privileged position of high culture and therefore looks with contempt at the appetite of the petit-bourgeois to rise above their station. In the end, this would mean that Haneke's project would simply be grounded in this patrician director's condescending attitude towards the *parvenu*, a critical position that I find untenable because it obscures the real problems with which Haneke's cinema wrestles.

What, then, does Haneke's focus on the middle class mean? As I mentioned before, Haneke is an auteur who truly reflects on problems of representation. The viewer who sees himself or herself mirrored by a film is not a neutral observer, but always already a representation of the middle class. The viewer's ideology is manifested by the practice of watching a "difficult art house film," which, in turn, effectively constitutes the viewing subject that misrecognizes itself as the cause of this particular practice. Indeed, as Slavoj Žižek reminds us, the middle class is actually a "non-class," an "embodied lie" whose self-image is not grounded in explicit values, but rather in opposition to the classless, hence faceless, entities below and above them, that is, the marginalized poor and the big corporations. Žižek explains that

> in psychoanalytic terms, the 'middle class' is a fetish, the impossible intersection of left and right which, by expelling both poles of the antagonism into the position of antisocial "extremes" which corrode the healthy social body (multinational corporations and intruding immigrants), presents itself as the neutral common ground of Society. In other words, the 'middle class' is the very form of the disavowal of the fact that 'Society doesn't exist' (Laclau)—in it, Society does exist. (Žižek 1999: 187)

The fetish of middle class denies the difference on which our postmodern culture is based, that is, the essential inequality of our society, and instead suggests that the utopia of a classless society is not only possible, but would already be fulfilled by it, if only those "other" forces chose not to threaten this perfect world order. The effect of this postmodern fetish is the projection and ensuing conflation of racism and cultural difference—if the others worked a little bit harder, they could be just like us. To put it bluntly, since a fetish covers a primal *Angst*, the castration anxiety kept at bay is not the fear that the middle class attributes to the fringes of society, namely the xenophobe fear that "those others" could take away what we worked so hard to achieve, but rather that the "others" actually do not want to be "just like us" at all.[14]

In this context, one of Haneke's most interesting characters must be Maria, the Rumanian beggar in *Code Inconnu*, who constitutes just such an other. Indeed, it is not by accident that she is more developed than the main character Anne, played by the international art house star Juliette Binoche, on whom the audience would naturally concentrate. At the beginning, Maria is as much a cipher for Jean, who wants to vent his frustration, as she is for Amadou, the son of an immigrant who reacts strongly to discrimination. And, of course, she is also a cipher for the European audience who encounters beggars like her daily in larger European cities. During the film, more and more facets of her character are explored—her pride in the house that is being built with the money she sends home, her role in her family's economy, the not-so-subtle pressure on her to return, and, finally, the humiliation she feels begging for money revealed during a harrowing confession to a fellow illegal immigrant. Another significant disclosure happens after she lies to a neighbor about her job in France. Driving away, one house after another in the main street of her village is shown in a state of construction; houses that, should they ever be finished, will strongly resemble houses in any prosperous part of Western Europe.

Here, and in other important revelations, Haneke forces the audience to provide its own frame of reference. The scene in which Maria finds a young gypsy in the place where she usually begs is filmed in a long shot while only the repetitive rhythm of Amadou's drum circle is heard. First, the viewer has to recognize the street corner of the first long take and understand that a gypsy has usurped Maria's spot. Then, when an Eastern European-looking man and a boy approach her and talk to her calmly, it is the knowledge of how these gangs operate—a knowledge that the film of course does not provide, but which is derived from newspaper articles and TV-features—that explains the situation. Certainly, a bad director would have attempted to raise audience sympathy for Maria by explaining the situation and creating an emotional impact through close-ups and point-of-view-shots, thus inviting identification with Maria as a victim. Haneke, instead, skillfully adds small facets to his portrayal of Maria such that, when Maria finds "her" street taken over by an organized gang of beggars, the whole significance of her deracination becomes clear because the other's frame of reference appears to be congruent with our own. These two frames, mirror images of each other, bring into relief a truly political insight: Maria, who wants to be like us, does not exist, and her space is always defined as a negation of other, so-called "positive," values—wife, mother, breadwinner, middle-class existence, etc. Maria thus constitutes a kind of answer to the initial question—what does Haneke's focus on the middle class mean?—in that she represents the hidden face of the middle class invoked by Žižek, that faceless, attribute-less grouping known as the middle class. Maria-the-other is actually the true embodiment of the middle class and Haneke's way of making us, his audience, face another, more troubling question: What if we, the audience who identify with Maria rather than simply feeling sorry for her, what if *we* do not really want to "be like us"? I will come back to this, but suffice it to say here that this is also Haneke's way of pushing the envelope of politics on a basic, existential level through cinematic means.

In every attempt to approach an oeuvre, especially one like Haneke's that seems homogenous at first glance but reveals itself to be fragmented when viewed up close, there are, of course, certain aspects that cannot be covered or are less deserving of examination for reasons of time and space. It should be clear by now that basing an analysis of film in the director's biography is, in my opinion, completely useless.[15] I will also not touch the question of whether Michael Haneke deserves the doubtful honor to be appropriated by the Austrian or by the German nation. To my surprise and dismay, such a debate has developed on the heels of the success of *Das weiße Band* at Cannes in May 2009, in both these countries—certainly a sad reminder of the ghosts of nationalism that still seem to haunt some sectors of the public. I agree wholeheartedly with the assessment of Robert von Dassanowsky who writes in his definitive book on Austrian Cinema that Michael Haneke's films "demonstrate his postmodern transnational hybridity as a German-born filmmaker in Austria who utilizes French casts" (Dassanowsky 2005: 254).

It also leads nowhere to speculate whether the individual member of the audience is driven by a certain "guilty displeasure" or genuinely appreciates films by Haneke, or even misunderstands the problematic. As I witnessed on several occasions in the classroom and at social functions in the US and Europe, it is certainly considered chic in circles that value cultural capital to profess a liking for Haneke's films, often in order to provoke a reaction. Sitting through *Funny Games* is now practically considered a rite of passage and noting the preference "for the original" is almost mandatory. Further, although this point might not be worth mentioning, there is an unfortunate tendency to blame directors for not fool-proofing their texts. Especially directors who deal critically with issues of violence are accused of inciting copycat crimes. After a public controversy, Stanley Kubrick banned his *A Clockwork Orange* (1971) for Great Britain. And Oliver Stone's *Natural Born Killers* (1994) was subject to a lawsuit for inciting a similar killing. The issue is simple but always problematic with regard to the real audience or the real director: as soon as violence is depicted, either in a very stylized, artificial way or with extreme realism, it is aestheticized, and thus subject to accusations of exploitation, regardless of the director's protestation. Concerning Haneke, I believe that the extreme nuanced shifting of frames makes an enjoyment "for fun" impossible.

The question of enjoyment aside, there is still the issue of emotion that, as I briefly want to highlight here, invalidates the charge that Haneke is engaging in an exploitative anesthetization of violence, along with politics, and racial and class stereotypes. It is noteworthy that Haneke's films, perhaps more so than any other fiction films, incite extreme hostility in viewers and critics alike. It seems clear that his critics are taking him seriously, as no journalist or scholar becomes as enraged by a sexist or racist depiction in a Hollywood blockbuster as they are by Haneke.[16] Haneke's austere style and his implication of the bourgeois viewer have repeatedly been compared to films by Luc and Jean-Pierre Dardenne (e.g., Wheatley 2009: 14). As Brian Gibson rightly points out in his insightful comparison, "the Dardenne brothers and Haneke draw attention to the camera and disturb the audience's usual comfortable distance in their recent films" (2006: 26). But while the former inspire a slowly growing, and certainly well-deserved audience, their films never elicit the strong emotional responses that Haneke seems to be able to trigger in some of his viewers. Paul Gilroy's short, but powerful dismissal of *Caché* in a special issue of *Screen* dedicated to this film can stand as representative for the many negative reviews; it is, certainly, one of the most articulate. Gilroy—a world-renowned scholar of race, racism, and nationalism—confesses to hostility and accuses the film outright of offering "only a shallow, pseudopolitical, or perhaps more accurately an antipolitical, engagement with profound contemporary problems that deserve—or demand—better treatment than an elaborate exercise in mystification can provide" (2007: 233). Looking closely at Gilroy's arguments, it becomes clear that his judgment of *Caché* relies on implicit assumptions of how an issue like race should be represented and what meaning such a representation should generate. Here, we come back to the form/content divide, discussed above: Gilroy assumes a difference of form (a fictional film that refuses a clear solution, thus functioning in a modernist mode) and content (the film is exploring issues of contemporary racism and of the return of the repressed colonial past). The politics of Haneke, instead, is exactly to avoid this separation in the first place, insisting that the chosen form of a representation is always already political. To put it bluntly, there is no value-free representation of an Arab character. Misconceiving Haneke's *politique des auteurs*, Gilroy must necessarily arrive at the wrong conclusions. For Gilroy, Haneke's refusal to provide his characters with clear psychological traits can only mean that he sets up a shallow, privileged cardboard-character as an easy target to divert attention from the fact that the racial other is still being depicted as a stereotypical, flat character. Majid's suicide is interpreted by Gilroy as the fantasy to get "the Arabs to do away with themselves," while Georges not being responsible for a crime that he committed as a 6 year old, according to Gilroy, can only mean that the Europeans are absolved of crimes that were committed sometimes generations ago, thereby reducing the historical mass murder of demonstrators by the French police to a simple plot-device (234–235). As such a reductive reading represents a typical misunderstanding of Haneke, I will return to accusations and misunderstandings like these in detail throughout this book. For now, it is enough to say that for Haneke, it would be unethical to claim to have an insight into the life of a man who was apparently the victim of horrible abuse and to reconstruct the events of the night when the demonstrators were killed and their bodies thrown into the Seine. And it is absolutely important to understand that for Haneke, the absolution of crimes is not on the agenda, given that the grown-up Georges acts unethically just as his mother did many years before him.

At this point, I have to divulge my own position *vis-à-vis* Haneke, not because I feel the need to follow in the footsteps of Augustine in a confessional mode and admit to my enjoyment of the Manichean world of genre-cinema prior to Haneke (I am still a fan of well-done genre cinema), but because films by Haneke cannot be watched with an emotional detachment. It is possible for me, for example, to watch a film by Sam Peckinpah with a professional distance and teach a class on "The Critique of Violence in Peckinpah" the following day, but this is not the case with Haneke. I also noticed that it is difficult in retrospect to differentiate between Haneke's films in all their fragmented proceeding and the plot that I am forced by his films to reconstruct after the fact. This, I think, is what sparked my interest in Haneke and could be called my own frame of reference. With Haneke, I noticed immediately that a distance, be it emotional or critical, is not possible, precisely because his methods are deceptively simple. Notably, none of the above-mentioned devices that Haneke uses are new. Tom Tykwer contrasts Lola's widescreen-world, filmed in saturated colors with her father's videotaped soap opera existence in *Lola rennt/Run Lola Run* (1998). In *Lost Highway* (1997) by David Lynch, disquieting videotapes that only show that there is a surveillance taking place are dropped off at the protagonist's doorstep. The aforementioned *Natural Born Killers* (1994), directed by Oliver Stone and written by Quentin Tarantino, is aimed at the audiences' complicity in the sensationalist representation of violence. The examples could be expanded to include the French and Italian auteur-cinema, especially Robert Bresson, the paragon of ethical filmmaking for Haneke. It is the way in which Haneke deploys these devices that makes for a powerful cinema where emotion, on screen and of the audience, takes center stage.

The brilliance of Haneke lies in the subtle shifts of perspective, the reframing, that he achieves with very traditional filmic means: voice-over, long takes, framing and close-ups. As David Sorfa discerns in his perceptive exploration of Haneke's domestic spaces, the home can quickly become an uncanny space in his films: "The place of safety (the *Heimlich*) is the very place of danger (the *Unheimlich*)" (2006: 98). Indeed, only a small effort is needed for the polite killers in *Funny Games* to gain access to the gated community and turn it into a prison camp. Expensive golf clubs, the perfect status symbol and emblem of unproductive leisure, can easily be deterritorialized, to borrow a term from Deleuze, and used to smash a knee-cap.

In these uncanny moments, Haneke shows himself as the master of inversion: while violence is normally represented as something that comes from the outside- that is, the domain of the other- Haneke is not content to show that we, in our misconception of ourselves as the "healthy social body," to quote Žižek again, also do violence to others—that is, only as a side-effect and unintentionally. Haneke restores the violence that is always already present in representation. If a deconstructive pun might be allowed here, Haneke literally re-presents, actualizes the violence that is hidden in the folds of representation. This, I think, is the source of allegations of hypocrisy for many critics who accuse Haneke of exploiting the violence that he critiques in his films. Even well-meaning scholars question whether it is possible to criticize violence with violent means. Here, I am tempted to quote Stanley Kubrick's Dr. Strangelove—"it is not only possible, it is essential!" The representation can only be destroyed from within, and it is the critic's job to unfold that process.

The violence that is re-presented in a Haneke film is not destructive; on the contrary, it produces a strong affect. In the brief comparison between Haneke and three post-9/11-films above, I mentioned the emotions of fear and rage that those films use in order to guide the viewer to an identification with the hero and to the cathartic fantasy of eliminating the alien other. In Haneke, emotions are a sign that life has become completely reified as they become visible in characters who cannot deal with feelings unless they are in commodified form. In *Der siebente Kontinent*, to take Haneke's first theatrical release as a prime example, kitschy, intradiegetic pop-music accompanies two key scenes. The families' dinner conversation—a string of clichéd exchanges while loud pop music and the traffic report are playing—is interrupted by a sudden nervous breakdown of the uncle that is embarrassing to his sister and his brother in law. While the mother clumsily attempts to comfort her brother, the little girl is watching. An emotional connection with this character is barely possible, because the brother has hardly been introduced. Instead, in moments like these, the emotion becomes abstract and the affect of grief is set free. To clarify this crucial difference in the cinema of Haneke, let us consider what a director of mainstream entertainment fare would do. Such a director would certainly try to make the audience feel sorry for the uncle, by explaining his situation—we could image a line that explains his grief for his dead mother—and by juxtaposing his sensitive side with his sister's coldness. Haneke, instead, steers the audience to feel for the situation: the cold light, the joyless intake of food, the mind-numbing music, and the inability to deal with emotions all serve to extract a feeling that is no longer bound to any diegetic character in particular, being bound instead to the entire scene.

A second example from *Der siebente Kontinent* is equally effective in contrasting affect against emotion—here, however, with a device that Haneke never used again. This shows that Haneke is actively working on solving problems, as I mentioned before, sometimes returning to the same methods, but other times abandoning them when they've served their purpose. In the last sequence, when the family overdoses on sleeping pills, the TV shows Jennifer Rush performing "The Power of Love," a song of cloying sentimentality whose lyrics provide an ironic counterpoint to the murder of Evi, the little daughter, that is taking place.[17] This pop-song is juxtaposed with one of the few moments of extradiegetic music in Haneke's entire oeuvre: when the little girl sees a ship that might be a vision in an earlier scene, Alban Berg's violin concerto "To the memory of an angel," can be heard. Again, in contrast to emotion, a pure affect is released that has nothing to do with the cheap emotions of commercial cinema. It seems, however, that Haneke abandoned the insertion of extradiegetic music entirely. There are in Haneke, of course, instances of intradiegetic music that carries over into another shot, thereby building an ironic counterpart—the scene where *La Pianiste*'s classical music is playing while she is sniffing used tissues in a sex shop booth comes to mind. But the effect achieved with a contrasting of extradiegetic classical music with cheap pop is maybe too commercial, too emotional, especially concerning the murder of a child.

I end this introduction on a personal note in order to facilitate the conceptual parsing of affect and emotion and bring into focus my own, already-mentioned frame of reference. It may not come as a surprise to the reader that I belong exactly to the class of people that Haneke features and targets, and that has certainly not much in common with the bourgeois high culture of Vienna a generation before mine: growing up in Germany in a working-class milieu where upwards social mobility was a clear goal, culture was certainly something to be appreciated, but was always considered a luxury, an acquired foreign good that could be proudly displayed. Although my parents and those of my friends were especially warm and affectionate, I occasionally caught a glimpse of families that could have served as a model for Benny's or Evi's families and where the brand of automobile, even more so than the father's job, quickly established who belongs and who doesn't. It is indeed easy for me to identify with the characters in Haneke's films, as opposed to characters in a Judd Apatow comedy, for example, even though the latter director is of my generation. The reaction of the father in *Le temps du loup* facing an armed squatter (who, judging by his diction and appearance, is obviously from a lower class), would probably be my own and that of most of my colleagues and friends. And which teacher of literary criticism doesn't dream of becoming a star like Georges in *Caché*, whose opinions receive a wide distribution and attention? Apart from the admiration for Haneke's immense skills as filmmaker, his films hold for me a strong emotional impact, maybe even more so because I am living in the United States, where a sudden loss of employment (with the ensuing loss of health insurance for the family) or an eruption of fatal violence is taken as a natural course of events.

Fascinated by Haneke's films and repulsed by the world they are depicting, I chose what I would describe here as a Deleuzian approach, looking for the moving image in Haneke's concepts in order to circumvent the pitfalls of an emotional entanglement and to arrive at a perspective where the *affects* that drive his cinema appear. For reasons that become clearer in the course of this book, Haneke's films resist theory. Perhaps because they are already concepts in motion, they show a kinship with the concepts of Gilles Deleuze, which, in turn refuse any application and exhibit their own resistance to systematization. If, in this book, Haneke appears quite Deleuzian as he thinks in moving images, there is nevertheless nothing hierarchical about the relationship. Reading Haneke alongside Deleuze is not to apply Deleuze to Haneke, or even Haneke to Deleuze; it is to deploy a certain manner of reading, one not given to system building or mastery, but to seeing the complexity of our contemporary situation depicted with the disarming freshness and simplicity that only cinema can muster.

The writings of Gilles Deleuze are notoriously difficult, which is often credited to his complex subject matters. Even though no other thinker is able to conceptualize better than Deleuze what is essential in cinema, that is, in Deleuze-speak, to bring out what will always be new about it, I must nevertheless admit to a hostile emotional reaction against the implied author Deleuze, whose convoluted style and shifting concepts signal for me an obvious disregard for the reader. Followers of Deleuze might point out that writing about representation is already a Deleuzian problem. Commenting in one medium about another always entails a conflict between percept and concept, between the conceptualization in one medium of what is perceived in another. In other words, the question is: how does one talk in one medium about the practices of another? Here, Haneke clearly has the advantage over Deleuze of conceptualizing representation in a representational medium, whereas Deleuze has to force everything into philosophical concepts. Still, my impression is that Haneke is indeed an ethical artist, that he does the best he can for his ideal audience, so to speak, while Deleuze writes only for one ideal reader, himself.

Afraid that personal emotions might impair my judgment, I chose not to make the attempt to meet the creator of the object of my study, nor watch the 2005 documentary film about Haneke by Nina Kusturica and Eva Testor, *24 Wirklichkeiten in der Sekunde/ 24 Realities per Second*, before I finished this book. Like his films, Haneke seems to inspire extreme reactions in people who meet him personally. Curious as I am about "the real Michael Haneke," I prefer to keep my professional distance for the moment.

Frame I

THE CONCEPTUAL FRAME OF REFERENCE

In this chapter, I first expand my main conceptual point, the shifting frames of reference, briefly introduced above, and then review theoretical concepts that inhabit related conceptual fields to Haneke and to which I return throughout this book. After discussing my concept of the frame of reference, I outline how a paradoxical thought from and of the Outside could look and what bearing this has on Haneke's cinema. Then, I discuss Haneke's cinema as a "Cinema of Cruelty," following Antonin Artaud and André Bazin in order to refute the notion that Haneke's cinema is a cinema of violence. This thinking of the virtual is political thought and, as Haneke understands and practices it, can help to overcome the compulsions of present-day politics, which is always a biopolitics in the sense in which Foucault describes it.

Shifting Frames

Caché/Hidden (2005), Michael Haneke's critically and commercially most successful film so far, begins with what must already be one of the most written about sequences in film history. These first five and a half minutes, consisting of a long shot filmed by a stationary camera from a slightly elevated position in a single long take—only briefly interrupted by a shot of a man leaving a house and looking for something—lay out the aesthetic and thematic groundwork for the film to follow: what appears to be a neutral shot of a middle-class Parisian neighborhood is suddenly revealed to be a recording by a fast-forwarding of the tape and two voices which—as the viewer has to deduct—belong to the couple who lives in the house that appears at the center of the frame. The credit sequence is then, in turn, mirrored by a coda that was mentioned in the introduction, also consisting of a long take that is filmed

FIGURE 2 Rue des Iris

in a long shot by a stationary camera and that forces the viewer to reconsider any prior assumptions and deductions about the plot. These two long takes from the beginning and the ending of *Caché* are truly emblematic for Michael Haneke's oeuvre. For one, most of Haneke's feature films contain shots that are retroactively revealed to be not neutral but to belong to somebody's point of view. In other words, these images have a different ontological status than the viewer had assigned to them based on the conventions of narrative cinema.

The crucial element required for the processing of information that a film by Michael Haneke provides, and, of course, for filling in the blanks where the film does not, is time. At the beginning of *Caché*, the viewer is forced to look at the shot of the neighborhood long enough after the credits (which are difficult to read, due to their small size and spacing) to ponder about the location: cars and houses appear French, a high-rise in the back points to a large city and a street sign— "rue des Iris" —affirms that we are looking at a street in Paris and there is time to understand that the street name is ironic. Then, voices of a man and a woman can be heard, but what they say makes no sense to the viewer: "So?" "Nothing!," "Where was it?", "In a plastic bag, in front of the door." After a cut, a man is seen leaving the house. The camera, positioned in the middle of the street, pans with him as he walks towards the intersecting street. The brief interlude, lasting about 55 seconds, also does not make sense. Then, the same shot as at the beginning of the film appears, by now a shot that we recognize. The sudden fast-forwarding, then, comes as a shock because the viewer is forced to acknowledge that it is not the usual looking *at* something that is at stake here, but a looking *with* somebody. And this somebody is looking at a video-recording of a prior event, something that the viewer could not have noticed, since the movie *Caché* itself and the surveillance video are shot in a digital format. That means that the here and now of the narrative time, as well as the materiality of the film itself—normally abstract and suspended elements of conventional filmic and literary narration—suddenly come to the foreground. Here, the viewer has to adjust the basis on which the text is interpreted, a basis that could be called an ontological basis, since it concerns the fictional reality. To explore a visual metaphor, we could say that what is adjusted in cases like this could be called *a frame of reference*. This concept of a frame of reference retains the basic movement on the side of the viewer when adjusting to this new grounding, requiring not only a reinterpretation, but also a reflection—on the basis of this reinterpretation—on the image given by the auteur.

To establish what a shift of a frame of reference is in Haneke, I turn to one of the most basic conventions of cinema: the film's "fictional universe," the lifeworld of the character that depends on the film's genre. When a character in a horror film gets up from the couch and tells his friends that he will be "right back," the audience rightly expects the filmically conventional slaughtering of this character immediately afterwards and waits for these expectations to be met by the filmmaker in a new and exiting way. Judging by their financial success, the fictional universes of the *Alien-* and *Predator*-series—melded, so far, into *AVP: Alien vs. Predator* (Paul W.S. Anderson 2004) and *AVPR: Aliens vs Predator—Requiem* (Colin and Greg Strause 2007)—to give another example, apparently work well together bringing premises or elements of one sub-genre to the other. The genre of Fan Fiction, where fans write their own stories that are set in a "Harry-Potter-" or "Star-Wars-Universe," clearly shows the playful acceptance of a "fictional universe."

Genre conventions have, of course, been parodied. Indeed, following Viktor Shklovskii we could say that a genre only comes into existence when its features are so distinctive that it can be parodied (1990: 192). And, as has often been quipped, the behavior that people display in the sub-genre of the romantic comedy would get them arrested in real live. The often-cited "willing suspension of disbelief," certainly does not mean that an audience is so naïve as to accept a film as the truth. However, this fictional universe is supposed to be harmonious in itself: the audience expects a coherent diegetic world where certain genre-rules are obeyed. It seems that one "unreal" element, what screenwriters would call the "basic premise" in a sales pitch, is the accepted rule. *Minority Report* by Steven Spielberg (2002) is set in a technologically advanced future that is entirely possible, while the one fantastic element of this film—the existence of people who can see the future—is added to this possibility as just such an element.

Michael Haneke runs counter to this rule by first referencing a genre and then introducing a premise that abruptly not only breaks the rules of the genre but of the medium itself. Both versions of *Funny Games* begin with a wide shot of a driving car from a bird's eye view that immediately brings to mind the now classic beginning of *The Shining* by Stanley Kubrick (1980). Then, in the following scenes, Haneke refers to other generic cues typical for the horror/slasher genre, such as a close-up on a knife and the turning of household items into instruments of torture, thus pointing in the direction of a well-established sub-genre, the "home invasion thriller." Then, after the killers have already addressed the audience directly, in the most infamous scene in *Funny Games*, one of the killers is given the power to rewind the film itself. The shocking element that Haneke introduces here is not the breaking of the fourth wall, which is not that unusual, especially in genres like horror that have become more and more self-referential in recent years. Nor does Haneke show a soundstage in order to point to the extradiegetic reality, which would be a typical device of *mise en abyme* for modernist *auteurs* like Ingmar Bergman or Jean-Luc Godard and is something that Haneke does only once, in *Wer war Edgar Allan?/ Who was Edgar Allan?*, an adaptation of a novel that he made for television in 1984. Instead, Haneke's jarring move in *Funny Games* is to give one of the characters authorial powers, effectively creating a short-circuit between the level of the diegetic character, the level of the narrator, that is, the camera controlled by the implied author, and thus the extradiegetic reality, the *hors cadre*.

Here, a comparison to *The Strangers*, a successful "home invasion thriller" that was already briefly mentioned in the introduction, helps to better understand the uniqueness of Haneke's move. The basic plot of *The Strangers* is not that different from *Funny Games*: preppy young people whose only motivation for killing is their sadistic pleasure get away and continue on their murderous path. However, *The Strangers* could easily be expanded into a series with rising body count and more expensive special effects, or it could end with a sequel where the genre-typical revenge takes place and the sadistic intruders themselves are killed by their victims' parents, as in the reversal of the home-invasion-thriller, *The Last House on the Left* by Dennis Iliadis (2009). Notably, the ending of *The Strangers* strongly suggests the possibility of a sequel: one of the killers claims, "It will be easier the next time!," while the "final girl," as the lone, female survivor in a horror film is known,[1] is still alive when she is found. *Funny Games*, however, could never have a sequel as the characters are already able to manipulate the diegetic world and restart as if they were players of a video game. The sequel is, as it were, already virtually there in a nod to a generic practice, taking that practice to a logical conclusion that becomes its own negation. Here, only the perceptive critic of *Les Cahiers du cinéma* understood Haneke's point of remaking his own film shot-by-shot. As Christophe Beney declares in his short review, there is no reason to stop with one remake. One could imagine a whole series of *Funny Games*, for example, "Funny Games Iraq" or "Funny Games China" (2008: 60). What would change in any remake of *Funny Games*, then, would be the extradiegetic reality that serves as a reference to interpret the images. The newer version triggers different connotations of the image of the tied-up and hooded boy because now a viewer cannot *not* think of the pictures from the Abu Ghraib prison abuse scandal that were ubiquitous not too long ago.

The changing socio-political context implicates the questions of class and intended audience. As mentioned above in the introduction, Haneke's cinema is very class-conscious. Class—that is, its representation and its reception—provides a crucial reference-point. The gated community, the SUV, boat and golf clubs appear as ostentatious signs of wealth in the first version of *Funny Games*, because these status symbols are still unusual in Europe even though they do not appear especially extravagant in the American context, where—at least before the recent economic downturn—the middle class was able to afford such luxuries. Some viewers in Europe certainly could not suppress a feeling of malicious delight in seeing a rich family being punished by their own kind. On the other hand, the musical guessing game would not appear that remarkable in the European context, but could be interpreted as a sign of elitism in the United States. While the set-design is carefully transposed to fit with the general taste of the class depicted—more rustic, as befitting a weekend retreat in Austria and the "sophisticated-yet-casual look"[2] after which the American middle class is striving—it is remarkable how easy it is to identify with either family. It seems, then, that Haneke's often-repeated statement—mentioned above in the introduction—that both versions of *Funny Games* were made as a wake-up call for the American audience, might indeed be a ruse to shake his European audience out of its complacency, because the Europeans will find that the ideal intended viewers of these films are not "the typical Americans" but they themselves. The film's title, *Funny Games U.S.*, which was released with this English title throughout Europe, could then be read as "*Funny Games* us," shifting the reference from the projection of the image of the 'ugly American" to us, the complacent middle class audience.

Haneke's move is not to invent a film with mutant powers to replicate itself in an infinite series of moneymaking blockbusters, but to create films that point inexorably in the direction of their extradiegetic context by way of shifting frames of reference that implicate the viewer, an inhabitant of that context.

The Frames of Narratology

With the above-mentioned shifts in the frames of reference, Haneke strongly points to the viewer's role in creating meaning, as well as the author's role in the creation of a text. In narratological terms, what happens here is a metalepsis as Gerard Genette defines it. In his most influential work, *Narrative Discourse,* Genette defines "narrative metalepsis" as a transgression insofar as the authorial voice draws attention to itself and its powers, claiming to be present as the narrated events unfold by, for example, announcing a shift from one location to another (see 1980: 234–235). As Monika Fludernik (2003) convincingly shows, this device has been used before the nineteenth century, where Genette places it, often with parodic intentions. For the sake of the argument of this book, I want to make clear the important difference between *mise en abyme* and metalepsis: a *mise en abyme* is an instance of a pointing to the fictional character of a text, for example by a zoom back that reveals a film set. But when a figure claiming to be the author crosses the frame that separates discourse and story and begins to act as a character, a metalepsis happens. The reverse—a character steps out of the intradiegetic world into "reality"—also happens. The obvious example that Genette picks is in his book on the metalepsis is *The Purple Rose of Cairo* (1985) by Woody Allen (Genette 2004: 60) where a character from an old film joins an adoring fan. A more recent example for such a crossing of the intra-/extradiegetic border can easily be found in films written by Charlie Kaufman, especially *Adaptation* (Spike Jonze 2002), where a character named Charlie Kaufman is introduced as the struggling writer of a screenplay. This narrator is then split into an art house-persona and a Hollywood-hack who threatens to take over the entire film.

The type of shift that Haneke employs is similar but places the accent on materiality of the film and the conditions of reception. Looking at two other examples of filmic metalepses that Genette mentions can be helpful in understanding the difference (Genette 2004: 65–67). Ernst Lubitsch's black comedy *To Be or Not to Be* (1942) and François Truffaut's famous self-referential *La nuit américaine/Day for Night* (1973) begin with a shot that appears to be the film itself, and that is suddenly, by an intrusion of the directorial voice, revealed to be a fictional scene that is performed in the diegesis—a stage where a play is rehearsed in the former, a film studio in the latter—pointing to the films' main topic of the porous boundaries of illusion and reality. Haneke follows this concept but pays attention to the materiality of the medium: in *Caché*, it is not only the voices that alert the viewer to the fact that a recording is being watched, but also—and especially—the additional fast-forwarding of the tape, the latter alerting the viewer that *Caché* itself is shot in a digital format and that there is no difference in film stock between the film and the surveillance footage.

To take another example, while the different fragments in *Code inconnu* consist of long takes—sometimes filmed with a static camera, sometimes with a dolly-shot—that avoid close-ups, the dramatic film-in-film, however, is edited like a Hollywood-movie, with typical shot-reverse-shots and point-of-view shots. When the film suddenly stops and a voice tells Anne and her colleague that the dubbing needs to be redone, the audience not only realizes that is was duped, but also that it fell for a run-of-the-mill scene that was not even especially well done. And *Benny's Video*, the film where Haneke uses this type of metalepsis for the first time in a feature film, begins with the videotaped killing of a pig that is suddenly rewound and then replayed in slow motion, thereby alerting the viewer that the video is being manipulated, therefore watched by an unknown person.

The boundary that is crossed in Haneke is not just the difference between intradiegetic and extradiegetic but between the world of the narration (narrative *discourse*) and the narrated world of the story (narrated *histoire*). Indeed, as Marie-Laure Ryan points out, this type of transgression should not just be seen as a simple rhetorical device, but should be called ontological (1991: 197). Insofar as the materiality of the medium and the reception by the audience are thematized, it is an allegory of the text itself that is produced. The allegorical character of this form of metalepsis underlines that the ontological shifts that happen in *Caché*, *Code inconnu* and *Benny's Video* should not just be understood as instances of simple self-referentiality as these appear now even in mainstream Hollywood productions, but indeed as a true metalepsis.

In the case of *Funny Games*, now, the killer breaks out of the story and transgresses into the world of discourse, controlling the film itself, a clear case of an ontological metalepsis. To return to the example already mentioned in the introduction, the mise en abyme of pairing real survivors with the actors that portrayed them at the end of *Schindler's List* leaves intact the implicit representational contract between teller and audience that promises that an event is told truthfully. The diegetic world is, of course, not necessarily real, but coherent and independent from the reality of the narrator and the audience. With his ontological metalepsis, however, Haneke links the transgression metonymically with another one, the mother's revenge, which the viewer is forced to see again in reverse. The disappointment of seeing the murderer resurrected and the shock of this breaking of ontological boundaries are closely connected, aiming directly at the genre convention and, most importantly, on how the audience normally deals with these conventions. Again, the decisive point here is time—a mise en abyme, shocking as it might be, works like a symbol, a timeless switch from one level to the next with its meaning still tightly controlled by an authorial instance. Walter Benjamin's famous definition from *The Origin of German Tragic Drama* grasps that: "The measure of time for the experience of the symbol is the mystical instant in which the symbol assumes the meaning into its hidden and, if one might say so, wooded interior."[3] Meaning and image are here in a spatial relation. An ontological metalepsis such as Haneke constructs it develops instead meaning over a period of time because it forces the audience to reflect on what they have seen, turning it into an allegory. In narratological terms, another discursive level is added that now assigns meaning to the first. A naïve belief in the existence of a pure histoire is thus destroyed and the deferred temporality makes a solution impossible: In the case of *Funny Games*, the audience is forced to witness the undoing of something it was longing for and must instead see the revenge-killing in which it rejoiced as an allegory for the problematic representation of violence: "Whereas in the symbol destruction is idealized and the transfigured face of nature is fleetingly revealed in the light of redemption, in allegory the observer is confronted with the *facies hippocratica* of history as a petrified primordial landscape" (Benjamin 1991: 166).

The gesture of guiding the viewer to challenge well-rehearsed viewing patterns by adding an authorial signature is an authoritative, self-referential statement, underlining that these images are not only given to the viewer, but that they belong to somebody else. To put it bluntly, the violence on screen is suddenly framed by a message identifying it as a representation, thus turning these shots into veritable emblems of representation: "this is *about* violence." Insofar as the image in Haneke always bears the marks of its mode of production, we could rightly call it a modern allegory. And it is precisely in this sense that Michael Haneke is truly a *modern* auteur.

An understanding of this emblematic nature of Haneke's films is crucial. As was mentioned above, there is reason to suspect that the public utterances of Haneke should be taken with a grain of salt, whereas the implied target audience seems to bear great resemblance to the main characters in the films. Here, a quick look at common narrative concepts can show how skillfully Haneke manipulates the narrative frames of his films. In *Caché* several other narrative frames open up or rather come into relief that are normally invisible in a movie that is geared towards telling a story. A successful auteur can serve here as a counter-example to Michael Haneke: the brand of popular comedies which have Judd Apatow's signature (either as director, writer, or producer) are targeted towards a very specific audience (white, male, heterosexual, college educated, 20–40 years old). The public image of Apatow as "funny, but honest guy" (see Rodrick 2007) enhances the image of the implied author that the films suggest. Recurring motifs in Apatow comedies, which have earned them the fitting moniker "dick flick," include language considered not politically correct, nudity, girls that would normally be considered too beautiful and smart for the main character, and constant vulgar jokes about sexuality, especially homosexuality. Generally, the camera in a Judd Apatow comedy does not draw attention on itself, that is, it does not reveal itself as a narrative instance, whereas the filmic text provides clear and stable markers for what is meant seriously and what is not. The frame of reference for films like these is assuring, insofar as it grounds the audience. The viewer finds a structure that always provides a position for the spectator with which he (!) can readily identify, not because the main character is so similar to the viewer, being slightly inferior (he generally is overweight and socially and professionally unsuccessful), but because this character has an ethical kernel around which the film is structured (only having sex with his true love, taking responsibility after a one night stand, etc) and which must always stay untouched by the satiric elements.

Consequently, the plot resolution is never ambiguous and rewards the main character for his ethics. Judging by newspaper reviews and posts on the web, individual viewers indeed find the sexism in these comedies offensive. However, in general, viewers accept the heteronormative structures that Apatow's films provide without questioning them.

In films by Haneke, on the other hand, an easy identification with the main characters, although encouraged, even programmed through the aforementioned class characteristics, is hampered by the complete absence of such a psychological kernel and the absence of any marker that would allow for an easy judgment of the character. This does not mean, of course, that the characters' actions stay unmotivated. But compared to most narrative films, even those that fall into the category of art house, Haneke's characters barely emote. This lack of an inner world is especially important for *Code inconnu*, where the main character is an actress who only shows emotions when she is acting. In her private life, her face does not betray any emotion. In films that follow the rules of Hollywood cinema, close-ups generally provide information about a character's emotions according to genre-specific formulas. Notably, we only see the face of the actress in close-up in *Code inconnu*, while in private, we never see the protagonists closer than a medium shot. Paired with the often-noted absence of extradiegetic music, the viewer is made aware of the spectatorial positions that films normally provide, but without generating such an awareness. Genre-specific psychological "explanations," such as the motivation to take the law into one's own hands in revenge-movies or the vigilante film, are plot conventions that are so established by now that they barely need an introduction. It should be noted, however, that the only stable frame of reference is the above-cited public image of Haneke as "Bearded Prophet."

With the first shift of the ontological frame in *Caché*, an additional narrator is established in the form of the person or persons unknown who operate the surveillance camera, as well as a narratee, as the fictional addressee of a story is generally known. In cinema, such an embedded narrative is, of course, nothing exceptional. In Jean Renoir's *Le crime de Monsieur Lange/ The Crime of Monsieur Lange* (1936), the fugitives tell their story—the major part of the films is thus a flashback—to a group of listeners who have to decide whether to allow them to continue their journey or turn them over to the authorities. The ideological position of the fictional audience is normally clear—in the case of a courtroom drama, for example—as is the spectatorial position, which jumps back along the fictional timeline and witnesses the events.

In *Caché*, however the implied viewer finds the spectatorial position strangely vague and undefined. The event to which the tape bears witness does not concern the content of the clip (a possible blackmail scenario comes to mind), but the very fact of being under surveillance. The narrator/camera-operator is never revealed and, most importantly, the narrator's ontological position remains unclear: if the camera is/had been there, Georges should have seen it, and it should be visible to the viewer on several occasions, for example at Georges' visits to Majid. A rewinding of the film reveals that the camera is so well hidden (*caché* in French) that it is invisible.

The important ending of *Caché* unfolds and complicates the narratological positions again. Contrary to convention, the ending is *caché*/hidden after the end of the credits—thus pointing to the implied author—and many individual viewers probably do not even notice that the main characters' children talk to each other in this long shot. If an individual viewer now observes this meeting at the edge of the screen, there is still the question whether he or she notices that the camera's perspective mirrors the set-up of the surveillance camera that is operated by an unknown force. Because there is no frame that helps to determine whether this last shot is filmed neutrally or is the point of view of the surveillance camera, the viewer has to decide the far-reaching implications for the plot. If the shot takes place at the level of the filmic lifeworld, the information that the main characters' children appear to know each other could mean that they conspired against Georges. However, since the *mise en scène* points to the modus of the surveillance camera, we could also assume that its operator is not only still unknown, but that the tapes were sent by the director who transgressed boundaries by entering into his own film.

The Truth of the Perspective

The consequences of the paradoxical question—"How do I represent the politics of representation?"—bring into relief the striking affinity that Haneke shares with so-called postmodern thinkers, especially Michel Foucault and Gilles Deleuze: this question indeed demands that the discourse describe itself from outside the discourse. Maurice Blanchot, quoted on numerous occasions in Deleuze, develops the notion of an outside that is paradoxically not exterior: "*le dehors non extérieur*," and "*le dedans non intérieur*," "the not-external outside and the not-internal inside," as it has been translated.[4] It is this "*dehors*," the limit and the base for thinking to which philosophy and art strive to point:

> Perhaps this is the supreme act of philosophy: not so much to think THE plane of immanence as to show that it is there, unthought in every plane, and to think it in this way as the outside and inside of thought, as the not-external outside and the not-internal inside—that which cannot be thought and yet must be thought.... (Deleuze and Guattari 1994: 59).

The "base of thinking," the "not-external outside and the not-internal inside," for the theater-director-turned-filmmaker Haneke is literally a stage, that is, the underlying plane on which the action, often played against a flat, immobile background, takes place. A quick example from *Caché*, filmed in a digital format that renders everything in flat, clear contour, can suffice here. When we see Georges and Anne interact in front of a wall of books in their living room, they frame a television screen on which news are playing. Georges in front of a wall of fake books on the set of his show echoes the impression of the first shot. The difference is that Georges now fully enters the space of the television becoming an accessory in somebody's living room, just as he himself had reduced the news about a war to background noise. A double articulation takes place here: underlying the foil of the space as it is represented by the film, the flat, postmodern plane that is *caché/*hidden emerges, however briefly. This plane is again put into relief by a switching of the frame of reference. What appears as an unmediated clip of Georges' show is suddenly stopped and we have to acknowledge that we were watching the show with Georges who is editing it. By not switching to an outside, an exterior, for example by the mise en abyme of showing studio equipment, Haneke here comes closer to this unthinkable base of philosophy, what Deleuze and Guattari describe as "that which cannot be thought and yet must be thought," than most other filmmakers.

A twofold question seems to arise here: Is there such an outside to Haneke? And, secondly, how can the viewer gain access to this not-external outside? The paradoxical status of this position makes clear that as soon as it is reached, there is a descent into a mode of universal history, of judging. To answer this two-part question, we need to understand how Deleuze thinks in and about images.

While I cannot provide an introduction to Deleuze here,[5] it is necessary to briefly outline Deleuze's and also Haneke's different thinking about cinema. Both come as autodidacts to cinema, as observers, often willfully ignoring the written and unwritten rules of the game.

The writings of Gilles Deleuze are, contrary to their influence on film theory, not geared towards an analysis or even understanding of film. His two volume work, *Cinema*, is primarily a work of philosophy. However, it seems that the works of both Haneke and Deleuze are aimed at solving problems of representation and movement and that both demand a different way of thinking about cinema, an ethical thinking from the point of view of the image. There are also affinities, as one might call them, that suggest reading one with the other. To begin with, Haneke's favorite films that he listed for the "*Sight & Sound* Top Ten Poll" in 2002 are also those that are prominently featured in Deleuze.[6] On a deeper level, it should be stressed that both refuse the binarism of a mode of "being against something," that is, a simplified dialectics that opposes another concept, such as "Hollywood cinema," even if they construct foils for their thinking. Instead, both thinkers place their texts in different traditions which they evoke and, sometimes playfully, challenge.

As mentioned above, all films by Haneke are ostentatiously framed by the rules of the genre to which they appear to belong, only to undermine the audience's assumptions. The above-mentioned post-9/11 film, *Le temps du loup,* clearly falls into the genre of the post-apocalyptic thriller. After the breakdown of civilization, a mother who lost her husband in an act of unprovoked violence must fight for the survival of her children, roaming a devastated landscape in search of shelter. Instead of the genre-typical showdown between the forces of evil and those who defend humanist principles, Haneke creates a lawless space that is completely emptied of any illusions about the existence of such core values to begin with. Before accusing Haneke of nihilism, as has predictably been done, we need to understand how exactly Haneke's cinema differs from others. Values like individualism, dignity and compassion that, for example, Spielberg's post-apocalyptic *War of the Worlds* promotes, are not what holds a mainstream film together. The point is one of representation as these abstract humanist values are truly embodied by the male hero who reacts to situations that he encounters in a given location and whose reactions drive the plot. For Deleuze, this basic formula is the predominant ideological form of realist cinema which he calls the "action-image" in his first cinema book:

> What constitutes realism is simply this: milieux and modes of behaviour, milieux which actualise and modes of behaviour which embody. The action-image is the relation between the two and all the varieties of this relation.[. . .] The milieu and its forces incurve on themselves, they act on the character, throw him a challenge, and constitute a situation in which he is caught. The character

reacts in his turn (action properly speaking) so as to respond to the situation, to modify the milieu, or his relation with the milieu, with the situation, with other characters. (1986: 141)

The point crucial for our understanding is that Deleuze argues here from the point of view of the image, that is, movement, from the many parts that contribute to the image's meaning, and disregards the narrative that is told by the moving pictures. For Deleuze, the decisive characteristic of "American cinema," as he calls it, is its conception of history, which is a universal history, treating all events and "phenomena," such as affluence and poverty, as a given (149). To put it bluntly, this type of cinema states that it is true that there are rich and poor people. Following Nietzsche, whose concepts of three different types of history Deleuze appropriates, Deleuze recognizes in American cinema three aspects of universal history. First, there is "monumental history," insofar as the stories center on the conflicts of great individuals and their clearly recognizable milieu, that is, the time and place of the story. Second, "antiquarian history," concentrating on "forms," that is, the wars, weapons, and machines typical for that time and place, which it makes accessible by translating them for the present. And, there is a third aspect that brings the first two together in what Deleuze calls "an ensemble," the "ethical judgment" that allows empathy but also a critical distance by allowing the viewer to see the whole, the big picture, so to speak (1986: 149–151).[7] A typical "universal history" about a struggling actress, be it a lighthearted "rag-to-riches" story or a drama about the perils of this profession, would depict the specific milieu that actualizes, indeed, makes present, the heroine's motivations—the small town, her childhood dreams of fame and glamour—and then move on to show the challenges that she encounters and how she reacts to these situations (career opportunities, relationship problems, success and failure, a choice between child and career, etc).

In contrast to this type of cinema, what holds the narration together in Haneke's cinema are not the firm boundaries of a realist text, but the flexible, dynamic and permanently shifting relations of intertexts. As he demonstrates in *Code inconnu*, lives are indeed connected, but there is absolutely no meaning in these connections, the "big picture" never emerges, just as the camera never shows us an event from different angles. In Haneke, maybe because of his experience as a stage director, filmic space is also conceptualized differently, even if the finished film might not look that different from other narrative films that follow "American cinema," to stay with Deleuze's term. I will return to a discussion of Haneke's filmic space in detail in Frame VII, but a scene from *Code inconnu* can serve here as a brief counter-example to the American model. The protagonist, a struggling actress, and her boyfriend, as usual named Anne and Georges, have a quarrel while shopping. Anne asks for advice concerning a little girl that is abused in the apartment next to hers, and Georges refuses to make a choice for her, accusing her of indecisiveness in general. Anne counters by asking Georges what he would do if she told him that she had been expecting his child but had aborted it. The story is not remarkable, as it is already obvious that their relationship is troubled. However, the almost 5-minute long scene is shot in one uninterrupted take, metonymically linking the actions of shopping, i.e., choosing between different products, to the troubled relationship and the topic of choice in general: staying in the relationship or breaking up, having a child or deciding to abort. The form also echoes the first sequence that introduces the film's topics and characters in a long take that lasts more than 9 minutes and stands in contrast to the Hollywood-style drama in which Anne has a leading role. While the scene still happens in a mode of realism—is looks as if it was shot on location with just the typical cold supermarket lighting—two milieux struggle here: on the one hand the couple as members of the well-educated, urban middle class and on the other the cramped space of a supermarket in Paris, preventing any actualization of either set. The modes of behavior also waver between poles, and thus never embody an essential emotion. In "American cinema," the same scene would have been broken up in at least several dozen shots, with point-of-view shots and close-ups, just as the inserted scene from Anne's film suggests. Also, a conflict between milieu and behavior would have been used for comic or dramatic effect, depending on the genre, but never in the way that the conflict is used here, in a very philosophical manner. To stretch the thought experiment further, in a melodrama, Anne's confession would probably have taken the form of an emotional breakdown triggered by her seeing a young woman with a baby, thus leading to a public display of emotions. In any case, it could not have been left open, as in *Code inconnu*, where the viewer never finds out if Anne made up the pregnancy or not, thereby withholding the possibility to judge her.

The above example should serve to alert us to the fact that the only way out of this deadlock—and others like it that constitute the stuff of which Haneke's cinema is made—is to think in terms of a certain kind of movement. The movement is not switching between positions. That is, we should not conceive the movement as weaving in or out, with or against mainstream cinema, but rather as one that encompasses both in an open-ended rapprochement. The emphasis should be placed on the shift that occurs when a frame of reference is opened up. Instead of a "whole" in the sense of a totality that is more than its parts—a universal history—the whole of the text here is a permanently changing effect of frames which never makes a claim to solve conflicts in favor of a higher order—not unlike a kaleidoscope. Further, the introduction of a new frame should not be understood as an addition, but as an unfolding of something that was already there. Of course, from the perspective of the viewer who needs to adjust to the information that this is somebody else's point of view this sudden change in the ontology of the image is experienced as a shift. But from the perspective of the text, the scene was always anchored in a character and the adjustment only unfolds what was hidden but present all along.

The figures of folding and unfolding, although they certainly have a strong metaphoric potential, need to be understood as a movement. A perfect illustration for this would be a classic Hollywood film where actions that are not relevant for the plot are cut. When a person leaves his house to goes to work, an average film shifts immediately from home to workplace, regardless of the means of transportation. Whatever happens in-between, however, is potentially there, only in a folded state—stepping out of the door, crossing the lawn, getting into the car, etc.[8] Unfolding, as Gilles Deleuze states in a book dedicated to the figure of the fold, *Le pli* (*The Fold*),[9] is not opposed to folding, but opens up new perspectives. Playing on the meaning of the word *pli*, French for "fold," Deleuze brings attention to the moment of unfolding what is normally suppressed. To illustrate with the example from above, Haneke unfolds the shopping into an allegory for the couple's relationship. For the cinema of Haneke this means that the unfolding of the im*pli*cit movements, the ex*pli*cation, does not show "the hidden truth of Hollywood cinema," that is, judge from an Archimedean point outside of mainstream cinema. His is a Deleuzian explication, which works on the completely different level of nonessential truth, a truly subjective point of view, limited not only in space but also in time. Instead of presupposing a metaphysical Truth that has to be extracted from the filmic text and to which each reader has a subjective relation, Deleuzian thinking achieves an extremely limited point of view that can give us a unique insight, albeit briefly. This is why Deleuze can talk "of perspectivism as a truth of relativity (and not a relativity of what is true)" (1993: 21). Deleuze elaborates in *The Fold*:

> The point of view is not what varies with the subject [. . .], it is [. . .] to the contrary, the condition in which an eventual subject apprehends a variation (metamorphosis), or: something = x (anamorphosis). For Leibniz, for Nietzsche,

> for William and Henry James, and for Whitehead as well, perspectivism amounts to a relativism, but not the relativism we take for granted. It is not a variation of truth according to the subject, but the condition in which the truth of a variation appears to the subject. This is the very idea of Baroque perspective. (1993: 20)

Deleuze differentiates relativism, that is, the commonly held attitude that everyone possesses an equally-valid personal perspective onto the truth, from the true point of view. Just as there is only one point of view from which we can recognize what a distorted, anamorphic Baroque painting shows, grasping the "truth of a variation" would be to understand what the world looks like from the perspective of—to take an example from Haneke—Eva, in all her incarnations in the cinema of Haneke. Her gazing at the dying fish in *Der siebente Kontinent* understands what she herself might not understand at that moment: that she is an object in her parent's possession. While Hollywood Cinema with its proclivity for innocent children would look at Eva and feel sorry for her, children in Haneke are not innocent. Far from it, they are innocent of the situation—a true shift in perspective.

ANTI-CINEMA AND THE VIEWER

As was pointed out above, Haneke does not operate in a mode of "counter" or "anti," even though his cinema could be described as "counter-cinema," as Catherine Wheatley has done. Wheatley's monograph, *Michael Haneke's Cinema: The Ethic of the Image*, a thorough study of the relationship of Haneke's cinema to its spectator, is based mainly on a distinction between first and second generation modernism.

Closely following Peter Wollen's influential 1972 article—after more than 35 years still a required reading for film students—in which he lists the strategies of counter-cinema, Wheatley situates Haneke's films in the tradition of Anti-Hollywood cinema. It is worth recalling Wollen's taxonomy in detail, which centers on Jean-Luc Godard who "has developed a counter-cinema whose values are counterposed to those of orthodox cinema." By taking, "seven of the values of the old cinema, Hollywood-Mosfilm, as Godard would put it, and contrasting these with their (revolutionary, materialist) counterparts and contraries," Wollen comes up with the following table:

Narrative transitivity	Narrative intransitivity
Identification	Estrangement
Transparency	Foregrounding

Single diegesis	Multiple diegesis
Closure	Aperture
Pleasure	Un-pleasure
Fiction	Reality

(Wollen 1982: 79)

Wollen's description can be directly applied to Haneke. The break with a straightforward narrative is made "to disrupt the emotional spell of the narrative and thus force the spectator, by interrupting the narrative flow, to re-concentrate and re-focus his attention" (81). The estrangement caused by addressing the spectator or other types of mise en abyme "breaks not only the fantasy identification but also the narrative surface" (82). Like the early Godard, Haneke foregrounds the material side of film by inserting black film "as an erasure, a virtual negation," thus destroying the illusion of watching unmediated reality (82). Wollen's next "virtue" concerns the character's diegetic lifeworld which is normally "coherent and integrated," while Haneke often points to the extradiegetic reality. Instead of a text that is closed upon itself, Haneke's films refer to other texts, genres, media. In short, instead of a single vision, we find competing discourses: "The film can no longer be seen as the discourse of a single subject, the film maker/auteur. Just as there are multiplicity of narrative worlds, so too there are a multiplicity of speaking voices" (86). The refusal of transitivity, an easy identification, a pretended transparency and a single diegesis with a clear closure leads to frustration, "un-pleasure" as Wollen has it, and the relation between "film maker and spectator" could be called "sado-masochistic" (88). Finally, anti-cinema makes clear that the film itself is a fiction. Wollen sums up the formula of bourgeois ideology according to Godard as follows: "fiction = acting = lying = deception = representation = illusion = mystification = ideology" (90).

Wheatley modifies Wollen's binary distinctions, arguing that there are two forms of modernism, one where the spectator is made aware of watching a movie, and a second where the spectator's role is in the foreground. As Wheatley elaborates, films that belong to the first generation modernism adhere to Bazin's principles and

> are aimed at restoring realism to the cinematic experience, maintaining continuity editing but doing so in such a way that the spectator is forced to engage rationally with the minutiae of the filmic image. They rely on what I shall term a 'benign' form of reflexivity, which allows the spectator an extended period of time to reflect upon the image and thus distances them from an action on screen. (54)

Here, Wheatley counts especially Haneke's glaciation of feelings-trilogy, with their fragmented and anti-psychological narratives, as indicative for this type of modernism. The second type of modernism, while still using the alienating techniques of the first type, is distinguished by a

> more direct, 'aggressive' approach to the spectator, which is explicitly metatextual. These works can be seen building on Eisensteinian montage techniques, rupturing continuity to jar the spectator into critical awareness. This second group of "aggressively" reflexive films is not concerned with distancing the spectator from the cinematic action, but with emphasizing their proximity to it. That is, where first-generation modernism only calls the spectator's attention to the film, second-generation modernism calls their attention to *themself*. (55)

In Wheatley's understanding, Haneke's French films, here especially *La Pianiste* and *Caché*, are aimed at raising an awareness of the spectator's role in the ideological apparatus of cinema as a passive consumer of images by foregrounding acts of watching and scopophilia (133) and by inducing negative emotions through a frustration of the spectator's expectations (87 and 153).

As Wheatley discusses Haneke's films one by one, she returns repeatedly to this distinction. Even though she never explicitly addresses the point, it appears that the two types of modernism should not be thought in opposition and ought rather to be imagined on a sliding scale. However, there still seems to be a dialectical tension between the two modernisms as Wheatley understands them, and it is here that the weak point of her study becomes clearer. The point of contention is, not surprisingly, *Funny Games*. While Wheatley applauds Haneke's intention to bring the spectator to the point of critically examining the system of narrative cinema, she points out what she considers a serious limitation: Haneke does this from within the system itself, that is, from within the generic framework of classic cinema. Her reasoning is worth quoting at length:

> The rigorous systems of control and the patent audience manipulation that his films demonstrate work at cross-purposes with the film-maker's humanistic intentions to position the spectator morally and to force them to examine the systems of control and manipulation that they so willingly submit to when viewing a mainstream film. In this way, Haneke's brilliance as a manipulator of audiences' responses threatens to undermine the very freedom his film seeks to accord them. (114)

This type of critique, of course, has been brought forth against Haneke on several occasions, especially by American critics who do not take kindly to accusations by a European intellectual of submissiveness to capitalist ideology. To her credit, Wheatley's critique is backed by an argument that tries to plot in the terms of modernism the "patent audience manipulation" that typically elicits critics' knee-jerk emotional reactions.

There are three assumptions that need to be addressed here, since they appear in different form in many critical assessments of Haneke. The first assumption concerns on the notion of counter-cinema. Wollen wrote his article in 1972, mostly basing his case on films from Godard's radical period. As the name of Wollen's concept implies, counter-cinema, as an Anti-Hollywood cinema, is always reactive and as such limited by a negative mode. The critique of Godard that Wollen develops in the final paragraphs shows this misunderstanding:

> The cinema cannot show the truth, or reveal it, because the truth is not out there in the real world, waiting to be photographed. What the cinema can do is produce meanings and meanings can only be plotted, not in relation to some abstract yardstick or criterion of truth, but in relation to other meanings. This is why Godard's objective of promoting a counter-cinema is the right objective. But he is mistaken if he thinks that such a counter-cinema can have an absolute existence. It can only exist in relation to the rest of cinema. Its function is to struggle against the fantasies, ideologies and aesthetic devices of one cinema with its antagonistic fantasies, ideologies and aesthetic devices. (91)

Godard—and Haneke as well—would argue that, indeed, cinema can show a true perspective precisely because the truth is not out there and instead needs to be generated in the filmic text in relation to other texts. This should not be confused with relativism, i.e., the commonly-held attitude that everyone possesses an equally-valid personal truth. Films such as those of Godard and Haneke avoid relativism by openly adopting an allegorical mode, permanently evoking a variety of references and intertexts. As was addressed above, Godard and Haneke create what should be called with Gilles Deleuze a "relativity of perspective" that grasps the truth of a perspective while eschewing the God's eye view of a metaphysical Truth.

It is my contention that Haneke, while certainly admiring the critical impetus of modernism, is aware of the limitations that Wollen mentions and of their proclivity for a Nietzschean *ressentiment*, and that he actively works on overcoming them. I will discuss Haneke's strategies concerning the "perspectival truth" in detail below, but a brief example can illustrate my point. While "orthodox cinema," to borrow Wollen's term, establishes children as symbolic bearers of a transcendent truth—they are innocent, they see through lies, they deserve our compassion—a real counter-cinema would not attempt to disprove this by showing that children are in general deceiving and cunning, or, in a more sophisticated form, show how the image of the innocent child is constructed and used for nefarious purposes.[10] Instead, it attempts to show the perspective of the child, which, though it might be flawed, is truthful. *Caché* clearly makes the point that Georges as a boy really felt threatened by Majid, even though this was objectively speaking not true. Haneke strictly avoids flashbacks and instead localizes the memories of the past events in the grown-up Georges' dreams and thus creates a truthful perspective. This true perspective, in turn, is set against other perspectives that claim to be truthful, for example Georges' and Anne's impressions that they are innocent victims of terrorism. Again, we find here an actualizing movement, a true re-presentation, a "bringing to the present" of a past event that is contrasted with the binarism of Georges' and Anne's world.

The second assumption, and one that seems to be shared by steadily growing scholarship on Haneke, including the *feuilleton*, is that he has "humanistic intentions," as Wheatley declares in the quote above. This assumption needs to be modified, because it implicitly suggests that Haneke promotes a return to values that were destroyed by late capitalism. Indeed, no overview of Haneke's films fails to mention the indictment of consumer culture. Roy Grundmann begins his discussion of Haneke's cinema and the debates surrounding it listing "the director's preeminent thematic concerns" as follows: "the alienation of the individual in the modern world, people's inability to communicate, a loss of the capacity for giving and receiving love, the brutalization of the young, society's constant need for distraction, and the steady rise of violence of the mundane as well as the spectacular kind" (2007: 6). Also, Haneke's methods of frustrating the viewer, for example through false generic leads, the strict avoidance of psychology or open endings, is rightly seen by most critics as a clear indictment of the viewer as consumer of violent images. Then, the recurring themes and the accusation of the viewer are, in turn, interpreted as the aforementioned call for a return to values. Here, however, Haneke's construction of movements that are not bound to teleology or transcendence overcomes exactly the type of thinking that is rooted in a "return to . . . ." Indeed, even though Benny in *Benny's Video*, to give just one example, is clearly the product of a bourgeoisie that embraces consumerism almost to the point of parody (the framed art prints, the stylish kitchen, the video equipment, a communication reduced to clichés, the pyramid scheme, and money instead of affection), the film does not suggest at any point that a return to values might be feasible or even possible, nor does it suggest that this lack of values actually causes Benny to kill the girl. Again, it is important to differentiate between a diagnosis of a problem, something that can be shown, the underlying political structures that fuel the system, something that has to be deduced from the text, and, finally, a strategy to truly overcome those structures by pointing in the direction of a new thinking. I will return to this point later.

The third assumption concerns the narrowness of Wheatley's book and the decisive weakness of other similar analyses of Haneke's cinema. It concerns the critic's position vis-à-vis a film and the refusal to think the image as a movement. A critic facing a Haneke-film from the outside, with an objective, critical stance will not find out very much, because this mode always entails a text's assessment by how well the task at hand is accomplished. As mentioned before, due to his style, Haneke has often been described as a modernist, that is, as somebody who works with the traditional means of expression of modern art in order to criticize the evils of modernity: fragmentation, alienation, senselessness . . . The typical judgment, then, returns not much: a young man runs amok, the film is told in a fragmented style, therefore Haneke is a traditionalist. From the perspective of the outside, this is entirely true. However, Haneke's films suggest a more Nietzschean approach, one that forces the viewer to disregard well-established routines of interpretation and dare to pass a judgment, and it is this that critics have misunderstood or omitted altogether.

In this context, Gilles Deleuze provocatively and unabashedly states that there are "bad" films and that there are "good" films. As is well known, Deleuze locates the decisive aesthetic break for cinema in Italian neorealist cinema (Badiou 2000; Žižek 2004). Deleuze explains in the first pages of his book *Cinema 2: The Time Image*, that, after the Second World War, good films no longer follow the logic of the action-image with its teleological narration. Instead, they are governed by "a principle of indeterminabilty, of indiscernibility: we no longer know what is imaginary or real, physical or mental, in the situation, not because they are confused, but because we do not have to know and there is no longer even a place from which to ask" (Deleuze 1989: 7).

These distinctions, at first glance, appear to be nothing but a more complicated version of David Bordwell's definition of art-cinema, first formulated in 1979 and worth mentioning here so as to grasp the critics' position. In his article "Art Cinema as a Mode of Film Practice," later integrated into a chapter of his influential *Narration in the Fiction Film*, Bordwell states that "art-cinema narration," is characterized by "the episodic format, the goal-bereft protagonist," a "narrow focus complemented by psychological depth," in short: "The marked self-consciousness of art-cinema narration creates both a coherent fabula world and an intermittently present but highly noticeable external authority through which we gain access to it" (1985: 209), a convention which takes "its cues from literary modernism" (1985: 206). While a classic Hollywood film is prone to providing clear answers, "the art film, like early modernist fiction, holds a relativistic notion of truth" (1985: 212). With this assessment, Bordwell seems to differ only slightly from Wollen's account, discussed above. In sum, for Bordwell, art cinema appears to be a genre whose primary characteristic is the creation of ambiguity, a term that he uses repeatedly.

For both, Bordwell and Deleuze, the French director Alain Resnais, famous for *Hiroshima, mon amour* (1959) and *L'année dernière à Marienbad/ Last Year at Marienbad* (1961) provides the prime example for their respective theses. It is useful to mention here their arguments as a way of better understanding Haneke vis-à-vis art-cinema. Bordwell begins his exemplary reading of one of Resnais' films by concentrating on the viewer, who "must draw upon tacit conventions of comprehension characteristic of the art film—objective verisimilitude, expressive realism, overt narrational intervention—in order to construct the fabula and identify the rules unique to this film's narrational work" (213). In other words, the viewer's reading is shaped by the expectations raised by art films in general and other films by Resnais in particular. So far, Bordwell's analysis could still be applied to Haneke's cinema. Ambiguity is a trait of all of the films under discussion here and they certainly embrace the moniker "art-cinema" by topic, film style and casting. Haneke is, without doubt, a "highly noticeable external authority," and the audience, in turn, is expecting certain Haneke trademarks: stylistic austerity, an open ending, modernist themes of alienation and reification . . .

In the last paragraph of his chapter on "Art-Cinema Narration," Bordwell is consistent enough to take his method to its logical end. He has the following to offer as a critique of *L'année dernière à Marienbad*:

> Constructed like a *nouveau roman*, the film solicits comprehension within an art-film frame of reference but goes beyond the limits of that paradigm. The syuzhet is so wrought as to make it impossible to construct a fabula. [. . .] Once there is no longer a fabula to interpret, once we have no stable point of constructing character or causality, ambiguity becomes so pervasive as to be of no consequence. Art-cinema narration self-consciously points to its own

interventions, but the aim is still to tell a discernible story in a certain way. These schemata are of no help when everything in the film may represent both subjective vision and authorial address. (232–233)

Bordwell's assumptions are not surprising and expressed here openly: a text needs some point of stability, otherwise meaning cannot be generated in an intersubjective and valid manner. As in Wollen, we return here to the problem of relativity. A filmic text that criticizes our postmodern predicament is supposed to have—regardless of its stylistic variety—a stable point to which a position of objectivity can be anchored. Otherwise, it would fall into meaningless relativism. Bordwell also admits that the schemata—syuzhet and fabula—are of no help in certain types of texts, and I would reiterate here that Haneke falls into this category.

Turning our attention to Deleuze's reading of *L'année dernière à Marienbad*, which is after the admirable clarity of Bordwell an admittedly difficult task, it is noticeable that Deleuze attempts to think from the (impossible) point of view of the filmic text. Indeed, the crucial difference is that Deleuze, unlike Bordwell, avoids the critic's position itself that allows the establishment of an oppositional definition in the first place. As the quote above shows, Bordwell is still vested in keeping apart the positions of (critical) spectator and text, a model that Deleuze rejects from the start (Deleuze 1989: 2–3). Instead of a descriptive juxtaposition that suggests at least the possibility of a dialectical solution, Deleuze indeed judges a body of film as "good," which he means in a Nietzschean way, insofar as they go beyond good and evil and adequately represent the crisis of (representational) realism. When looking at *L'année dernière à Marienbad* (or a Haneke film for that matter) from the outside, the film's extreme ambiguity must appear confusing. As Deleuze underlines, indiscernibility does not mean confusion (1989: 9). In a *good* film, the "subjective vision and authorial address," that Bordwell mentions converge to the point of indiscernibility, as he also concedes. Deleuze tries to think precisely from this point of indiscernibility, or, to put in other words, to think while keeping it intact. In this sense, Deleuze's project is more ambitious than Bordwell's because Bordwell still wants to hold on to a firm objective position, while Deleuze would deny that a film could be analyzed objectively, because the film replaces its object, as he declares (1989: 7 and 10). To put it bluntly, for Bordwell, a film analyzable in his terms is always about something, while for Deleuze, a good film is on the way to becoming a representation of representation. Deleuze declares that "the essence of cinema—which is not the majority of films—has thought as its higher purpose, nothing but thought and its functioning" (1989: 168).

Here, we return to the above-quoted "base of thinking," the "not-external outside and the not-internal inside," and the paradoxical, twofold question whether Haneke makes accessible, albeit briefly, an outside and how one might account for the viewer's access to it. It appears that the question that guided this inquiry was, indeed, based on the premise of the possibility of an outside position. With Deleuze, we can now determine that perspectivism is a movement towards a true perspective, something that is created mutually by viewer and text, and that such a position is not strictly speaking "outside." It is, rather, a passing by, a recognition after the fact, an intuitiveness inspired by the shifting of a frame of reference that helps us to understand the truth of a perspective.

It should also be noted at this point that Deleuze mentions Artaud as a "forerunner" (Deleuze 1989: 169), a point to which I will turn in the following section.

A Cinema of Cruelty

In 1975, François Truffaut edited articles by André Bazin into a book to which little attention has been paid. Its title, *Cinema of Cruelty*, plays on Antonin Artaud's well-known "theater of cruelty," and here Bazin credits Erich von Stroheim, Hollywood's silent film pioneer, with the invention of a cinema of cruelty (1982: 11). In the short article on Stroheim, originally published in 1949, Bazin admires Stroheim's oeuvre as that of a true *auteur*, that is, "a startling vision of the world seen through a prism colored by consciousness—or rather by the unconscious" (1982: 6). Interlacing his arguments in his usual impressionistic style, Bazin does not treat the films by this Austrian-born director as a singular, timeless text, but points out that these films can only be understood as a new way of narrating that came after Griffith had already revolutionized the way cinema tells stories:

> Stroheim's work appeared to be the negation of all the cinematic values of his time. He will return the cinema to its main function; he will have it relearn how to *show*. He assassinated rhetoric and language so that evidence might triumph; on the ashes of the ellipse and symbol, he will create a cinema of hyperbole and reality. (1982: 8)

With regard to Haneke, two important points emerge here. In claiming a return to cinema's main function, it is Bazin's insight to insist that the cinema of cruelty is not a reaction to mainstream film. First and foremost, the cinema of cruelty is a "post-cinema," insofar as it returns cinema to the essential function of showing movement by eradicating rhetorical devices that imply the transcendence of time, especially the manipulation of time in the form of an ellipsis and the timeless power of symbols. Secondly, this pedagogical labor is inherently cruel—again, it does not react to an established way of telling stories, but kills and exorcises. I invoke this discussion here because it is instrumental for seeing how we might think of Haneke's cinema beyond the counter-cinema paradigm that was the subject of the previous section.

Bazin's main points are directly inspired by Artaud, and as a French intellectual of his generation, he assumes a thorough knowledge of Artaud's concept of a "theater of cruelty." Artaud's ideal theater is indeed decidedly unpsychological, unnarrational, and uneconomical, that is, not an anti-theater that reacts against certain prevalent traditions but a theater that completely abandons psychology and the economy of narration. Looking at Artaud's polemic manifesto program through the lens of Bazin, we begin to see emerging a clear parallel to Haneke's cinema, especially in Artaud's key essay "Mise en scène and Metaphysics." Here, Artaud begins by analyzing, or, better, reading a painting in which he finds "ideas" that are "metaphysical," a "spiritual profundity" that is inseparable from the form and the content. Artaud also sees here, among other things, "an idea about Becoming," an idea about "Fatality."[11] Artaud claims that this is how theater could be, leading to his demand for a "*poésie dans l'espace*," a poetry of and in space (46/232).

The omission of some rhetorical devices, of course, does not automatically mean that a text is essentially different from a commercialized production, as Bazin himself admits. However, here we have to understand Bazin's argument as one concerning the text's realist perspective, that is, as a subjective, but truthful "prism colored by consciousness." In Haneke's case, as has been mentioned above, the outcome might not look very different from classic Hollywood cinema—there are still discernible plot elements, shots, cuts, montage . . . . But unlike a cinema that subordinates these elements to the most economical telling of an event, the cinema of cruelty shows events in their materiality. Here, Bazin states that Stroheim is not interested in narrating an event, but in "the presence in space of simultaneous events and their interdependence on one another—not a logical subordination as with montage, but a physical, sensual, or material event. Stroheim is the creator of a virtually *continuous* cinematic narrative, tending toward permanent integration with all of space" (1982: 10–11). The spectator's position in such a continuous cinematic narrative is therefore limited to the perspective of the event. An example in Haneke's cinema would be the morning routine in *Der siebente Kontinent*. Instead of the neutral telling *of* an event—"a family is getting ready for the day"—the single events (getting up, brushing teeth, getting dressed, eating breakfast) are integrated into a tableau that is comprised of the family's private spaces (bedroom, bathroom, kitchen). The close-ups on the objects of use (the alarm clock, the toothbrush, the food) are framed in such a manner that the spectator is forced to take the true perspective of the objects, creating the truly strange impression that the people are handled by the objects. In other words, what could be a case of "kitchen sink realism" is turned into realism in Bazin's sense.

The most important question for a reading of Haneke—regarding violence in relation to cruelty—remains unanswered in the collection of Bazin's articles. Artaud also does not furnish an easy answer to the questions of cruelty and what that might be in theater or, by extension, what it might mean for cinema, but at least he does not mince words about what makes bad theater: "[A] theater that subordinates *mise en scène* and production—that is, everything that is specifically theatrical—to the text is a theater for idiots, crazies, perverts, grammarians, philistines, anti-poets, and positivists, in short, a theater for Westerners" (50/234). Keeping in mind that Artaud's theater *is* metaphysical, but does not express metaphysical ideas, as Artaud underlines in his "Second Manifesto," the task is to subtly create "temptations" and "drafts of air around these ideas" (107–108/243). The immediate question here is, of course, what does Artaud mean with these cryptic injunctions?

One answer to this question has emerged before in the reading of Deleuze: such a theater of cruelty must be perspectival. Instead of showing *the* truth about a situation, it must lead the audience to a point from which the truth of a perspective can be grasped. This process is painful because it shifts the responsibility for an ethical interpretation onto the audience, but it does not necessarily entail scenes of cruelty.[12] A scene of cruelty might distract from the task at hand and trigger emotions rather than free the affective power necessary in such a shift of perspective. Indeed, creating "drafts of air around ideas" will make sure that the viewer has to actively fill those gaps and blanks left by the conceptual airing-out.

The "temptations" that Artaud mentions seem to be very subtle and depend on the skill of the director. By their nature, these elements are very difficult to pin down; still, insofar as they temporarily create true perspectives they are crucial for the film. One such temptation is the just-mentioned morning routine in *Der siebente Kontinent*, where the impression is created that the objects handle the people. Also, Haneke's skill as a director of actors is well-known. Arguably, actors like Daniel Auteuil and Isabelle Huppert deliver some their best performances, creating deeply-nuanced characters despite the lack of psychological motivations. Other points can be made with less certainty and must remain suggestive "drafts." Here, I just would like to draw attention to doors in Haneke. In a commercially produced film, doors are always part of the action—people enter or leave. In films by Haneke, the often open doorways that sometime frame an action seem to exert a pull—neither do they shut out, nor do they exactly usher in characters entering characters entering. We might credit this to Haneke's experience as a director for the theater, where it is, of course, essential how characters inhabit or occupy the space of the stage, intruding upon it or being swallowed up within it. These drafts, then, would involve the situation or event, and thus on a basic level space and movement, two Deleuzian preoccupations explored by Haneke.

As stated above, the cinema of cruelty is aimed at events in their materiality. A further example will help us to understand in what sense Haneke is cruel, and to elucidate the connection between event and space. His *71 Fragmente einer Chronologie des Zufalls* could justifiably be called an essay on cruelty. Indeed, different spaces are inhabited by their respective form of cruelty, a cruelty that is notably forced by the unwritten rules of the milieu. The embarrassed teller in the bank treats her father like a customer, because she is already in a position of power (she is called to countersign) and does not want to jeopardize her career by acting "unprofessionally." The security guard's wife is cruel to her husband, at first questioning his mumbled declaration of love because it never happened before. The childless couple, of course, acts responsibly by adopting, but they are cruel towards the children that they do not choose. The event that is already announced by the title card at the beginning of the film, the murder-suicide in a bank, however, does not stand out as the cruelest event, but only as the most violent and unmotivated. It is therefore instantly turned into a mediatized event, just as the other violent events that appear on TV are turned into immaterial events.

Against this foil of "news," consisting of clips and sound bites without any deeper analysis, especially the obscene pictures of civilians killed in the Bosnian War that are lined up like game after a hunt, the viewer has to actively arrange the fragments of cruelty into a picture. This is the "*poésie dans l'espace*," demanded by Artaud. Arranging the fragments into "the big picture," must fail, however, as any search for an explanation will lead to nowhere: Why did the student snap? Was it really just the pressure of his rough trainer? Is this a tragedy? This is one of the basic lessons of Haneke and Deleuze: any attempt to grasp a whole, any retrospective "oh, that's what it was!," establishes an onto-theological perspective that they both reject. Instead, the viewer has to acknowledge that the whole is a permanently changing image. To slightly paraphrase the quote by Artaud from above, the viewer is forced to come to terms with ideas of fatality and to create ideas about becoming.

The space where these ideas are acted out, that is, where they move, is still the three-dimensional space of the stage or the potentially existing filmic space. This stage should be understood as a plane of immanence as Deleuze and Guattari describe it. In the above-cited passage from *What Is Philosophy?*, Deleuze and Guattari state that the "supreme act" is not to attempt to think the plane of immanence as an essence but, rather, "to show that it is there, unthought in every plane." In the French text, the word is "*plan*," which, apart from "plane," can mean "plan, outline, map or blueprint." In cinematography, *plan* designates a shot, with the same meaning as in English, the space that is being shown, as well as the duration. With this sense of *plan* in mind taken from Deleuze/Guattari, a shot in Haneke should be described as containing, or being traversed by, the dimension of the "not-external outside and the not-internal inside."

At this point, we might consider how cruelty—deployed by Haneke and conceptualized with Artaud and Deleuze—serves to destroy the cliché, another important concept for film studies and for Deleuze. To do this, I turn again to Deleuze's *Cinema Two* and *Francis Bacon: The Logic of Sensation*. In the book on Bacon, Deleuze concentrates on the figure of the artist. As he explains, the painter does not start out with an empty canvas, but on the contrary, the labor is to clear away all the clichéd images that already surround us: "We are besieged by photographs that are illustrations, by newspapers that are narrations, by cinema-images, by television-images. There are psychic clichés just as there are psychical clichés—ready-made perceptions, memories, phantasms" (2003: 87). While here the cliché is a kind of visual detritus, in *The Time Image*, Deleuze grasps the cliché from the point of view of the viewer, as a quasi-automatic reaction, a trained response to an event.[13] These trained reflexes are hard to break: "We have schemata for turning away when it is too unpleasant, for prompting resignation when it is terrible and for assimilation when it is too beautiful" (1989: 20).

By changing paradigms in this chapter, from anti-cinema to cinema of cruelty, I attempted to simultaneously perform that which I set out wanting to define and explain: the shift in frame of reference. Ultimately this kind of paradigm shift illustrates precisely what is meant by a shift of the frame of reference. At this point in the book, I have shifted the frame of discussion, accounting for characteristics in Haneke and in terms typically employed by criticism (cliché, plan, genre, violence, etc), but from a different stand-point. As a critic, my aim is to renounce trying to give "the big picture" or to account with finality for narrative loose ends or to answer questions from the objective point of view. Instead, the "big picture" becomes a kind of moving, kaleidoscopic image, narrative loose ends are seen as implicated on a different plane, and the myth of the objective point of view is dispelled in favor of a perspectival truth. Indeed, I hope it is clear that I take seriously the idea of the medium thinking itself and allow for the emergence of subjective perspectives with their truths. The latter is precisely what a shift in frame of reference allows us to do, be it with regard to a specific sequence in a film or to broader questions that traverse the entire Haneke oeuvre.

Frame II

A MOVEMENT THROUGH HANEKE'S OEUVRE

The object of this frame is an introduction to Haneke's films as well as a review of scholarship on Haneke, organized around groups of films or specific films presented in chronological order. In the following pages, I move through Haneke's films with a certain critical velocity and with a view to setting up Haneke scholarship as a foil to my argument. I begin with some general remarks about Haneke scholarship, its basic preoccupations and their tenor, which allows us to garner certain critical points to be revisited in detail in the sections that follow. As I indicated in the introductory frame, I introduce a reading that is not opposed to the interpretations that I briefly outline here, but one that takes them as a foil in order to unfold another Haneke, one about whom little has been said.

Looking at Haneke's oeuvre from the typical film critic's or cinema scholar's point of view, recurring topics and a tendency toward coldness are immediately perceptible already to his early critics. He is said to furnish, "an examination of sickness, alienation, suicide, the concept of guilt and suffering, of communication (that is, non-communication) of anti-realistic types of narration, of violence and the representation of violence" (Horwath 1991: 17). Not surprisingly, this account has been repeated elsewhere in comparable form. In *The Guardian* Peter Bradshaw lists Haneke's "classic themes of guilt, denial and violence as the mysterious symptom of mass dysfunction" (2009). Thomas Assheuer, who also edited a volume of interviews with Haneke (Assheuer 2008), writes in the German weekly *Die Zeit*: "All stories are completely different, but all are of identical implacableness. They circle around anxiety and guilt, around forgetting and repression and, above all: around a violence that does not come from the dark, but from brightness, the common" (Assheuer 2009: 58). Roy Grundmann gives a similar interpretation of Haneke's intentions: "His aim is to debunk the desirably normal as the oppressively normative that gives rise to violence and dysfunction in the first place" (2007: 6).

A second point emerges in critical assessments of Haneke—the implication of the viewer. John Wray writes in a feature on Haneke with the witty title "Minister of Fear": "Over the last two decades, the director has developed a reputation for stark, often brutal films that place the viewer—sometimes subtly, sometimes explicitly—in the uncomfortable role of accomplice to the crimes playing out on-screen" (2007). Libby Saxton's concise survey of Haneke's cinema in a recent book dedicated to European auteur directors provides a similar appraisal, pointing to the self-reflexive elements in Haneke: "In recurrently casting their protagonists as spectators, as subjects defined by visually mediated encounters, his films reconfigure self-other relations in terms of ways of looking and viewing practices" (Saxton 2008: 86–87). This point is shared by journalists and scholars, most of whom also remark on Haneke's clear refusal to psychologize his characters. In an article, first published in 1996, Karl Ossenagg observes that we should speak of figures rather than full-fledged characters in Haneke, because they serve for the projection of the viewer's sentiments (2005: 123). While I would agree with the point that Haneke's characters are only figures whose role it is sometimes to serve as foils, it must be emphasized that there is no identification in the normal sense that is taking place. In other words, a viewer can feel *for* the victims in Haneke's films, but he or she does not feel with them, as it is always clear that these are the viewer's own feelings.

This ethical difference might also help to explain a paradox in Haneke's oeuvre, the interesting phenomenon that the actors under his regime deliver some of the best performances of their career and that he is especially successful directing children. Here, Haneke follows his idol Bresson (Haneke 1995/1998), who grasps this difference in two aperçus in his famous *Notes on the Cinematographer*: "*Metteur-en-scène*, director. The point is not to direct someone, but to direct oneself." In the following note, Bresson argues against the use of actors and, instead, propagates "the use of working models, taken from life. BEING (models) instead of SEEMING (actors)" (1997: 14). The French word for director, *metteur-en-scène*, would literally translate to "one who puts onto stage." Bresson's aim is twofold here, and I invoke it as it resonates with Haneke's directorial practice (or praxis even). On one level, he describes the director as an artisan. The director is not someone who tells someone else what to do, but a painter or sculptor who works with a raw material. On another level, the stage as material becomes a plane where truth *is*, not a make-believe situation that communicates the truth to the audience in a sender–receiver model.

Most critics situate Haneke firmly in a European context. According to Richard Combs, Haneke is "working his way towards a definition of himself as a European filmmaker, towards a definition of a new European art cinema" (2002: 28). Roy Grundmann sums up Haneke's main topic: "At the core of Haneke's analysis of European malaise is his interest in the inverse relation between material wealth and social bonds: The more prosperous society becomes, the more tenuous are the ties between people, particularly between parents and their children" (2008). German critics note the same pre-occupation: "The motif of the self-destructing nuclear family is a constant in Haneke's work." This critical appraisal by one of Germany's leading film-critics, while tending to agree with Grundmann's assessment, comes with a caveat. Citing accusations of taking his audience hostage, the critic objects that, "indeed, one can pose the question, whether this dramaturgical cleverness with which 'Funny Games' takes apart the conventions of cinema, is not infected by what it wants to denounce" (Kilb 2002: 48). Amos Vogel, after acknowledging "Haneke's iconoclasm and profound moral seriousness," voices a similar objection:

> "All filmmaking inevitably entails control over the spectator; it is the degree and the kind of control that will vary from filmmaker to filmmaker, from film to film. Haneke's stated intention to have the viewer come to his own insights and explanations presupposes in its purest form, a level playing field that cannot exist" (1996: 75).

While Vogel is certainly correct in pointing out that a work of art can never be a Habermasian exercise in noncoercive communication, we should not forget that the realization happens over time, that is, the viewer will maybe "come to his own insights" after the film is over or in a discussion about the film. It also seems that Vogel overlooked the crucial difference between spectator and viewer—in Haneke, the viewer is educated to critically assess the omniscient spectatorial position that the average film provides. In other words, the film caters to a spectator who languishes in the powerful grasp of two intersecting myths, those of the omniscient director communicating with the full-fledged spectator.

From the traditional perspective of the survey of scholarship and a retrospective of the oeuvre, a type of evolution is noticeable in Haneke's feature films among which I count *Fraulein*, which certainly exceeds the frame of TV-film as a virtual Haneke feature film. With *Fraulein*, as

I show in the next chapter, Frame III, a mode of overcoming is introduced in Haneke's oeuvre. Certain stylistic features, such as the TV news and the "watching with," appear here for the first time and find their way into most of his later films. Already in *Fraulein*, but more so in *Der siebente Kontinent*, a tendency towards a clear structuring principle can be found that Haneke seems to have abandoned later.

This principle—or more precisely, the mode of application of this principle—is obviously inspired by the French and Italian cinema of the fifties to the early seventies. The parallel to other European cinemas is something on which critics have also remarked. I invoke it here as a way of differentiating the mode of application of the principle of structuring that Haneke shares with the European filmmakers from the mode consistently applied by Hollywood cinema. As the brief references above to Steven Spielberg and the comedies of Judd Apatow show, mainstream film, regardless of whether it is about "serious" topics or considered a harmless comedy, is still centered on a kernel, something that gives meaning to the film and introduces a transcending momentum. Spielberg's films, for example, are openly centered around humanist values: "Whoever saves one life, saves the world entire," as the motto for *Schindler's List* (1993) puts it. These values always find a symbolic expression in his films. In *Schindler's List* the coat of the little girl shining red in a pile of clothes in the otherwise black and white film signals her death at the hands of the Nazis and stands for the inhuman nature of the regime. In *Catch Me If You Can* (2002), the pursuing agent is clearly a father figure for Frank, the con-artist, whose troubled family life—symbolized by a glass of spilled milk in a scene with strong oedipal undertones—is to blame for his crimes.

Filmmakers like Jean-Luc Godard, Roberto Rossellini, or Michelangelo Antonioni instead structure the form and content of their films around central but not necessarily dialectically opposed principles, often exploring metaphoric meanings and thereby working in an allegorical mode against the metaphysical kernel of Hollywood cinema. A brief look at two films that Haneke counts amongst the films that influenced him can help to understand my point (Sight & Sound 2002). The young boy in *Germania anno zero/ Germany Year Zero* (Rossellini 1948), without doubt a blueprint for the children in Haneke's films, functions in such an allegorical mode. Clearly, Edmund who killed his own father does not stand as a symbol of innocence; however, as was pointed out above concerning the truth of the perspective, he is innocent of the situation. The film's topic, the moral disorientation after the war, is reflected by a camera that disorients the spectator, avoiding establishing shots and continuity.¹ *L'eclisse* (Antonioni 1962) takes place under different clouds: the mushroom cloud of a possible nuclear war, the fascist past in the form of buildings and, above all, the capitalist gamble. Opposed to these reactionary forces is the heroine whose character, in turn, is allegorized by the wind that is constantly blowing.

Haneke is clearly influenced by those filmmakers, especially the above-mentioned Robert Bresson, whom he praised in an article he wrote for the German conservative daily *Frankfurter Allgemeine Zeitung* in January 1995, crediting him—in a very Deleuzian manner—with inventing "the 'dirty' image" in art house cinema.² While Haneke certainly takes a lot from Bresson—the fragmented narration, the refusal of identification with the characters—he clearly goes beyond his role model by additionally integrating "the fragmentary, subjective concept of Viennese impressionism, the distancing effects of Brechtian theater, and finally, the rejection of the false totality of art that Walter Benjamin saw as a strong contribution to the aesthetic/political aim of fascism" (Dassanowsky 2005: 254). Still, as Stefan Grissemann notes, Haneke stylistic austerity and his avoidance of exposition and lengthy dialogue should also be seen as a reaction to the rather conservative Austrian film at the time (Grissemann 1991: 133).

While opposing forces similar to those in the classic French and Italian films can be found in Haneke's early films—which brought him the moniker "the last modernist"—these conflicts become less and less obvious in Haneke over the course of the years, and need later on to be actively searched for by the viewer. This, as I argue here, is due to Haneke's overcoming of a form/content divide, latent in his modernist phase, which leads to a growing rift between the position of the spectator, a position that becomes increasingly problematic for Haneke and the viewer who has to supply ever more and ever more external knowledge in order to understand what is going on. Again, this should be described as an important shift, as the films become more com*pli*cated, to borrow Deleuze's pun. In other words, the esthetic-political becomes more prominent the more folded the films become. Still, Haneke retains one distinctive stylistic trait from *Fraulein* on: the first sequence establishes a pattern—again, more openly in the early films and folded-in in the later ones– that already contains the entire film and that has been called "synecdochic,"³ but that would be better described as allegorical since it reflects the means of production of meaning conveyed through allegory. All opposing patterns return in the last scene of the film, where they finally merge into one and become image.

Films for Television

Probably due to a lack of availability, the films that Haneke made in the 10 years before Fraulein have received very little critical attention. As practically every German-speaking filmmaker, Haneke started out directing films for television, taking advantage of the relatively generous system of subsidies and the general openness of German and Austrian state television channels to aesthetic innovation.

These films should not be dismissed as early exercises by a late bloomer. On the occasion of a retrospective of early Haneke films organized by the German Goethe Institute in the US, Scott Foundas remarks that these TV-productions are certainly films in their own right (2007). In retrospect, Haneke's films for the small screen clearly show first signs of topics typical for Haneke—the tribulations of middle-class existence, self-destruction, the inability to communicate—and also of Haneke's cinematic style—fragmented narration, lack of psychological motivation, self-referential position of spectatorship. As Andrea Pfandl observes, in films like *Drei Wege zum See* (1976) and *Wer war Edgar Allan?* (1984) Haneke's "clear tendency towards a depletion of narrative continuity, the unity of space and time" follows the model of the French nouveau roman (1996: 205). More importantly, we see here not just an attempt to translate from one medium to another, but to look at the problem that the literary texts attempt to solve. Not coincidentally, both texts deal self-consciously with the topic of a crisis of the self, a well-established, if not ubiquitous literary sub-genre.

Drei Wege zum See consists mostly of medium close-up to medium long shots, from a stationary camera—with just a few long shots, notably, a pan over the mountainous region around the lake and one of the lake itself—and is kept in grey tones, without much contrast. *Drei Wege zum See* features an omniscient voice-over, flashbacks and extradiegetic music—devices that Haneke later abandoned. Notably, this film still provides some psychological clues, especially establishing parallels between the men in the protagonist's life. At times, the same event is shown twice, from different perspectives, or a brief flashback appears suddenly within a flashback. As in his later films, the viewer is forced to deduce plot elements from implicit clues in the film. Some topics appear here that return throughout Haneke's oeuvre: the middle class milieu from which the protagonists break out (here a small town in rural Austria), the signs of modernization and a general feeling of loss and uprooting and problems of representation, especially the presentation of violence.

Ingeborg Bachmann, in "Drei Wege zum See," begins her lengthy short-story directly with a self-referential statement: "On the map of trails for the Kreuzbergl area published by the Klagenfurt board in 1968, ten different trails are listed. [. . .] The origins of this story can be found in topography since the story's author believed in this hiking map." Haneke uses a voiceover to read the lines at the beginning of the film. He also follows the literary source directly in exploring the topography of the main character, Elisabeth, a successful photo-journalist whose midlife crisis is experienced as a crisis of meaning.[4] Haneke remarks in an interview that Bachmann's story already has "a filmic structure, the plot is organized according to associative-dramaturgical aspects" (1995: 12). Both, literary source and adaptation, follow the protagonist through spaces where time is out of joint and that seem to be disconnected from the outside: her childhood home where she is pressed into the role of the unmarried daughter by her ailing father; a hotel in London, where she is stuck for several days; the forest blocking access to the lake; her stylish apartment that she uses to keep her much younger lover; and, finally, the airport where she meets what could have been the love of her life. Those spaces and dwellings "show a sinking into the steadily intensifying lostness of exile," as Birgit Flos writes in her excellent analysis of *Drei Wege zum See* (1991: 168). The windows that appear prominently in many scenes never open to a view, but show dark courtyards and walls. Indeed, all spaces that Elisabeth briefly occupies, especially the transitory spaces of hotel rooms, appear restricting and claustrophobic, but so does the *Heimat*, the *petit-bourgeois* hometown of Klagenfurt.

FIGURE 3 Window to the Soul

Well-established *topoi* are cited and then dismissed in book and film: for example, the forest and the empty path are, of course, a common romantic image for a search for the self—only that in "Drei Wege zum See" the highway that is being built turns all these paths into dead ends. Here, Haneke very cautiously transposes the image from text to screen by drawing attention to the camera work: the forest is made abstract by avoiding establishing shots and by adding overly loud birdsong on the soundtrack. The construction site takes the form of a gaping abyss that suddenly opens at Elisabeth's feet, Haneke having opted not for the customary point-of-view shot, but for a showing of Elisabeth from below and then slowly zooming back until Elisabeth is a tiny figure on top of a vast cliff. When Elisabeth realizes that an old acquaintance whom she accidentally meets at the airport represents what could have been, virtually, another, maybe happier life, the camera jumps 180 degrees, signifying this realization.

The problem that fascinates Haneke is clearly that of the relationship of time and space and their representation in memory, but also the problem of the representation of violence. Different spaces trigger different memories, which in turn are recalled, made present. When the protagonist stumbles and twists her ankle, she remembers that she twisted her ankle after receiving the shocking news that her ex-lover had committed suicide some months before. This, in turn, brings back memories of their troubled relationship, especially his tirades against the hypocrisy of her trade. After claiming that photo-journalists like her are needed to shake up and wake up the complacent citizens of the west, Trotta, her lover, answers: "The only ones who are awake are the ones who can imagine it without your help. Do you believe that you have to photograph those destroyed villages and corpses so that I can imagine war, or those Indian children so I know what hunger is? What kind of stupid presumption is that?"[5] This accusation will resurface almost 25 years later explicitly in *Code inconnu*, where Georges, returning from Bosnia, faces similar questions from a friend. But already the "glaciation of feelings" trilogy—and here especially *71 Fragmente einer Chronologie des Zufalls*, and *Benny's Video*—asked the same question more or less directly. *71 Fragmente einer Chronologie des Zufalls* begins with a long excerpt from the evening news and also ends with the news, and in *Benny's Video*, after being exposed to a litany of atrocities from around the world, the mother asked by her husband "what's new?", answers absentmindedly, "nothing . . ."

The difference is that in the Bachmann-adaptation, closely following the short story, Trotta is literally and metaphorically a very ambiguous character. He plays the role of the world-weary, cynical, and arrogant intellectual to the point of caricature, an *artiste manqué* who lives in a kind of inner exile. The figure of von Trotta is also an openly disclosed intertext to the novel *Radetzkymarsch* (1932) and the related *Die Kapuzinergruft* (1938), Joseph Roth's swan songs to the Austro-Hungarian multinational monarchy. In those novels, as in Bachmann's short story, the Trotta-family of Sipolje, a fictional village in Slovenia, symbolizes the pillars of an obsolete society. The last generation, then, clearly sees the decline of the empire, but is too weak to break the strict rules of the stratified society, not unlike Elisabeth's father and her lover. The attack on the integrity of journalists therefore comes with a caveat, as it is framed by the worldview of the disappointed romantic. In retrospect, then, the late nineteen-seventies, like the end of the Austro-Hungarian empire, appear as the beginning of the end, where, even though it becomes increasingly apparent that the news are nothing more than a spectacle, a journalist could still believe in his or her mission when telling the world about atrocities committed in Vietnam or Algeria. Now, as Haneke seems to point out with even more emphasis in his later films, "the news" on television caters only to our basest instincts.

Wer war Edgar Allan?, filmed about 8 years after the Bachmann-film, is a loose adaptation of Peter Rosei's eponymous novel, first published in 1977. The production-design is noticeably richer than in the other films Haneke made for television. According to Michael Haneke, the film was initially planned for the big screen, but rights for the music he used—a short clip composed by Ennio Morricone from Bernardo Bertolucci's *Novecento/1900* (1976)—made the film prohibitively expensive for a theatrical release (Haneke 1995: 13). This fragment, a haunting, neo-romantic piece, plays repeatedly on the soundtrack, especially during the shots that show the picturesque beauty of Venice. The ostentatious use of this musical fragment seems to be inspired by Jean-Luc Godard's use of a similar sounding piece by Georges Delerue for *Le mépris/Contempt* (1963), his famous adaptation of Alberto Moravia's novel.

Wer war Edgar Allan?, the short novel by the Austrian author Rosei, is a playful examination of many different genres: crime novel, parody of a *Bildungsroman*, confession of youthful sins, travel narrative ... The narrator reconstructs his stay in Venice at a time when he indulged in drugs and increasingly lost connection to reality and where he met Edgar Allan, a mysterious American, who might have been the boss of organized crime in Venice or a figment of the narrator's imagination. While the novel immediately raises doubt about the validity of the narrator's reminiscences, the film begins with a genre reference by evoking the mysterious atmosphere of a "whodunit" with an establishing shot of a police procedure in Venice. Haneke explains that he and Rosei "wanted to turn inside-out a book that is actually set completely in the head, completely inside" (Haneke 1995: 12).[6] Haneke does not use voice-over to render the first-person narration of the source.

Compared to other Haneke films, *Wer war Edgar Allan?* appears relatively conventional. To underline the doppelgänger-motif, the protagonist and Edgar Allen switch places in nearly identical shots of the café where they often meet. A mysterious whistle—a few bars from "Bella Ciao"—can be heard from off-screen on several occasions. A recurrent visual motif of horses, some as statues, some painted, gives a surreal touch but does not provide a key to the mysteries that drive the film: Who was Edgar Allen? And: Does he really exist? There are two notable instances of mise en abyme. What appears to be a travelling point-of-view shot from a gondola shows what appears to be the famous statue of the Four Horses of St. Mark's on a barge. When the camera tracks the departing barge in a 180-degree pan, the main character appears standing in the gondola.[7] In a more memorable scene, the narrator tells the story of Edgar Allan Poe's "Hop-Frog" straight into the camera. While he tells the story, the camera moves back, revealing a large soundstage on which props from the film are scattered: a phone booth, a gondola . . . This mise en abyme, however, appears about half-way through the film, when it is already clear that Edgar Allen might not be a criminal mastermind, or that he might not even exist. Further, the space that opens up to the retracting camera is a theatrical space, not a cinematic one. Symbolizing the protagonist's cluttered state of mind, it does not appear especially shocking.

FIGURE 4 A State of Mind

Rosei's novel works with framing and reframing, drawing on an atemporal network of quotes, references, and loops in order to render the narrator's world. The adaptation emulates this by repeating and rhyming shots and by long travelling shots that establish metonymic connections. Willy Riemer states in his comparison of novel and film: "This technique of establishing connections, though patterned after Rosei's incremented texts, is only partially successful, since it depends too much on the camera for providing necessary links" (2000: 193). Indeed, none of these devices appear again in Haneke's oeuvre, and this type of approach seems to be a path that he later abandoned.

Haneke directed two other films for television between the above-mentioned adaptations. The two-part film *Lemminge/Lemmings* (1979) is a portrayal of Haneke's own generation and the small-town milieu. The first part, *Lemminge, Teil 1 Arkadien/Lemmings, Part 1, Arcadia*, is set in a small town outside of Vienna—Wiener Neustadt, Haneke's hometown. It is "Fall of 1959," as a title card informs us. Violence, the influence of American culture, and the pressures of tradition are the topics of the first part. With Paul Anka's "Lonely Boy" blaring on the soundtrack, we see cars being vandalized. The tone is still lighthearted, with a fanciful shot into a car mirror showing an unsuspecting policeman on a bike, followed by two dark figures running away. The next scene opens on two girls, writing a homework assignment on the fourth commandment: what does it mean to honor your parents? Here, we find for the first time a sign of an allegorization in Haneke, if only in nascent form. We also find misleading clues as to the genre: the grand-bourgeois family is dysfunctional to the point of caricature and Haneke explores their dark and joyless mansion with a camera that suggests Orson Welles and film noir. Still, the film provides its protagonists with a lot more psychological depth than later Haneke films, primarily by vividly portraying them as suffering from the *Zeitgeist* of the late fifties. The patriarchal regime of the Leuwen family, ruled by the handicapped father and supported by a meek mother, severely scars the children, who have the ostentatiously Germanic, that is, Wagnerian, names Sigrid and Sigurd, and who vent their frustrations in petty acts of vandalism. The other members of the loose set of friends to which the children belong render equally well the socio-economic aspects of the town. Indeed, their characters are sketched to the point of being archetypes.

Apart from allegorization, there are other reasons to consider *Lemminge, Teil 1* the first "real" Haneke. "It is a film with the span and depth of a great novel, but the sensory thrall of great cinema—very bold in its use of long takes and punctuated by moments of almost unbearable emotional intensity," as Scott Foundas writes (2007). The topics of suicide, or better, self-destruction and murder-suicide, a general glaciation of feelings, and the malaise of the middle class appear here not just in nascent form. Also, some of the recurring visual motifs are discernible: When Sigurd is caught, he commits suicide in front of his sister, who, in turn, does not appear to be affected at all, just as Georges is not in *Caché*. In some scenes in *Lemminge*, the perspective is closer to a perspectival truth than the omniscient perspective of a traditional filmic narrative. The latter perspective still dominates the portrayal of the relationship of Fritz with his teacher's wife. But when Evi and Christian decide to lose their virginity, Haneke manages to bring out the affect of embarrassment in this potentially ridiculous situation by focusing on the small gestures, avoiding the omniscient perspective.

Lemminge, Teil 2 Verletzungen is set 20 years later, contemporaneous with the time of the film's making. A viewer hoping to find—after the repressed fifties and the supposedly liberating years of the late sixties—self-confident, happy people will be deeply disappointed: even though all of the characters have a career in the first part, they are frustrated and depressed. The hopes of the characters, as well as those the audience had for them, are crushed. The second part of *Lemminge* should be considered Haneke's first Foucauldian film because he pitilessly attacks the institutions of modernity: the priest is a tortured alcoholic, the teacher a helpless weakling, Fritz a nihilistic doctor, Christian a frustrated commissioned office in the army, and the demure Evi is now a reprobate, cheating on her husband . . .

More so than in *Drei Wege zum See* or in *Wer war Edgar Allan?*, the viewer of *Lemminge* receives important information only after the fact. The disclosure that Sigrid's and Sigurd's parents are handicapped because they saved their children's lives comes only at the end of the first part. And a viewer will spend a good deal of the second part trying to figure out who is who, because Haneke does not introduce the grown-up characters at all and did not cast actors who look anything like the young actors from the first part. Compared to most of the films that appeared on German and Austrian state television of that time, Haneke's two-part portrayal of a generation is, of course, outstanding. However, compared to his later films, *Lemminge* suffers from a stylistic mix—the emerging auteur seems to be still caught in the clichés of traditional filmmaking. The most prominent cliché here is the overt oedipal theme. Fritz, who sees a surrogate father in his teacher, sleeps with the teacher's wife. Sigurd masturbates while watching the maid change, but then hits her in a sadomasochistic display of power. The castrating figure of Sigrid and Sigurd's father is still present through his death mask, a mask that the clumsy priest breaks. And the impotent officer, after the botched murder-suicide attempt, has his raised left arm in a cast in a parody of the Hitler salute when he shouts at the recruits while his children silently watch. In his critical assessment of *Lemminge*, Claus Philip rightly claims that Haneke still lacks the sovereignty that distinguishes him later on (1991: 173).

Variation oder "Daß es Utopien gibt weiß ich selber!"/ Variation or "Utopias exist, yes I know" (1983) begins with two allegories, one concerning the viewer, the other the plot. The first is told while the camera shows aerial views of a city. The viewer finds out only later that this is from an interview that Ann conducted of Georg, a progressive teacher. He tells a story about his sister's childhood fears concerning angels that are very large and can even peer through the windows of high buildings. Obviously, this is a parable concerning the position of the spectator, who is invisible and in a position to intrude everywhere. The second allegory uses an intertext. After watching Goethe's play about a man caught between two women, "Stella," Georg agrees that the threesome that the young Goethe had in mind as an ending is a lot more appealing than the double suicide that ends the later version, but he also concedes that this tragic ending is a lot more realistic. His middle-class existence as a teacher who lives with his wife and his sister is shaken up when he meets Anna, the journalist who lives in a relationship with an alcoholic woman, a frustrated actress. As Michael Palm explains in his analysis of *Variation*, the film "receives its melodramatic substance from the tension of a simulation game" that is introduced with the well-known metaphor of life and theater: "Haneke receives his reagent from the logistics of a causal connection of situations and events" (1991: 178). Indeed, the characters appear as mice in the maze that Haneke lays out for them and no character, neither the lovers nor their spurned partners, are portrayed in an especially sympathetic light. Furthermore, Haneke casts very plain looking, middle-aged actors in the roles, dressing them in unglamorous clothes. This is in contrast to the high theatrical and the Hollywood tradition, where only young and beautiful people fall madly in love, and it counterbalances the "melodramatic substance." Haneke works here mostly with medium close-ups, with abrupt shots and countershots to isolate the characters in their frame.

Variation is also Haneke's most light-hearted film as we observe the characters struggling with the rules of the game and their own emotions from a distance. Here, the key scene is surely the meeting on Eva's insistence of all parties involved. Instead of the utopia that Georg hoped for—he still seems to care for his ex-wife—the spurned lovers have fond a new energy and seem to be quite happy alone. At the end of the film, Georg receives Anna's note, telling him that she needs time to think things over. He goes to see Woody Allen's *Annie Hall* (1977), a film that critically examines the genre of the romantic comedy and that might be seen as yet another variation on the related topics of love, relationship and commitment.

Die Rebellion is a short novel by the Austrian journalist and writer Joseph Roth, that appeared first in installments in the summer of 1924 in *Vorwärts* ("Forward"), the newspaper of the Socialist Workers Party of Germany. Roth leads an unsettled life, constantly defying categories of nationality, class, and religion by switching identities throughout his life. Michael Haneke adapted the novel in 1993 for the ORF, the Austrian state television. Haneke's eponymous adaptation begins with documentary footage from the funeral of Austrian emperor Franz Joseph in November 1916 and of World War One, showing soldiers from different nations charging while their respective national anthems are playing in cacophony on the soundtrack. These anthems are important for an understanding of the film: one of the songs that the main character's organ plays is "the National Anthem." At the time the story takes place, this was the old imperial anthem of the Austrian-Hungarian empire, "Gott erhalte Franz den Kaiser" ("God Save Franz the Emperor") by Franz Joseph Haydn. Set to lyrics by August Heinrich Hoffmann von Fallersleben, the melody was appropriated by the German Reich and became "Das Deutschlandlied": "Germany, Germany above all/Above everything in the world . . . ." The melody is used prominently by Haneke throughout the film to suggest a continuity between Austria and Nazi-Germany.

Even though Haneke uses excerpts from the literary source verbatim or only slightly amended for the voice-over narrator, he does not use any explanation of motivations that the novel provides, especially for Andreas' sudden rebellion, a verbal confrontation with a bourgeois gentleman. In the novel, for example, the narrator informs us: "An inexplicable hatred has its way with Andreas. Perhaps it had been in him a long time, buried beneath humility and respect" (Roth 1962: 53, 1999: 62). In Haneke's adaptation, we see Andreas' face in close-up, but he betrays not much emotion. While Andreas gets into a violent altercation in the novel, hitting a conductor, his opponent and even the policemen with his crutch, Haneke's adaptation tones down the physical side of the confrontation. Haneke also completely skips over a sub-plot in the novel that explains—and satirizes—at length the bourgeois gentleman's psychological character.

Instead of these psychological explanations, Haneke mostly manipulates the color. Andreas Pum's dream of a secure postwar existence in form of a small store or as attendant in a park or a museum—images that are shot in bright colors—is destroyed by political upheaval. Later scenes appear especially washed-out and drained of color. During one of his outings as an organ grinder, he attracts the attention of a recently widowed woman. Slowly, but noticeably, the film becomes more and more colorful during the courtship, almost turning into a "real" color film during the protagonist's happier days.

The wedding picture is the last full color picture before Pum's downfall. Haneke uses a common convention here: as soon as the cameraman sets of the flash, a freeze frame indicates that a moment has been preserved in the form of a photography. The frame then fades from color to sepia, foreboding Andreas Pum's death. The following sequence begins with sepia-toned historical footage of a large demonstration, in which Haneke skillfully splices shots of the characters. The rest of the film stays in the same sepia tone, until the last sequence, Andreas Pum's death; his dying vision is again filmed in color.

FIGURE 5 Before the Fall

As Haneke himself points out, the adaptation is an experiment in style:

> In *Rebellion*, I intended to reproduce the process of reading which is fundamentally different than that of film-vision, of "tele-vision." While reading, an image appears in my head, in film it appears first on the screen, thereby cutting into my fantasy. Generally, I attempt in my work, to give the viewer a chance for the type of distanciation that reading allows. My primary concern with the Roth-adaptation was not to lose in the transposing in another medium this possibility of an interaction between the work of art ("Kunstprodukt") and the other recipient. Here, the factor of time is of decisive importance. The reader determines the speed of reading, the director determines that of watching a film. Therefore, the point was—using a *Timing*, befitting language and absolutely atypical for television, by doubling image and sound and other forms of alienation—to create that type of possibility for distanciation for the observer of the screen that is inherent to reading. The images should not block the way to individual fantasy. (Haneke 1995: 13)

However, the novel's key scene, Andreas' rebellion, is told relatively straight forward, raging from medium long shots to medium close-ups and do not leave time for the viewer's fantasy. After the shouting-match between Pum and the gentleman, a conductor quickly takes the side of the gentleman and asks Andreas Pum to leave. He refuses and is dragged out by force, while the other passengers call him "Jew" and "Bolshevik." A policeman is equally unimpressed by Pum and finally takes his organ-grinder-license away. It seems that Haneke solves the aesthetic problem years later in *Code inconnu: Récit incomplet de divers voyages* (2000), where a similar scene abruptly ends after a continuous shot that last over 9 minutes.

Haneke's 1996 adaptation of Franz Kafka's *Das Schloß/ The Castle* is his last work for television, so far. After the success of Haneke's feature films, *Das Schloß nach Franz Kafka* was given a limited theatrical release in Europe.

Haneke follows the plot of Kafka's novel closely, even ending the narration mid-sentence and finishing the film abruptly with the sudden appearance of a white title card: "At this point, Franz Kafka's fragment ends." The film is set in what appears to be a snow covered, stormy German village in the early nineteen fifties. The camera dollies alongside the walking characters, never allowing for an establishing shot, and always staying on one side of the snow covered path. As in other literary adaptations by Haneke, the dialogue is mostly taken verbatim from the source. Equally, the text for a voice-over narrator who fills in background information or replicates what is shown on the screen is taken directly from Kafka. Haneke removes, however, some references to the count, instead mentioning "the castle" as the abstract power that presumably hired K. Here Haneke seems to aim for an allegorical reading, stressing the biopolitical motives in Kafka's novel.

FRAULEIN—EIN DEUTSCHES MELODRAM/FRAULEIN (1986)

As mentioned above, this is the first time in Haneke's oeuvre that fully allegorizes the entire film already in the first scene. *Fraulein*, shot in black and white (with a notable exception), begins with a shot of a billboard, advertising *Baron Münchhausen* with Hans Albers. The announcement "in color" is clearly visible. As the camera swoops down and retracts, the sounds of a fifties doo-wop song and happy banter can be heard. While we see a couple of young people in an American convertible and a German-made three-wheeler, the credits in red appear: "Fraulein—a German melodrama." From the music and the situation, we must assume that this is West Germany in the mid-fifties.

The different intertexts, mostly concerning German film genres as diverse as Nazi propaganda films, fifties kitschy musicals, the Heimatfilm and the German New Wave appear throughout *Fraulein*. An attentive viewer will realize that *Baron Münchhausen*, by Josef von Báky (1943), is a film commissioned by Joseph Goebbels to celebrate the 25th anniversary of Ufa—the largest German studio—and that is was re-released after the war. Hans Albers is, of course, one of Germany's best-known actors. Playing almost exclusively characters who encounter challenging situations but whose heart is always in the right place in mostly action-oriented films, he could be compared to John Wayne. Albers' career began in the early thirties and seamlessly went from being Nazi cinema's biggest star to many roles in West-German cinema and television. Here, Haneke contrasts Hans Albers' character with the title character's husband, Hans—a point to which I return in a detailed analysis in the next chapter.

The black and white film stock and the camera set-ups suggest films of the German New Wave, referring to the early films by Wim Wenders, Werner Herzog and Rainer Werner Fassbinder. Haneke also establishes a strong connection with the *Heimatfilm*, a genre of escapist films that was always a staple of German and Austrian cinema, but that became especially popular after the war. These colorful films are set in bucolic spaces that were spared the destruction of the war. At one point in *Fraulein*, a poster announces the famous *Schwarzwaldmädel* (Hans Deppe

1950) with Sonja Ziemann, the first German post-war Heimatfilm that strongly influenced the genre. At the same time, the very unidyllic life of the film's main character, Johanna, points to the *Antiheimatfilm*, a series of Austrian and German films that portray the countryside as a parochial breeding ground of bigotry.

The complex relations that Haneke establishes with other films allow the mood set by the light-heartedness of the first scene to be replaced later by the melodramatic tone that the film's title announces. *Fraulein* often uses films or the practices of film-going as commentary or even, on occasion, as comic relief. When the family returns after waiting for the father at the train station in vain, he is sitting at the family's cinema under a billboard that announces "Ronald Reagan in *Law and Order*." The film intensifies these self-referential aspects by often showing a movie-screen or the rapt audience watching a film, and, as I will discuss in detail in the next Frame, by establishing an intertextual dialogue with those films. It is not always clear, however, what a specific reference to a film means. In one instance, we see Johanna's daughter crying while watching a 3D projection of *Creature of the Black Lagoon* by Jack Arnold (1954), intercut with her telling her mother that she will marry her American boyfriend and move to the US. Indeed, many film-clips and filmic references that appear in Haneke's films do not fulfill a specific function and their form and content might just be red herrings.[8]

The most important innovation for Haneke is the direct targeting of the spectator's position. Already his two-part *Lemminge* withheld crucial information from the audience, especially concerning the identity of the characters as the story jumps ahead almost 15 years. In *Fraulein*, however, the viewer searches in vain for a stable position as the main character descends into madness. Stability begins to slowly slip away. The film never reveals the exact date and time when the action is taking place. The viewer has to deduce from cars and other information how much time has elapsed. A newsreel about Grace Kelly marrying the Prince of Monaco, for example, dates the closing scenes to April 1956. Most importantly, though, the end of *Fraulein* is also the beginning of an important shift of frame of reference insofar as the film not only suddenly turns to color, but is colored by the film *Baron Münchhausen* that inexplicably appears in color on a TV-screen in a French bar in a framing that suggests that we are watching with the main character.

As this topic will be discussed at length in the next chapter, I will not go into details here.

DER SIEBENTE KONTINENT/ THE SEVENTH CONTINENT (1989)

In *Der siebente Kontinent*, Haneke's first film to be given a theatrical release, the main theme is quite obvious, as blindness and insight are immediately introduced, followed closely by another, related motif, that of showing/not-showing. The latter becomes apparent as the camera refuses to show the protagonists' faces for a considerable length of time. The insertion of black film, signaling the absence of an image and not-seeing, is also immediately noticeable. In this film, the length of the inserts of black is relative to the length of the preceding scene. In later films, for example in *71 Fragmente*, all black inserts have a length of about 2 seconds. As Bernd Rebhandl explains in his perceptive reading of this practice: "The black film negates cinema as a medium of representation, but the former affirms the latter as technique of projection" (2005: 85). Since under certain circumstances black film can serve to affirm cinema rather than just negate it, as Rebhandl suggests, in Haneke the absence of representation signaled by the black film is as important for the film as what must necessarily stay unsaid and unseen in every act of representation.

The father's face can only be seen about 11 minutes into the film, and even then it is barely visible in a long shot. The film's first close-up is granted to Eva when she feigns blindness. The teacher, of course, is blind to the fact that the girl has psychological problems, something that conveniently falls out of her sphere. She orders the girl to open her eyes, because, as she puts it, she needs to see what's wrong. The mother who runs an optician's shop is introduced with an extreme close-up of her eye. Trained only to see medical problems, she examines a customer whose head is fixated in a device. The script of *Der siebente Kontinent* gives the telling instructions: "Overall, the scene has the character of a subtle rape" (Horwath 1991: 58). The customer, unmoved by the examination, prattles on about a cruel joke that he and his friends played years ago in high school on a girl who looked ugly because of her thick glasses. And after Eva's mother finds the newspaper article with the headline "Blind, but never again lonely," she stares out of the window with an empty gaze.

In her astute analysis of allegory in *Der siebente Kontinent*, Eva Kuttenberg states: "The television set and its broadcasts emerge as the optical master allegory; it reliably fills the void, provides companionship throughout life *and* death, and remains the only object 'surviving' its owners" (Kuttenberg 2010: 308). Indeed, all of the film's visual motifs return in the last scene where they finally merge into an important allegory of blindness: the dead Georg is staring at the TV-screen that shows nothing but white noise.

As Kuttenberg remarks, the allegorizing in the film extends to the smallest detail: "Repeated shots of the beautiful fish tank allegorize a largely mute family devoid of personality but quite pleasant to look at" (2010: 293). Kuttenberg's perceptive reading culminates in the following analysis:

> The bizarre family banquet in the partly destroyed home suggests a historic inversion from consumerism to the postwar years in rubble and allegorizes postwar Austrian attitudes of turning one's back against the past. The family enacts the famous Paul Klee painting *Angelus Novus,* turned into a cultural icon by Walter Benjamin, for whom this figure was the angel of history pushed into the future by a fierce storm called progress. (Kuttenberg 2010: 300)

The first part of Kuttenberg's analysis is certainly convincing. The accumulation of goods is the success story of the economic boom of the post-war years. And the destruction of those accoutrements of a middle-class existence in *Der siebente Kontinent* is the opposite of what a liberating act is supposed to be. The famous slogan of the late sixties and early seventies, "Macht kaputt, was Euch kaputt macht" ("Destroy, what destroys you!" from a song by a political rock band), was carried by a sense of liberation of self. Haneke, who seems to be critical of such ideas, pursues this motto to the bitter end—first an inversion, then an implosion of history.

The second part of Kuttenberg's interpretation, the link between Walter Benjamin and Michael Haneke, needs to be amended. While it might be true that the family turns its back on history, both personal and history proper, just as the Austrians did earlier, and that it effects a kind of reversal, saying that it "enacts" the *Angelus novus* doesn't say much about the family's complex relationship to time, especially once the family has crossed the threshold of death, or how time functions in Haneke—all important aspects announced by the very allegory invoked by Kuttenberg. Important for my argument is especially the dead father's gaze and the shot/countershot structure of the last scene, interrupted by images from the film: the animated billboard, the mother, Evi, the fish . . . After both the TV and the father die, the father's gaze is freed as a disembodied gaze that now sees/shows images from the film.

This scene thus not only calls for a more thorough discussion of Benjamin, who is only mentioned in a cursory manner by Kuttenberg, but it can also provide a direction for an understanding of the image in Haneke. Walter Benjamin writes in the famous fifth thesis on the "Philosophy of History": "The true image of the past flits by. The past can be seized only as an image that flashes up at the moment of its recognizability, and is never seen again. [. . .] For it is an irretrievable image of the past which threatens to disappear in any present that does not recognize itself as intended in that image." Perhaps it would be more accurate to say that, in a partial allegory, the family symbolizes the Austrian refusal of the past, but that it simultaneously allegorizes something much richer and more abstract: the loss of an attitude to the past that treats it as alive and answers its moral demands. The father's vision is precisely that which invites such an interpretation. The images of the fish, Eva, the mother that "flit by" for the father's gaze to behold are just such a past, invoked by Benjamin, that here doesn't threaten to, but *is* actively disappearing in a present that embraces death and is the renunciation of everything past and present. The flat, inanimate present of the family's death is, significantly, also a refusal of responsibility and decision-making that the clamoring past always casts our way in the form of an ethical demand that amounts to an injunction to act. Furthermore, to shift the discussion slightly to the practices that Haneke expects of the viewer vis-à-vis the film ethic announced by Benjamin and to come back to the question of the image, the image is not the individual shot that we need to remember, but the very movement of retrieving it and deciding upon its meaning. In other words, what the viewer needs to understand is indeed that he or she is the addressee of this image which is not safely removed in a "past," but demands the responsibility of decisions. I would therefore strongly disagree with interpretations that see these images as a flashback or a type of rewinding (e.g., Horwath 1991: 13). There *must not* be a flashback in Haneke because it implies an all-encompassing perspective, a point to which I will return later.

As mentioned in the introduction, *Der siebente Kontinent* features some devices that Haneke abandoned later. The juxtaposition of high and low—Jennifer Rush's "The Power Of Love" on TV and Alban Berg's violin concerto "To the memory of an angel" as intradiegetic theme— is one of the most noticeable among such devices. Indeed, it seems that this is Haneke's most symbolic theatrical film, with clear-cut similes that do not ask for too much imagination from the viewer. The shot of Evi's dreadful physical education class, framed in a medium shot that shows just the bodies and not the heads, is obviously meant to represent the hurdles that the children have to take later in their educational and life career. As Jörg Metelmann puts it, advancing in one's career "is a type of leapfrogging, some get stuck, others advance quickly" (2003: 72). There are other metaphors, often visual, for example the wriggling fish that die in close-up symbolizing the family. There is also the service department that arrives and declares that it is against the law not to be reachable by telephone—the pun here is that the word "Störung," in the department's name, *Störungsdienst*, literally means disruption, dysfunction or disturbance.

The problem, however, seems to be that these symbols acquire a life of their own. They distract the viewers and steer their interpretation, instead of bringing into relief the moment of making meaning. The carwash, for example, is a space that is symbolically loaded: the cleansing, the life in a bubble, the car—both as sign for the family's financial status as well as the individual traffic and its inherent peril, the de-individualized death on the highway. It is therefore not surprising that the family's suicide has been interpreted symbolically, by the theologian Gerhard Larcher even as "an almost festive attempt of a metaphysical annihilation."[9] Here, Metelmann is absolutely correct to insist in his discussion of Larcher's reading that the family's end is "dirty" and "sordid," "dreckig" and "schäbig," as he puts it, and that "the immanence of the nuclear family's cosmos" does not leave any hope for transcendence (2003: 84). Adding to Metelmann's clear-sighted analysis, I want to stress the Deleuzian aspect of the family's refusal to live by its choices. The nuclear family here—as indeed all the families in Haneke's cinema—acts in bad faith by erecting a bad immanence, a shutting out the outside world in the vain attempt to resurrect what has long been lost in postmodernity: the difference between public and private space.

Coming back to the beginning of the film and the allegory that is presented here, we should not come to the conclusion that the unsaid and unseen is more important than what is immediately accessible. One important refusal to show is apparent in the use of close-ups, a shot that in mainstream-film is conventionally used to show emotions. As Gottfried Schlemmer explains in his short, but fruitful reading of *Der siebente Kontinent*, in Haneke, a close-up does not just show a deadpan face, but, rather, "das *Nichts*," the nothing, the void. Here, as Schlemmer discovers, Haneke also goes a step further than the critical cinema of the sixties and seventies, where close-ups still gained meaning in the context of their situation. In Haneke, gazes and gestures are tied to essentially meaningless acts of consumption (128). It is also important, as Schlemmer notes, that movements in space always cancel each other out—the garage door opens in the morning and closes in the evening (129). In terms of frame of reference, it needs to be added that the audience has to provide this missing context.

Schlemmer, like most critics, forgoes a deeper analysis of the decisive innovation at the heart of Haneke's cinema, the movement. At this point, a return to Deleuze, who fittingly calls the close-up the "affection-image," is necessary. As Deleuze underlines, the affection-image should not be misunderstood as a close-up *of* a face, but indeed as an essential relationship, because "the close-up is the face." Again, only a careful, perspectival reading from the perspective of the image itself can help to understand this paradoxical statement, keeping also in mind, of course, that we are talking about "good" films (Deleuze's example here is Ingmar Bergman's 1966 *Persona*). Contrary to what one could expect, the human face in close-up does stress the characteristics of a person but actually loses the connections to the individual, it becomes abstract. The affect that we can read in this face is therefore not bound to the individual thus filmed. Nevertheless, the face shows an expression. Deleuze elaborates further: "The affect is independent of all determinate space-time; but it is none the less created in a history which produces it as the expressed and the expression of a space or a time, of an epoch or a milieu (this is why the affect is the 'new' and new affects are ceaselessly created, notably by the work of art)" (Deleuze 1986: 99).

This statement will need some unfolding, as affect is crucial for the cinema of Haneke. The first step is to recognize that the human face in close-up is not an abstract, transcendent embodiment of an emotion but that it expresses an affect. This affect in turn is nothing

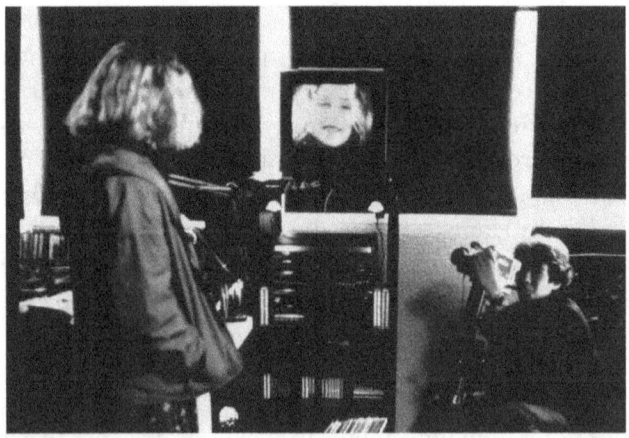

FIGURE 6 The Close-up is the Face (from *Benny's Video*)

personal: when we see Eva's face for the first time, her face does not signify innocence—a bad film would have certainly juxtaposed the teacher's annoyance with the girl's fear, inviting us to identify with the girl because we might remember similar confrontations we had with a teacher. Instead, in this scene, the affect is "the expressed and the expression" of the specific milieu—the run-down school, this part of Austria, the confrontation with the classmates, the overworked teacher, the power structures, the class, the gender . . . in short, the *dispositif*. But this affect is not bound to the specific time and place ("Linz, Austria, 1987," as the title card tells us). The crucial point here is that Eva's face does not betray any emotion that might move the viewer. Instead, the viewer is affected by the image of the little girl face-to-face with the expression of inquisitive authority. In moments like these, Haneke is also very Foucauldian as we witness the affective forces of knowledge and power *in actu*.

At the very end of the film, as I mentioned above, the initial differentiations—seeing/not-seeing, showing/not-showing—converge in the images that appear in Georg's dead gaze onto the dead screen. The movements and forces that we witnessed before come to a standstill. However, there is notably a sustained internal movement of reverse patterns: the more the family empties itself, the more agitated the movement becomes in the picture of the rocky beach that is first seen as a static picture on the billboard next to the car wash and that ends animated, with waves crashing.

FIGURE 7 Dead Gaze in *Benny's Video*

Benny's Video (1992)

Haneke's following film, *Benny's Video*, was released with an English title (the correct German spelling would have been "Bennys Video"), thus alluding to the Hollywood-films that Benny constantly watches. *Benny's Video* again establishes several opposing forces, as well as a stylistic pattern in the first minutes of screen time. *Benny's Video* is also noticeably more complex than his prior films, showing Haneke's mastery of handling several diegetic levels. The first scene already unfolds a complex struggle for authorial authority. As we watch a video of the slaughtering of a pig with a stun gun, shot with a handheld camera that suddenly stops and slowly rewinds, we have to adjust the frame of reference on several different ontological levels: (1) this video is a recording of a prior event, because it is; (2) watched and manipulated by somebody else, and is thus indeed *Benny's* Video; (3) the video-recording is that of a real event—there is obviously no trick involved and a pig was really killed for the film; (4) it was not only killed for the film we are watching, but; (5) the rewinding of the film, resulting in the "resurrection" of the pig, aiming obviously at the moment of death when the bullet enters the pig's head, aestheticizing the killing, and thereby raising ethical questions; (6) finally, the overarching esthetic-political question here is not only who controls *Benny's Video*, but the relationship between reality and the possibility of its representation. In addition to these dizzying, interlocking frames, a second motif is established with the sister's pyramid scheme, capitalism in its worst form, which I discuss in detail in Frame IV. Also, with this new topic, a formal distinction is established: only the video format can serve as the equivalent of a flashback. The video thus actualizes an event that was recorded before.

While the film's topic sometimes appears too obvious, resting on "motives from the bourgeois picture book of moral decline" (Kilb 2005: 70) and containing biblical references (Metelmann 2003: 92–93), it seems to be more a film of transition that already asks from the viewer to reflect on his or her viewing habits and that contains practically all of Haneke's distancing devices. The sudden shift from "looking at" to a "watching with" was already mentioned above and I discuss Benny's flight in/to Egypt below in Frame IV. The film, more so than the films prior, forces the viewer to remember situations, camera angels and phrases. The understanding that Benny's plea to leave the door open that, at the time, made him seem young and vulnerable but was actually a ruse that allowed him to tape his parents' conspiracy requires the viewer to remember the situation. First, we see a video-recording from a dark room. The voices can barely be heard. Only after a while do we realize that this is a recording Benny made in secret of his parents' conversation concerning the girl's body. Suddenly, two louder voices can be heard. After a hand in close-up removes a tape from a video-recorder, the whole meaning becomes clear: Benny was showing his video to the authorities, finally emancipating himself from his parents. As is usual for Haneke, *Benny's Video* does not provide so much a closure, as it closes the topics brought up at the beginning of the film. The ending repeats the struggle for authority and decides it in favor of Benny.

Asked by the policeman why he decided to turn himself and his parents in, Benny answers "So halt . . ." ("'cause so"). Benny's "so halt" echoes the "so halt" that his victim uttered shortly before he killed her and makes this phrase appear as a haunting memory. This memory is set against another ghostly repetition, the real killing of a pig, just as the killing of the father in *Le temps du loup* is set against the real killing of a horse in and for this film. Haneke subsequently follows this pattern throughout *Benny's Video* and in other films too: as soon as something "real" is represented, it is reproduced in another format. The atrocities that take place in another country are immediately mediatized.

71 Fragmente einer Chronologie des Zufalls/71 Fragments of a Chronology of Chance (1994)

The third and last installment in Haneke's glaciation trilogy begins with an inter-title telling us matter-of-factly that on December 23, 1993, the 19-year-old Maximilian B. shot 3 people in a bank and then himself. This title card is followed by a clip from a TV-News and the inter-title "12 Oct. 1993." As the first few minutes indicate, this film explores questions of space, that is, continuity and contiguity in real space as well as in the fake space of the media. The clip, in this case, a short report on the war in Bosnia and an incident in Haiti, links the geographical locations in a metonymic manner as it connects the fragmented space and unfolds it in its bad virtual reality, a point I address below in Frame IV. As a countermovement, we experience more than we see the illegal intrusion into the national space of a young Romanian boy that Haneke films in the dark and, for the first minutes, without a countershot— a xenophobe's nightmare of the penetration of "our" territory. While the film explores a plethora of symptoms of our postmodern condition, the new achievement in this film is an allegorization of space.

Or, to be precise, it is a juxtaposition of the two above-mentioned movements of metonymy and penetration in the space of allegory.

Haneke's first move is to work against the cliché of assigning a meaning to the individual fragments. Instead, as I have mentioned above, he explores the essential biopolitical cruelty of every space—the bank, the dinner table, the subway station, the orphanage, the dorm—thus lifting these typical spaces to the status of an allegory. Deleuze calls this type of space *espace quelconque*, "any space whatever," as it has been translated, because the space depicted could indeed be "any space." There is always the danger, though, that such a space is read symbolically as standing for something, for example, the bank as sign for the loss of genuine human interaction and its replacement with money. While such an interpretation is not wrong per se, it severely limits the political impact of Haneke's analysis because it limits the *allegorical* power of the space conveyed by its being a blank, *any* space whatever. This replaces Haneke's political impact with the mode of a "return-to" something, for which—it needs to be stressed again—there is no evidence at all in Haneke's films.

As always with Haneke, we need to pay attention to the details in order to understand how these spaces are built. Philip Brophy, for example, draws attention to the sound design: "Throughout *71 Fragments*, characters are acoustically framed by a mix of omniphonic and telescopic sound: irrespective of visual cropping, we audit the totality of their space—shunting trams, droning freeways, congested arcades, emptied parklands" (2006: 16). Another example would be the scene where the girl grabs the anorak and hides in the bathroom. There is an abstract quality to this shot, with large, black spaces framing the girl so that she appears more like an expressionist painting—not a disturbed girl who is desperate that somebody might take this prized possession away, but the affect of despair. These spaces are constructed, not given.

When such an "any space whatever" is constructed, the next move can take place: reterritorialization, to borrow a term from Deleuze. Here, the example of the Romanian boy is instructive. He cleverly uses the space of the subway station to whatever purpose suits him. If the station comes with the designation to be any station, it seems that the boy is changing the caption: this is a library, supermarket, playground! To extrapolate a bit, the media has a similar effect on the events that it mediatizes, and there is a danger that derives from this de- and re-territorializing power of the media. The violent even that touches the people "that were at the wrong place at the wrong time," is immediately

FIGURE 8 The "Any Space Whatever" (from *Der siebente Kontinent*)

mediatized and turned into an "any event whatever." The only contiguity is the continuity of the news, a space where the trials and tribulations of a washed-out pop star are as important as the killing of three people in a bank or a few civilians killed in a war in another country. A clear example here is an extremely unusual shot that draws attention to itself, especially after only showing the shooter and not his victims: when the student leaves the bank, the camera shows him briefly directly from above. This bird's eye view signals that this event can only be witnessed from the outside. Rendering this event with the bird's eye perspective is at once an acknowledgment of the power of the media as well as Haneke's refusal to mediatize the event depicted. Haneke returns to this shot repeatedly in *La Pianiste*, showing just the keys and the hands from above.

FUNNY GAMES (1997) AND *FUNNY GAMES U.S.* (2007)

Funny Games, in both its incarnations, is foremost a scandalous film. The controversial (mis-)understanding of the film as one that celebrates violence is something that is anticipated by the film and built into it before its release. Designed to create, and indeed having caused a scandal at the festival at Cannes where Wim Wenders famously left the screening, it is certainly Haneke's most controversial and formalistic film. Michel Cieutat, whose clear-sighted analysis of the first *Funny*

Games was included in a collection dedicated to "50 films that created a scandal" (*50 films qui ont fait scandale*), covers both aspects. As Cieutat writes, the fear of being confronted with "insupportable scenes," is strong, so that some viewers might overlook the film's goal: "to denounce the often-used attraction for the staging of the spectacle of violence (*la 'mise en spectacle' de la violence*)." The construction of *Funny Games*—the "constant mise en abyme," as Cieutat writes—makes it impossible for the spectator to safely identify with only the victims, but forces him or her to "attempt to anticipate the frame of the plot and thus to project oneself into the psyche (*esprit*) of the criminals" (2002: 204).

For Thomas Assheuer, the scandal at the heart of our culture is the completely reified modern subject. As he writes in an early review of the film, before the slaughter of the family at the hands of the killers, to whom he attributes "fascistic neutrality," comes the "death of imagination, the withering of human fantasy in the memory of language, a deadly process in the depth of com-passion (*Mit-Leidenschaft*) and emotion" (2007). Assheuer is careful not to confuse Haneke's denunciation of postmodern relativism with a call for a return to a time where family values supposedly still existed. More than just middle-class conventions, these are "social myths" as Gabriele Wurmitzer calls them, calling attention, for example, to the myth that politeness, safety and criminality arise entwined among the underprivileged (2010) Indeed, the "language games" expressed through the "rules of polite conversation" are corrupt and empty (Metelmann 2003: 135) because they are corrupted by the "brutal competition" of capitalism as Benjamin Schacht writes.[10]

The reviews concerning both versions of *Funny Games* show an interesting pattern, with European critics engaging *Funny Games* on its own terrain and British and American Critics harping on Haneke's supposedly condescending attitude towards his audience. Even a critic as seasoned as Mark Kermode, for example, dismisses both versions as empty exercises (see Kermode 1998, 2008) and Anthony Lane in *The New Yorker*, feels "patronized" and not so subtly suggests that the film is actually a call for vigilante justice (2008: 92). In *Film Comment*, Nathan Lee seems to share the same feelings when he concludes his review of *Funny Games U.S.* with the following assessment: "*Funny Games* is *Hostel* for the NPR set, a prolonged joke in the best possible taste" (2008: 28). It seems that many Anglo-Saxon film critics were not able to follow the shift, or better, the rift that Haneke opens up between spectator and viewer that Cieutat and Assheuer attempt to grasp.[11]

The classic pattern of spectator-identification implicitly asks that we accept the victim's point-of-view. In *Funny Games*, this does not work; on the contrary, we need to identify with the torturer, a shift in perspective to which the European viewer might be more used. This, I think, is the source of the negative reception and rejection in America as opposed to the studied consideration by European critics. Concerning the strong negative emotions that Haneke elicits, I would also venture to say that Haneke's accusations are leveled against the ideal-ego of the "chattering classes" to whom journalists and scholars belong as liberal, educated and embracing multiculturalism. To stay with the Freudian/Lacanian framework, it could be said that Haneke's films operate from the perspective of the "ego-ideal," allowing the middle-class subject to look at itself, showing its repulsive side, thereby causing guilt and an aggressive reaction. Haneke is making a class provocation, invoking precisely the viewers who would not go see his films as a way of subtly underlining their class, which is not that of the typical Haneke viewer. Further, he is, in an opposite move, bridging that gap by suggesting that the typical viewer is just as complacent about violence, just as unreflected, as the consumer of cheap thrills.

LA PIANISTE/THE PIANO TEACHER (2001)

The film begins with an entrance onto a scene: the door opens and Erika quietly steps into the dark apartment, where, at first, only the babble of the television greets her. Immediately, she is interpellated: "Bonsoir, ma fille!" ("Good evening my daughter!"). What follows is a well-rehearsed theatrical ritual, a theater of cruelty. Erika bought a dress, her mother tears it up, Erika attacks her physically, and tearfully they make up. In her review of the 2001 Cannes festival, where Isabelle Huppert was unanimously awarded the prize for "Best Actress" and Michael Haneke received the "Grand Prize of the Jury," Manohla Dargis succinctly sums up Erika's farcical existence: "Erika, trained to become a concert pianist, condemned to teach those for whom she feels contempt, lives alone with her mother, a harridan who is at once her jailer, her only family, her single friend. The pair even sleep in the same room, side by side like husband and wife, twinned corpses fast on the rot" (2001). For the rest of the film, the piano teacher will in vain try to direct the play that is her life, caught between two extremes, that of the performer and that of the voyeur: "The characters of this film live in the nowhere, in the overstuffed or whitewashed nothing, in spaces, in which *one sees* (video cabin, drive-in cinema), or those in which *one is seen* (concert stage, music room)" (Grissemann 2001: 18).

Even though the film leaves out some important plotlines of the novel on which it is based, it should still be considered a congenial adaptation of Jelinek's text. In his comparison of literary original and filmic adaptation, Willy Riemer points out several interesting transpositions that Haneke undertook. Instead of using flashbacks to fill in the audience on the back story of Erika Kohut's youth, her past and several female students of Erika's are combined into the character of Anna Schober: "Kohut's childhood experiences are not remembered, but demonstrated with Anna" (Riemer 2007: 274). Other changes concern the location:

> Instead of Kohut's voyeuristic pursuit of sexual experience in the meadows of the Prater, Haneke relocates the sequence to one of the few remaining drive-ins in Vienna. At the peep show Kohut does not watch women exposing themselves (as in the novel), but rather videos of hardcore. With this change by Haneke, the exposition of Kohut's perversion is combined with a critique of media culture wherein the media replace real life. (Riemer 2007: 273)

While Riemer is right in pointing out these changes as an indictment of a culture that deals in obscene images at the expense of the "real," a point that he omits is the modus of choice. In the sex shop, Erika has to pick one out of several performances offered. She picks the one that could be described as the most phallocentric, where a woman lying backwards on a table orally stimulates a man. At one point, the action is filmed from above, mimicking the signature shot of *La Pianiste*, the bird's eye view onto the piano keys with just the hands visible. The extreme angle of these shots—already adopted in *71 Fragmente*—draws attention to itself by distorting the perspective. It seems, then, that Haneke assigns the character of an event to both, equating the real music (this is obviously a real performance) with real sex (this is really a pornographic clip).

Erika's reaction to the real of music and sex seems to be a real perversion, a "*père-version*" ("father-version") as Lacan's famous pun suggests. "Dressed in a trenchcoat with tan kidskin gloves, her costume evokes the proverbial pervert," observes Harriet Wrye (2005: 1208). However, Erika does not simply adopt this position in order to take on an unnatural sexuality. In the incestuous family relationship—a matriarchal nightmare—the daughter does not replace the father in the mother's bed, but rather seems to fuse with him, a point that the novel

FIGURE 9 *La Pianiste* – bird's eye view

Die Klavierspielerin makes. In a detailed description of the novel's many intertexts, Karl Ivan Solibakke writes that in Jelinek's novel, "the politics of gendering becomes a critical issue when mother and daughter adopt a lifestyle that is an unstable mimesis of the patriarchal structure found in modern capitalist societies" (2007: 252). Another way to put this is to say Erika Kohut is the breadwinner and master of the phallic instrument; consequently, she sleeps in the marital bed, replacing her impotent, mad father, at one point even trying to rape her mother. The supplanting through fusion with the position of the father leads to her inability to script her own life because she never entered the symbolic order.

Jean Wyatt states in her excellent article that in the Kohut's "domestic interior, no third figure, no representative of the social/symbolic order, no law exists that would afford protection against maternal jouissance" (2006: 456). Jouissance, as Wyatt explains, is static, while desire is constantly on the move, searching for satisfaction to no avail. For Wyatt, this difference finds its emblematic expression in the first encounter of Erika and Walter Klemmer, when Erika and her mother build a petrified dyad in the cage of the elevator, while the athletic Klemmer runs up the stairs. All attempts by Erika to escape the dyad by forceful "expulsion" of the "maternal object" by cutting it or by throwing herself into a relationship must fail, because she is completely caught in the maternal jouissance, "the antithesis of romantic love, which is of course based on the belief that only the beloved can complete the self" (Wyatt 2006: 469).

The maternal jouissance manifests itself in a subversive displacement of meaning. The pornographic representation of the real, the money shot, is turned into vomiting. Catherine Wheatley observes: "The 'money shot' here becomes something disgusting and obscene, not a moment of satisfaction, but a moment of repulsion and rejection" (2010: 347). Here Wrye is correct in pointing to the many motivations that lie behind the teacher's act of violence against her student Anna (2005: 1208). There is definitely more at stake than just the "lust for revenge" that Grissemann sees in her actions (2001: 20). Jealousy is certainly a factor, but Erika might also act under orders of her mother, who told her that nobody must be better than her at Schubert. Judging by her reactions to the visit of Anna's mother, monstrous just like hers, Erika is also aware that she spared the young girl a fate similar to her own.

The film also addresses the problems of obscenity and censorship. As Wheatley points out, Walter's black clothing and large frame both resemble and effectively act as the black rectangles that censors often place over genitalia in film, blocking out the act so that we cannot see either her arms or his penis (Wheatley 2010: 346). This inclusion of a sequence that effectively 'pre-censors' itself serves a purpose in Haneke's commentary concerning censorship, and more broadly, obscenity vis-à-vis moral codes. The scene foregrounds obscenity in a programmatic way. Ending her analysis, Wheatley writes, "What is truly obscene about *La Pianiste* is not that it offends accepted sexual morality, but that by foregrounding the ob-scene—by way of its linguistic derivation, that which can't, or shouldn't, be seen—the film leads the spectator to ask whether "accepted" sexual morality itself is offensive" (Wheatley 2010: 353).

The meaning of the ending—Erika walks out of the frame after her symbolic self-castration—brings up the question of the problem that Haneke attempted to solve with this film. Judging by the first scene, *La Pianiste* is a movement through the psycho-sexual state of a character without falling into the explanatory mode of psychologizing. Instead, the character's mindset is unfolded as a stage where everything is performance of the thwarted forces of desire.

Le temps du loup/The Time of the Wolf (2003)

Apart from mostly neutral reviews and a few scholarly articles, this film has generated the least interest, despite its star cast. As mentioned, it follows the genre of the post-apocalyptic thriller, without, of course, the leader/hero that customarily appears on the scene to save humanity. Notably, it is the only feature film by Haneke that does not show a television set displaying the news of armed conflicts from around the world because Central-Europe, normally on the receiving end of catastrophic news, has become a war-zone, due to some unknown catastrophe, and a source of such news. In Saxton's assessment, *Le temps du loup* is "Haneke's most concerted attempt to date to confront us with the material realities of the distant catastrophes that we in the western world are accustomed to witnessing only on the small screen" (2008: 100).

Again, the beginning encapsulates the aesthetic devices of the entire film. The first shot shows a minivan approaching through a peaceful, wooded area towards the slowly retracting camera. The framing, the retracting camera and the deep focus shot suggest not tragedy, but a car-commercial. Stepping inside a dark cabin, the family finds an armed squatter who shoots the father point blank. As in all Haneke films, the brutal killing is shown as an echo, an effect on somebody and not as a deed by somebody: the children turning their heads and Isabelle Huppert's character wiping her husband's blood off her face before she throws up. The next scene shows the mother and her two children alone on an empty street, without any information regarding how much time has passed.

As all other films by Haneke, *Le temps du loup* has a striking visual leitmotif. Whenever Eva asks her mother for advice, the mother just stares at her, her face betraying no emotion. For the viewer, who cannot help but to identify with Eva, the film's only full-fledged character, this film is arguably one of Haneke's most punishing films: when the

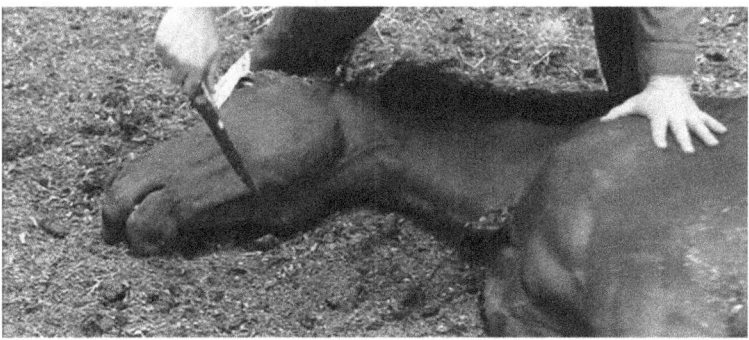

FIGURE 10 Real Blood

father's killer arrives at the compound and an ensuing shouting match promises a cathartic confrontation, Haneke suddenly cuts to the slaughter of a horse that takes place nearby. The killing of an animal— the horse is shot, then its jugular vein cut—is clearly not a trick. Here, Haneke seems to employ a metonymic and metaphoric displacement by which the viewer's thirst for fictional blood is answered by real blood.

CODE INCONNU: RÉCIT INCOMPLET DE DIVERS VOYAGES/ CODE UNKNOWN (2000)

The full title translates to: "*Code Unknown: Incomplete Tales of Several Journeys.*" Like, *72 Fragmente*, the film consists of loose fragments (in this case, 39 plus a prologue and an epilogue). That is, there are no sequences in the traditional sense. The scenes are shot in one continuous take (with four notable exceptions). The most outstanding long take here is the more than 9-minute long sequence shot right after the brief charade of the deaf-mute children, an incredible technical feat that draws attention to itself. Each facet ends as abruptly as it begins and is separated by black screen that lasts approximately 1 second, so that we cannot technically speak of jump cuts. Most "tales" do not provide crucial information until mid-scene or can only be understood in retrospect, demanding considerable powers of concentration from the audience.

Indeed, *Code inconnu* is the film that shows Haneke's reflected view of the middle class best, as I pointed out above concerning the figure of Maria, the Romanian beggar. As in his other films, some of the protagonists move from the countryside to a big city. Anne, around whom the majority of the film is centered, is dating Georges. While Georges chose the dangerous and certainly also glamorous profession of war photographer, his younger brother, Jean, is trying to break free from the influence of their father, who wants Jean to take over the family farm. The beginning of the film's action consists of the complex tracking-shot, which was mentioned above, where the tangled mixture of racism, class and sexism are introduced. Jean's double and antagonist is Amadou, a second generation immigrant who chose a job in social services as teacher in a school for deaf-mute children. Amadou's father, who like Jean's remains nameless in the film, is an African immigrant working as a cab driver. While Jean's petulant manners point to an arrested development, Amadou emotional reactions to real or perceived injustice are probably due to his experience growing up as a member of a minority. Notably (and contrary to Haneke's often-cited anti-psychological stance), the motivations of all characters can be explained. It is, for example, only natural for Anne to take Jean's side in the quarrel because she knows him. However, both fathers stay absolutely empty characters.

CACHÉ (2005)

If *Le temps du loup* is Haneke's least discussed film, *Caché* is certainly the film that generated the most scholarly responses, and the film that most openly invites the theoretical scrutiny. Since I return to *Caché* several times in this book, I limit myself here mostly to the review of scholarship. The film, as reviewers immediately noticed, evokes the genre of mystery thriller and disappoints viewers, refusing the resolution that the average "whodunit" normally provides. The title, *Caché* or "hidden," hints at hidden secrets that need to be brought to light, and most commentators also point to the puns involved, since the homonym *cachet* can mean tablet (as in the sleeping tablets that Georges takes at the end), as well as official seal; *avoir du cachet* means "to have clout," an obvious comment on the Laurents' lifestyle. All these genre markers steer the viewer to expect a mystery thriller, in the line of films by Claude Chabrol, who also often uses puns and a self-conscious style and whose films often focus on the hidden crimes of the bourgeoisie.[12] Paul Arthur comments: "As in previous films, the director's manipulation of genre expectations—a twisting of formula that never stoops to parody or quotation—redirects the hermeneutic energies of the thriller inward toward the protagonist's flimsy identity and outward to his enveloping social context" (2005: 26). This social context is, at least at a first glance, contemporary French society and its problems with racial integration. Credited with uncanny prophetic powers after riots erupted in the fall of 2005 in the dilapidated housing projects surrounding Paris, *Caché* has been framed in the discourses of postcolonialism as a signaling of the return of the repressed via the very representation of the other that was meant to block it out. Ranjana Khanna, in a special issue of *Screen* dedicated to *Caché*, concludes that *Caché* "is ultimately a film about anxiety in relation to a history of colonial violence and the technology associated with it" (2007: 243).

Max Silverman, in the same issue of *Screen*, reads the film with Frantz Fanon, stating, "In the postmodern climate of contemporary France, the device *par excellence* for screening out the real is the image" (2007: 247).

The image as Haneke constructs it is perhaps most intriguing as a filmic device. Haneke famously shot *Caché* in a high definition digital format that erases difference between the film's diegetic world and its recording by the surveillance camera, hence the confusion of the last scene that makes two mutually exclusive readings possible. As in the case with the ending of *Der siebente Kontinent*, two frames of reference not only overlap each other, but intrude into each other's ontological level. In Martine Beugnet's words, this intrusion is "the inscription of trauma, via the video image, in the body of the film itself" (2007: 228). In this sense, *Caché* might be the solution to a problem that occupied Haneke since the beginning of his filmic career: how to express the violence inherent in every representation regardless of its content.

In *Caché*, Haneke deliberately invites comparisons with his prior films. Georges' mother is played by Annie Girardot, who gives a memorable performance as monstrous mother in *La Pianiste*. The shift from "watching" to "watching with," of course, echoes the beginning of *Benny's Video*. And the background noise of the television, ignored by the characters and displaying images of news footage and other entertainment, appears in most of his films. But the casting of Juliette Binoche, who is shot here in a similar manner as in *Code inconnu*, might be the most obvious reference and clearly influences our judgment of her character in *Caché*. Accused by her son, Pierrot, of having an affair with Pierre, she denies it. Her character's flirting in *Code inconnu* points to the possibility that she is lying, making us suspicious of her in *Caché* as well.

The upper-middle-class couple, Anne and Georges, does not live in a gated community as their doubles in *Funny Games* do, but their house, armed against intrusion from the outside, appears like a prison. Elizabeth Ezra and Jane Sillars point out that "the composition of shots of its exterior puts its vertical barred windows centre frame; horizontal bars cut across shots; the iron gate clangs." Ezra and Sillars continue this analogy, remarking that "Georges's and Anne's grey, shapeless clothes are reminiscent of prison uniforms and have nothing of the chic glamour of outfits worn by French characters of their milieu in countless other contemporary films" (2007: 216). Giuseppe Mecchia notices that the Laurent's are "slightly worn out in their appearance, and all in all unglamorous in their baggy clothes and slightly overweight bodies, but fundamentally at ease with themselves and their life" (2007: 137). This comfortable life, as I have remarked above in the introduction, is the very incarnation of a middle-class dream, with a tastefully decorated house full of books and enough space to entertain their racially diverse and similarly cultured friends. They also both work in well-paying, creative, fulfilling jobs—Georges is outright famous, Anne's boss is "a friend," which makes for a pleasant work environment and job security. Indeed, the Laurent's would be the poster couple for a marketing effort promoting culture: Anne is an editor and Georges the host of a show that discusses new books. Under the gaze of Haneke's camera, this utopia begins to appear as a façade, and the work of the characters in the domain of culture increasingly takes on the tinge of the commoditization of culture. As many reviewers remarked, the living room with its rows of books looks just like the studio with the fake book spines. Only another image can access this flat, sterile environment and contaminate it, forcing Georges to leave his island in search of the origin of these dirty images. Indeed, as Sureyyya Evren notes: "Throughout the film, George is forced to enter the realm with which he does not want to have any kind of direct contact or contiguity" (2005: 445). In other words, he is confronted with the realm of the other.

As always, the perceived source of violence is the other. Confronted with the footage from his first visit at Majid's that shows him as the aggressor, Georges presents himself, in a telling re-presentation, not only as a simple victim to his boss, but as a victim of terror ("terreur"), a term that sounds ominous after 9/11. Here, Georges exerts damage control by reframing the threatening videos as a reaction to an unprovoked violent action. Florence Jacobowitz perceives Georges' motivation as follows: "Georges has no control over the illicit videotapes and, unlike his television program, cannot mediate or filter what is represented, thus his power is threatened" (2006: 62). This control over the meaning of images is at the heart of *Caché*. The censorship extends to friends, as the dinner party shows. An absent friend who is sick and needs an operation is dismissed as somebody with whom they were "never that close," for the benefit of her husband, now dating a girl named Marianne and present at the dinner. The Marianne of French national lore is, of course, the emblem of the French republic, representing universal values of freedom and tolerance, values that, as Ezra and Sillars remind us, are invariably trotted out in the course of public discussions regarding the cultural difference of citizens from the former colonies (2007: 217).

In the context of the battle over images, the talk show that Georges edits, or censors, for easier consumption is especially important.

Immediately preceding the key scene of *Caché*, Majid's suicide, Georges' drive for mastery over the image is introduced with a shift—what appears to be live footage from the show stops suddenly in a freeze frame, with Georges' voice heard, complaining that this is "too theoretical." The topic is Arthur Rimbaud—France's premiere poet-cum-*enfant terrible*—and how his sister controlled and censored his work and thus his image. This talk show on censoring is, in turn, censored by Georges in the editing room. Giuseppina Mecchia points out an important intertext, explaining "that Pierrot's angel face, his long unruly hair, disquieting eyes and sulky expression bear a striking resemblance with the different portraits of the young Rimbaud. [. . .] Majid's son, who appears to be between 16 and 18 years old, [is of] an age that symbolically [. . .] will always be the one of the young French poet" (2007: 139). This intertext could indeed point to the combined authorship by Pierrot and Majid's son of the harassing videos and drawings.

While Haneke certainly disappoints viewer expectations—by preventing, as in the example above, a clear conclusion concerning the authorship of the videos and drawings—he uses the viewer's search for clues to direct their attention to other aspects of his films. As in *71 Fragmente*, the sound design is extremely important. As Ezra and Sillars bring out a hidden clue, their observation is worth quoting at length:

> The birdsong from the film's opening shot is identical to the birdsong in the penultimate scene, the flashback to Georges's boyhood home when the young Majid is taken away by force; in the farmyard, we see chickens but we hear sparrows. In fact, the soundtrack in these two scenes sounds the same (including footsteps crunching and car doors slamming) but for one thing: Majid's screams have been removed from the opening shot. When Georges replays the scene in his mind's eye at the end of the film, after having witnessed the adult Majid's suicide, he finally allows himself to hear the violence of the past, which manages to break through not only the birdsong, which becomes louder and louder, but also Georges's own psychic barriers. The cries Georges hears may also be interpreted as an expression of his own feelings—not the pain of victimization, which belongs solely to Majid—but the shame of having suppressed the memory of Majid's cries, and his own role in eliciting them. The cries in this scene not only show the leakage of the past into the present, they also remind us that while collective responsibility creates the possibility of the avoidance of guilt, shame—that intense, hidden, individual emotion—can reconnect us to that guilt. Shame has the power to animate history and to reveal to us our part in it. (Ezra and Sillars 2007: 220)

Indeed, the audience has to search for clues not only in the picture, but in the text understood globally as image, sound, intertext and frame of reference.

Caché is full of allegories, some easier to identify than others. The "Iris" in the "Rue d'Iris" refers obviously to the iris that controls the amount of light that reaches the retina or, in photographic terms, to a camera's aperture. Ezra and Sillars explain that "in Greek mythology, Iris, the goddess of the rainbow, carries messages to humanity from the gods communicating to the human plane from the non-human" (2007: 219). The video certainly has the quality of such a message. Other allegories are well-hidden in the film and might be more subversive. Maurice Yacowar draws our attention to the prominent painting in the Laurent's house that "serves as an emblem for the family members' respective subconscious, Georges as he digs up memories, Anne as she confronts her empty and dishonest marriage, and Pierrot as he faces his parents' guilt" (2006: 231). The many real and fake books that are prominently displayed allow for an allegorical reading: "books cannot open up other perspectives or the past, because they are never opened" (Ezra and Sillars 2007: 216). The most interesting allegory appears when Georges takes refuge at the movies after Majid's suicide. The posters tell their own, virtual stories:

> *Ma mère* (my mother—one of the adults responsible for sending Majid [Maurice Benijou] away), *Deux frères* (two brothers, or Georges and Majid), *La mauvaise éducation* (bad education—what Majid's son informs Georges that Majid suffered as a result of being ejected from Georges's family home) and *Mariages* (marriages—the family melodrama hinted at when Pierrot accuses his mother of having an affair with her colleague), which seem to spell out the various domestic and allegorical configurations in which Georges is implicated, as well as the various narrative and generic routes down which *Caché* as a film could have gone. (Ezra and Sillars 2007: 217)

It seems, then, that *Caché* has a fascinating double nature: Haneke's most accessible film, but also the most densely layered that demands from the viewer a constant rewinding and reviewing and leads him on a search for clues that always ends in frustration. The viewer, educated by other Haneke films, will also notice that certain phrases are echoed, just as Benny repeated the girl's "So halt!" The first words we hear are "Alors?" ("So?") and Anne's answer: "Rien!" ("Nothing!"). "Alors?" is repeated by Georges when he interrogates his son, then mirrored during the dinner sequence when Anne asks Georges why he stayed out so long, "Alors?" and he lies "Rien!" Finally, it seems that Anne now takes over the power of the interrogative "Alors?" She asks Georges who he thinks is behind the tapes and then, in a later scene, pressures him to reveal the history of Majid, asking "Alors?" no less than five times.

If *Caché* represents the struggle for representation, the film should be read as an allegory. Libby Saxton argues that "Georges's consistent failure either to face up to the uncomfortable truths buried in his past or to redeem himself through ethical action in the present can be read as an allegory of France's uneasy relationship to its colonial history and especially the legacy of the Franco-Algerian war" (2007: 11). This is reading that Giuseppina Mecchia also shares. Concentrating on the French colonial past, she remarks on Georges' "continued refusal to accept responsibility for it. In this respect, Georges clearly stands for the whole of France" (2007: 134). For Max Silverman "*Caché* is a commentary on a France (at least in the form of Georges) so incapable of dealing with difference unless it is kept strictly at arms-length, and so anaesthetized against its own guilt and responsibility in relation to past events, that only a dismantling of the erected barricades will open up hidden truths" (2007: 248).

This certainly justified reading would, however, severely constrict the film's effect by limiting it to a specific nation and a specific historical situation. I would argue here for a more abstract view, insofar as this film could be remade in practically every urban setting throughout the first world. What is extraordinary about the Laurent's is that they are not bad people, being more akin to the parents in *Funny Games U.S.* They are the very personification of the cultured middle class that I have already mentioned above. Unlike the majority of journalists, teachers, professors in the humanities and other people who work for the cultural industry, Georges and Anne receive the monetary compensation that they feel they deserve and are content with it. In short, they are living a utopian existence and—educated as they are—it seems that they are fully aware of it. Here, they differ from Georg and Anna in *Benny's Video* who are clear representatives of Peter Sloterdijk's "cynical reason," rationalizing their cover-up, well-knowing that it is wrong, as Jörg Metelmann shows in his succinct analysis (2003: 93). Georges and Anne, instead, really believe in their innocence and their status as victims. This, I think, is a clear critical refinement on the part of Haneke, who portrays Benny's cynical father such that we could still distance ourselves from him. I would therefore not agree with Jacobowitz who attests to Georges' "racist attitude" in his altercation with the young black man (2006: 63). *Objectively speaking*, both parties are to blame—Georges did not watch his step and the bicyclist rode against the sense of traffic. What Haneke underlines here is that in our postcolonial, post-racist society—be it in France or elsewhere in the first world—it is impossible not to notice the race and the class of the people involved. A figure like Georges, unable to face the past, is easily encountered all over Europe.

DAS WEIßE BAND: EINE DEUTSCHE KINDERGESCHICHTE/ THE WHITE RIBBON (2009)

Das weiße Band, "a German children's tale"—an examination of the roots of fascism that also won Cannes festival's Ecumenical Prize for its humanist content—was a surprise winner of the Palme d'Or in 2009. Among many other prizes, the film won the "Golden Globe" for the "Best Foreign Language Film" (2010) and the 2009 European Film Award. Haneke's latest film at the time of this writing appears to be a return to a project that he had apparently planned for a long time, a return to German-language film and also a return to several topics from that period.[13] The film features several interrogations that closely mirror the interrogation of Evi by the teacher in *Der siebente Kontinent* that I discussed at the beginning of this section. More so than in most films since *Der siebente Kontinent*, in *Das weiße Band* the "close up is the face" in its affective power. For example, the interrogations by the pastor of his sons that take place on two occasions are mirrors of the same affect and should not be seen as the two sides of the pastor's character, but as a sign of the milieu. In one scene the father coerces the older son into confessing that he masturbated, while in the other, he allows his younger son to keep a bird that fell out of its nest, sternly admonishing him to take responsibility for it. Again, the affect is "the expressed and the expression" of the specific milieu (the authoritative father, the *dispositif* of the rural community) and should not be seen as tied to the specific time and place of the story. The danger—and I come back to the point of this film's danger in the final chapter—and also its promise is that *Das weiße Band* is set in 1913, concentrating on the generation that came of age during WWI, experienced the troubles of the Weimar republic and then supported Hitler. In a European context, this frame of reference will be seen as an explanation of the rise of Fascism, a promise that the film's narrator openly formulates. The first reviews generally stress this point. Andrew Lane writes in the *New Yorker*: "This out-of-the-way spot, with its fields of cabbages, is one of the thousand crucibles where history is being forged" (2009: 66).

Any story—film or historical novel—that is set in the past, especially one that takes place at the eve of an important historical moment, will be read as a comment on those events since it invites the recipients' historical hindsight. In other words, such a text will invite the relativism of the omniscient perspective of the later generation. *Das weiße Band*, set in the year preceding World War I, is Haneke's first period picture for the big screen and Haneke is obviously aware of the danger inherent in the genre. The question seems to be whether Haneke can really avoid such a reading. In the light of Haneke's oeuvre, *Das weiße Band* appears certainly strangely conventional insofar as it provides a romantic subplot, as well as characters with more psychological depth than Haneke's other films. The crisp black and white photography with a deep focus is modeled after period pictures and, according to a promotional interview with Haneke, the cast was painstakingly chosen for their authentic look.[14]

At the time of this writing, the film was not yet released and, apart from some brief reviews after the film won the Palme d'or at Cannes, there were no in-depth analyses of this film. I was thus not able to gauge whether the film will be a critical and commercial success, and if it will generally be interpreted as a period picture. In the following, I will therefore address the different frames that Haneke establishes and how these frames counteract relativism.

The pecking order appears to be well established in this isolated village of *Das weiße Band: Eine deutsche Kindergeschichte* (the full title translates roughly to: "The White Ribbon: A German Children's Tale"), with a triumvirate of notables ruling over their flock. However, this story could also be called, after Foucault's famous book, *Surveillir et punir: naissance de la prison* (the original title translates to "To Surveil and Punish: The Birth of the Prison," it has been published as *Discipline and Punish: The Birth of the Prison*): everybody seems to be under surveillance and under a constant threat of punishment in the form of torture and imprisonment. No relationship, be it class, gender, or filial seems to be exempt. Even the Baron, on whom everybody depends in this isolated community, cannot prevent his wife leaving him for another man. For the most part, the film consists of short fragments of interpersonal encounters and exchanges that introduce the main characters and map the power structures. Power is foremost patriarchal and clearly hierarchical; the slap in the face is its expression. However, violence also appears in the related form of the psychological pressure that the Pastor skillfully exerts. The violent events, in turn, appear as vengeance for the pressure exerted by the authorities.

While the village indeed appears to be a prison, the birth of something more sinister is announced at the beginning of the film, when the narrator assures us that he has "to tell the strange events that happened in our village, because they might shed light onto some occurrences in this country."[15] This promise to provide an explanation for the rise of fascism in Germany—the narrator is in his early thirties in the film and the frail voice belongs to an old man who thus must have survived both World Wars—will be disappointed, as the film invites neither a symbolic nor an allegorical reading. The violent events that puzzle the villagers are no mystery for the viewer who, in spite of some red herrings, quickly figures out that probably the children vent their frustration in acts of violence. The larger mysteries, however, stay unsolved. The sudden disappearance of the Doctor, the Midwife and their respective children is overshadowed by the outbreak of World War I. More important, though, is the narrator's puzzling promise of clarity regarding National Socialism that the film does not fulfill: The society exists as a strange hybrid of feudalism and capitalism, as the village produces wheat for the landowner and—cut off from the outside—keeps the cyclical lifestyle of agrarian communities, adhering to a strict faith in the patriarchal order, something that is certainly not specific to Germany. Notably, no reference to Germany or the German nation is ever made and the few remarks concerning nationalism that can still be found in the script did not make it into the film. The film could be remade into "The White Ribbon U.S.," or "The White Ribbon France" without much change and it appears that Haneke poses the German question, the "how could it happen?," only to show that there is no German exception. Certainly, there are no structures to be found that could be called protofascist, such as anti-Semitism, nationalism or militarism. Indeed, the question that *Das weiße Band* poses appears to be: how could it *not* happen?

FIGURE 11 The Interrogation

Because there is nothing that is exceptional for the time about this community, and nothing that could "explain" the later process of German history, *Das weiße Band* can only be understood as an examination of biopower. The related topics of interrogation and punishment structure the film's story, as well as the mise-en-scène: those in power demand the truth from their subjects. However, instead of the mise-en-scène of a more traditional film, Haneke finds an interesting expression for this type of relationship. Often, one character is seen from behind, blocking the left half of the screen, with only the other party in focus. It should be noted that there is no symbolic element is this distribution. When the Baron snaps at the hapless Tutor, the latter is blocking the view, looking down on the Baron who is standing on a lower landing. The deep focus photography of the film and the spatial arrangement make the Baron appear small and distorted, even though he clearly wields the power as employer and father of the missing boy. In other interrogations, the subject is in focus, while the shoulder of the interrogator blocks the left fourth of the screen, sometimes even half. However, the schoolteacher, who is not a skilled interrogator, does not receive this shot in his repeated—and futile—attempts to find out the truth.

Frame III

A MARRIAGE OF PAST AND PRESENT— THE OVERCOMING OF FASSBINDER

Not since the days of Rainer Werner Fassbinder has cinema seen the disgust, hatred, and immense contempt for the middle class and today's consumer capitalism that the viewer encounters in the films of Michael Haneke. While the public image of the two directors could not be more different—here the well-spoken intellectual, there the abusive *enfant terrible*—it is remarkable that, rather than expressing raging emotions, the films by Haneke and those by Fassbinder are governed by a cold will to dismantle the foundation of the bourgeois society they are depicting. It is this coldness, paired with a sophisticated use of intertextual quotes from and references to other media that translates into a technical brilliance and deserves a closer look.

In this chapter, I discuss the specific use of intertextual quotes and references in films by Fassbinder, especially in his 1978 film The *Marriage of Maria Braun* (*Die Ehe der Maria Braun*), and Haneke's answer to *Maria Braun*, the 1986 made-for-television-film *Fraulein—ein Deutsches Melodram* (*Fraulein—a German Melodrama*).[1] Both films reflect critically on several *Wunder* or "miracles" of the 1950s cherished by the public imagination: the *Fräuleinwunder* (as the plucky, sexy, and versatile young woman of the age was known), the so-called *Wirtschaftswunder* (the economic miracle) and the German victory of the 1954 world soccer championship that became known as *das Wunder von Bern*, "the Miracle of Bern." *Fraulein*—the last film before Haneke's debut as a director for the big screen—is, apart from a novel by Joseph Roth set in the aftermath of World War I: *Die Rebellion/ The Rebellion* that Haneke adapted in 1993 for Austrian television, the last period picture before Haneke's award-wining *Das weiße Band*. The intertextual strategies that

Haneke shares with Fassbinder, as well as the critical apparatus that he develops in *Fraulein* for the first time in his career have remained remarkably stable. This is especially noteworthy since Haneke declared that he planned *Fraulein* as the "attempt of an 'anti-film'" under the impression of the "indigestible mendacity" of Fassbinder's *Maria Braun* and *Lola* (Grissemann and Omasta 1991: 198). It is not my intention to speculate whether Haneke's vision of a woman's life in the fifties made 4 years after his prolific colleague, almost 3 years younger and internationally famous, had died, is a work of mourning or one of exorcism,[2] but, rather, to point out that the creative encounter between these filmmakers shaped Haneke's oeuvre so decisively that it could be called a veritable overcoming of Fassbinder.

The ideas of this chapter are developed in three steps: First, I compare the use of quotations and references of both films under discussion to those of films that could be called postmodern. I show that these references in *The Marriage of Maria Braun* and *Fraulein* introduce a mode of permanent questioning. Then, in a brief comparison to a German film that covers a similar topic, I show that both, Fassbinder and Haneke, not only refer to images from Germany's collective memory, but that they deliberately misquote them in order to open a critical space, and that Haneke, in turn, elevates these images from the intertextual and intermedial to a truly "intermodal" level by including the medial *dispositif*. Fassbinder—who overloads his images with meaning to the point of collapse—and Haneke—who adds the dimension of shifting medial framing—both direct their efforts against a reconstruction of history that bans images into a sealed-off, distant past. In the final part, I discuss the complex intertextual mechanisms that are at work in *The Marriage of Maria Braun* and *Fraulein* with the help of Gilles Deleuze's concept of the virtual. As I argue, the purpose of inserting quotations and references in the films of Fassbinder and Haneke is to open up an interstitial space between different texts, that is, an ethical space that forms between different media. This intermedial space facilitates a critique of the dominant culture without resorting to that dominant culture's favorite tool, the transcending perspective, opening instead a space where the question of ethics, and with it, politics, can arise.

In *The Marriage of Maria Braun*, Fassbinder makes references to images from Germany's past, such as the famous "Stunde Null," the hour zero of Germany's unconditional surrender and the beginning of the new Germany after the Second World War. We also hear original speeches by the German chancellor Adenauer broadcast on the radio.

These broadcasts, in combination with changes in costume and décor, provide the only framework for gauging how much time has passed. Likewise, Fassbinder refers to different film genres—the melodrama, the *film noir*, and the German musical of the 1950s—by quoting typical markers such as costumes or stylistic devices such as music or the close-up on a half-shaded face. More so than the genre of the *Trümmerfilm*, films that show the spirit of survival in the rubble of the destroyed cities, *The Marriage of Maria Braun* refers clearly to the "genius film," a standard genre in Nazi cinema that portrays historical figures as already following National-Socialist ideals. These films focus on "visionary Germans," whose life should serve as inspiration.[3] Telling the incredible rags-to-riches-story of Maria Braun, Fassbinder's film instead ironically portrays the heroine as a genius entrepreneur, a post-war capitalist *avant la lettre*. With an evening dress bought at the black market, Maria obtains a job in a nightclub reserved for soldiers, where she picks up Bill, a black GI who supplies food to her family and teaches her English. Unexpectedly returning from war, her husband Hermann surprises the couple. Maria kills Bill, but in the ensuing trial Hermann takes the blame. The English Maria learned from Bill proves to be useful when she impresses a French businessman, Oswald. At first hired only as a translator, she quickly becomes Oswald's right hand and mistress. Unbeknownst to her, Oswald and Hermann strike a deal: Hermann leaves for Canada, not to return until the terminally-ill Oswald is dead. In turn, Oswald will leave the company to Maria who will remain his mistress until his death. In 1954, Hermann can finally return to Maria. He tells Maria about the deal and the distressed Maria forgets to put out the gas stove on which she often lights her cigarettes. While the report from the final game of the 1954 Soccer World Championship blares on the radio, the house blows up. It is unclear whether this is an accident or suicide.

The title of Michael Haneke's film refers to the song "Fraulein," featured in the film as sung by Chris Howland (1958), a German cover of an American cross-over hit, a country song from 1957 by Bobby Helms. The title also brings to mind the 1958 film of the same title by the German émigré-director Henry Foster, a thriller with melodramatic turns that was partially filmed on location in the ruins of Berlin and Cologne and that ends with the heroine's emigration to the US at the side of the American officer whom she hid from the Nazis. *Fraulein* repeats some of the plot structure of *Maria Braun*, but the somber realism of its black and white images stand in stark contrast against the ironic candy-colors of Fassbinder's film.

In the mid-fifties, Johanna runs a small-town cinema that also screens American films in English for GIs. She has a passionate affair with André, a former POW from France who stayed on in Germany. Her daughter is dating an American officer who drives around in a shiny Cadillac convertible, while Mike, the son, is a typical *Halbstarker*, a rebel without a cause, who is impressed by André's career as an amateur wrestler with the stage name "The Black Mask."

To *Maria Braun*'s radio broadcasts, Haneke answers in *Fraulein* by directly inserting clips from period films and newsreels, which—as in Fassbinder's film—provide the only means for the spectator to guess how much time has passed. By way of these inserts, Johanna's husband Hans—returning like *Maria Braun*'s Hermann from captivity long after the war is over—is compared to the Hans portrayed by Hans Albers in a famous *Trümmerfilm, . . . und über uns der Himmel/. . . and the Sky Above Us*, directed by Josef von Báky in 1947, who also directed *Baron Münchhausen* (1943), a film from which several clips are shown in *Fraulein*. Unlike the strapping hero in *Münchhausen*, and unlike the hero from . . . *und über uns der Himmel* who regains his son's trust and also his moral bearings, Hans in *Fraulein* returns home physically and spiritually broken. He is not able to connect to his son who gets into trouble for stealing from the US army and blows himself up when caught. The miracle that seems to provide a happy ending for Haneke's Fräulein is ambiguous as the film suddenly shifts from black and white to color: After killing her bedridden husband by removing his intravenous tubes, Johanna takes the Cadillac convertible and drives to France in search of André, who left without a word and who, as it turns out, is married and told his family that the Germans kept him long after the war was over. While making love, she tells André that she has killed Hans. Intercut with her confession to a German police officer are scenes from a bar where Johanna has stopped after leaving André. A TV shows pictures from the war in Algeria. Suddenly, a familiar fanfare makes Johanna look up: on the French TV, its frame still black and white, a scene from *Münchhausen* dubbed in French appears in color. A countershot shows Johanna now, also in color. André arrives and tells her that copying her, he, too, has killed his spouse. The gesture of cutting somebody's throat is performed by Münchhausen on the TV-screen. Johanna begins to laugh and her laughter is heard over the last images of *Fraulein*, which coincide with the ending of the film-within-film *Münchhausen*. This *Münchhausen*, however, appears to be a shortened version that ends with the hero's escape.

Genre and Self-Reflexivity: Dialogue with Past Images

Looking at the genres that both *The Marriage of Maria Braun* and *Fraulein* evoke, as well as the many references to other film and media, one realizes that the constitution of genre rules and the function of a quote or reference is double: apart from its aesthetic function if recalling or citing, it tends also to (re)constitute genre rules. This is significant because genre and quotation are structurally related as we will see in the analyses to follow: a reference refers to something preceding and a quote obviously repeats what has been said before. Furthermore, both implicitly refer to the context in which this "original" existed, thereby disturbing the order of time with this actualizing movement of an insertion. The relationship of the quote and the new context is, then, also a self-reflection of the system, insofar as the reader of the text needs to consider this new relation, reflecting on the old. While it is certainly often the case for literature, the much more expensive art form of cinema always entails a thorough self-examination of prior products to gauge what made a certain film successful. Rick Altman can thus describe "film-making," in his *Film/Genre*, "as an act of applied criticism" (Altman 1999: 44). As Altman points out, this auto-observation identifies semantic elements, like "common topics, shared plots, key scenes, character types, familiar objects or recognizable shots and sounds." Those "building blocks," in turn, are "coordinated" to build "plot structure, character relationships or image and sound montage," in short, all the syntactic elements (Altman 1999: 89). The semantic elements, as Altman describes them, appear right at the beginning of *Fraulein* by evoking the immensely successful genre of kitschy musical film of the fifties: the first image shows a billboard for *Baron Münchhausen* with the smiling face of the film's star Hans Albers; while the camera swoops down and retracts into a panoramic long shot, the first chords of a fifties pop song can be heard along with some friendly banter—a group of friends in a three-wheeler truck and a Cadillac convertible who head out for a day of fun. The audience expectations thus raised will be disappointed, as the retro-look gives way to stark realism as soon as Hans returns from captivity.

A self-referential evocation of genre is, of course, by now standard in Hollywood-blockbuster films.[4] The strikingly frequent appearance of quotes from and references to other media, films and genres in films by Fassbinder and Haneke seem, at first glance, to fit into the same strategy employed by films like *Scream*. However, comparing

Fassbinder's and Haneke's strategy of self-referential quotes and references to the strategy of films that make quotes and references a central element of their plot, one instantly realizes that, although always aiming at one or more preceding texts, the quotes in Fassbinder and Haneke are going somewhat astray, insofar as they question the spectator's mastery over the text. *Scream* (Wes Craven 1996), now considered a classic of this sub-genre of films, in which pastiche and the playful manipulation of genre are the rule, can serve as counter-example to clarify this strategy of misquoting. Postmodern Films like *Scream* play on the spectator's knowledge of the above-mentioned semantic and syntactic elements, clearly providing the pleasure of "getting it" in addition to the genre-typical thrills. In one scene in *Scream* a couple of teenagers, all avid fans of horror films, are watching a classic of the genre, the movie *Halloween* (John Carpenter 1978), in which characters, in turn, are watching horror films from the fifties, while the killer, equally versed in the genre, is stalking those teenagers. This self-referential quote is quite complex: it refers to conditions of the genre's consumption, since most horror-films are now seen at home. It also comprises the history of the genres since Jamie Lee Curtis, who can be seen in the clip the teenagers in *Scream* watch, was the "scream queen" of the seventies and early eighties, while Drew Barrymore not only is the scream queen, but plays that role in a heightened, self-conscious form in the film *Scream*. And the surprising development that the character this well-known actress portrays should get killed off about 5 minutes into the movie clearly refers to *Psycho*, where Hitchcock disappoints the audience in a similar way. But even a viewer who does not recognize all of these quotations[5] will still enjoy the self-referentiality of the film as a "being in the know," a tongue-in-cheek acknowledgment that "we, the filmmakers, know that you know that we know that you have seen all these films . . . " Thereby, the spectator's mastery over the text is not only confirmed, but elevated to the level of the above mentioned syntactic elements of the genre to which this text belongs.

Already in Fassbinder's first feature film, *Love is Colder than Death* (1969), the ice-cold killer wears the same outfit as Alain Delon in *Le Samourai* by J.-P. Melville—himself copying Bogart. The pimp Franz (played by Fassbinder), before committing a hold-up, wants "a pair of sunglasses, like the policeman in *Psycho* by Hitchcock." The well-known *Angst essen Seele auf/ Ali: Fear Eats Soul* is an homage to *All That Heaven Allows* and its maker, Douglas Sirk, who, before his emigration to the US in 1937, was the master of melodrama in the German cinema.[6] *Fontane Effie Briest* is filmed to look like an old silent movie and has intertitles, while *Lili Marleen* is filmed in the style of Ufa entertainment films. Fassbinder's films *Veronika Voss* and *Lola*, which with *Maria Braun* constitute the other two films of the so-called "German trilogy," have—apart from working with quotes as well—cross-references to each other.[7]

Haneke, in turn, appears to be less obtrusive than Fassbinder, as his film style does not directly imitate prior film styles. However, Haneke refers to other films by showing film posters or advertisements and especially by evoking genre markers in practically all of his films—in his earlier films for television as red-herrings to play with audience-expectations (calling up, at first, a noirish family mystery in *Lemminge I*), and, especially in his later films, to blatantly break them. For example, *Funny Games* (1997 and 2007) begins with an aerial shot of a car that reminds the spectator of *The Shining* (Kubrick 1980), while the static shots of the isolated house and the subsequent intrusion by sadistic killers echoes other slasher/horror films, especially the home-invasion-genre and the influential *Straw Dogs* by Sam Peckinpah (1971). While in the latter's controversial show-down an American visiting Great Britain has to savagely kill the intruders to prove himself a man, the killers in *Funny Games* cripple the man of the house right away and even have power over the film itself: after the mother is able to shoot one in a genre-typical revenge, the other killer finds a remote control with which he rewinds the film. The "final girl"—as the massacre's last survivor and another stock character of the horror/slasher-genre is known—is not able to turn the tables with a knife that appeared prominently in a close-up at the beginning of the film but is instead unceremoniously thrown overboard, thus violating yet another genre-rule, the "plant and pay-off," as Alfred Hitchcock famously called it.

Apart from the recurring names (the parents are always named Ann/Anne and Georg/Georges) and actors, a signature shot of the *auteur* Haneke that appears in most of his films and that adds a meta-level to the filmic text should be mentioned here as it plays a prominent role for the first time in *Fraulein*: a television screen, often centered in a shot, that displays its news-footage of civil wars in other parts of the world unnoticed by the characters.[8] This footage, framed by the TV-screen, as well as by the narration itself, refers to the reality of the "real world," as much as it draws the spectator's attention to the topic of violence and its medial presentation that are one of the central points in Haneke's films.

Critics, however, have for the most part understood neither the nature of these quotes and references going astray nor their potential to create a critical space where philosophical questions of ethics and politics can arise in a manner more pertinent than if they were simply thematized by the films. Because of these authorial, self-referential gestures that distance the spectator, critics of Fassbinder and Haneke generally either dismiss both directors as playful, postmodern artists that exploit society's problems of fragmentation and violence by making violent and fragmented films, or they interpret these self-referential quotations and references along the lines of a Brechtian heritage. Gemünden (1994: 70, also 58/59 and 64), for example, talks about "Fassbinder's attempt to wed Hollywood-melodrama with epic theater," and Moeller (1984: esp. 105 and 112) sees a strong relation between Fassbinder and Brecht. Jörg Metelmann links Haneke's programmatic "anti-aesthetic" —he refers here to the infamous and often-quoted statement by Haneke "I want to rape the audience into autonomy" — to the importance the active involvement of the spectator plays in Brecht's epic theater (156–159).

It appears, then, that depending on the critic's stance towards self-referentiality, Fassbinder and Haneke are either hypocritical postmodernists (the film critics' position) or, indeed, *bona fide* critical artists, i.e., modernists, a position to which most film scholars seem to adhere. However, Fassbinder, who himself declared that acting is the only profession he really knew, would never have used any superfluous alienation effects because an epic theater needs direct contact with the audience, something of which Haneke, a theater director of long standing, is also well aware. Furthermore, the classification of Fassbinder and Haneke into the pigeonhole of "postmodernism" seems highly problematic, if by "postmodernism" one means only the retro-look and playfulness of today's blockbuster movies. This does not mean that Fassbinder's and Haneke's films are not political in the way Brecht's theater is. On the contrary, it means that both directors found similar ways to transpose, or rather, translate, this program into the medium of film by introducing a mode of ethical questioning through a permanent shifting of the boundaries between original and quotation, what I will refer to below as framing and re-framing.

Framing and Re-Framing

Returning to the above-mentioned "film-within-film"-moment in *Scream*, it could be said that the television screen here frames the classic films of the genre, just as quotation marks set the borders of a literary quote.

As in *Scream,* the direct quotes in *Maria Braun* and *Fraulein* are framed by an intradiegetic source, in the former a radio, in the latter the screens of cinema and television. While all three films, *Maria Braun, Fraulein,* and *Scream,* use clearly marked references to and quote formal aspects of other films and media, there is an important difference in the way intertextuality functions in each one of them. *Scream,* by parodying the rules of the genre while simultaneously following them, evokes a nostalgic feeling for a more innocent past when teenagers could still be scared by a low-budget film like *Halloween.* It could be said that it is not simply an innocent mythical past that is created, but a *look* onto "the good old days" that obviously never existed. None of the reactionary gender roles or the psychosexual implications of the horror-genre are subverted (Neale 1980: 61). On the contrary, the more references are recognized, the more imaginary mastery over the filmic text is gained by the spectator without eliciting a critical distance, causing instead a fetishistic denial of difference. *Scream* can thus not only spawn *Scream II* and *III,* in which the plot of *Scream* is now adapted for television, but also the parody of the parody, *Scary Movie I* through *IV.*

As Kristeva explains in her groundbreaking article "Word, Dialogue and Novel," parody still results in a "strengthening of the law" because the structures that carry the power-relations not only stay intact, but even appear natural (Kristeva 1980: 80). How, then, can *The Marriage of Maria Braun* and *Fraulein—a German Melodrama,* films that deal with some of post-war Germany's most cherished memories, avoid the ideology of a blockbuster like *Scream?* Unlike a parody, the true subversive power of a "carnivalesque" text, as Kristeva calls it, stems from the ambivalence of a quote which "gives a new meaning while retaining the meaning it already had" (Kristeva 1980: 73). As was mentioned above, a quote is a deliberate recourse to something pre-existing that is made present and whose actualizing movement disturbs the order of time. A carnivalesque text introduces, or better, inserts, a mode of questioning which is directly addressed to the spectator, opening up a dialogue: What is the relationship of old and new meaning? What happens with the new meaning when it is actualized?

From the first scene on, *The Marriage of Maria Braun* stresses that this interstitial zone has to be created by the spectator in the uncanny gap between original and quotation. The peculiar way in which the first image of the movie is framed and reframed shows Fassbinder's strategy for opening a dialogue between filmmaker and spectator: What at first looks like an inserted picture of Adolf Hitler in medium-close up turns out to be a painting that has been blown-away in a bombardment. In the space of a second, the seemingly extradiegetic insert is revealed to be intradiegetic. We, as spectators, must deduce that it was a blown away painting which now reveals a scene through a hole in a wall in a medium long shot from the *outside* of a building and that, therefore, the camera must have jumped 180 degrees, since the Hitler portrait obviously hung inside a room. Retroactively, we now identify the film's first image as a close-up of the typical Hitler-portrait that hung in every state-run building. Furthermore, the soundtrack, barely discernible over explosions, gun fire, and a crying baby, gives us the necessary information—a wedding ceremony is taking place—so that we can deduce further that the time must be shortly before the end of the war and that we are indeed witnessing the marriage of the title, Maria Braun's marriage, with its burlesque beginning—the husband has to wrestle down the fleeing clerk to obtain the required signature. With this striking rhetorical operation Fassbinder establishes a link between the emerging post-war Germany and the title character's marriage, which is metaphorical and allegorical alike: the title, by ways of paradigmatic substitution, alludes to "the marriage of Eva Braun," Hitler's mistress, whose short marriage did not outlast the Third Reich. This allusion to Hitler's marriage, the literal and figurative "fall" of the Hitler-portrait, the impeding end of the German Reich and the sound of the crying baby all signify the "birth of the new Germany." However, because of the over-determination, this all-too-literal illustration is also shown *as* image in its constructedness. What Fassbinder achieves with this permanent framing and reframing—one that clearly demands a considerable amount of reading and reinterpreting from the spectator—is an emblematic illustration, a slowing down of the classic Freudian construction of the fetish with its double articulation of metonymic *Verschiebung* (displacement) and metaphoric *Verdrängung* (repression). The unraveling of the movements of displacement and repression are repeated throughout this film. Another significant substitution appears at the very end of *Maria Braun* and brings the film to a full circle. At the very end, even after the logo of the film stock appears, extradiegetic portraits are inserted—negative photos of all German post-war chancellors in their historic occurrence (except Willy Brandt, whom Fassbinder held in high esteem). In an aesthetic shock, the status of the initial image, the portrait of Hitler, chancellor of the Reich, changes again and becomes a point of reference which needs not only to be remembered, but indeed becomes a kind of paragon. *Reichkanzler* Hitler is the blueprint for the post-war chancellors, who,

Figure 12 In Color

being his negative images, his negation, will always affirm the fascist legacy.[9] Such is the damning critique and political statement of Fassbinder.

With *Fraulein*, Haneke introduces a similar circular mode. The first black and white shot of the film shows the aforementioned billboard of Albers in his role as Münchhausen, with the line "*Farbfilm*" (in color) prominently displayed, while the last sequence containing shots from the end of *Baron Münchhausen* is, literally, in color. The origin of these colorful images is, however, perplexing, because it is not quite clear in which medium they are supposed to appear—a point to which I will return later. All other film clips that are inserted in *Fraulein* are always retroactively framed by their medium, as was mentioned before. Especially in the first sequences of *Fraulein*, a reaction shot shows the enchanted faces of the movie-watching crowd, or a point-of-view shot from Johanna includes the curtain around the movie screen. When a letter from the association of war returnees causes the family to purge the house of André's trophies and his pictures, a sad tune ("Es weht ein Wind von Norden") is playing. After a cut, the tune is revealed to be intradiegetic, as we see the key sequence of . . . *und über uns der Himmel* in Johanna's cinema: Hans who gave up his selfish criminal dealings is visibly pulling himself together and walks out of the frame into a still uncertain future, while in the background women are busily clearing the rubble. This revelation is structured so as to force us to

FIGURE 13 Watching Hans

compare one "Hans" to the others and to confront the message of this first *Trümmerfilm*.

Perhaps more subtle than Fassbinder, Haneke unravels a double articulation of metonymic displacement and metaphoric repression whose function needs even more meticulous unfolding. The *Trümmerfilm*, as has been pointed out, is in itself a sophisticated genre that rests on the dialectic of filmed and filmic space to explore the crisis that befell public and private spaces in the rubble of the destroyed cities (Kirchmann 2007: 282–283). Often, but not always, shot on location, the genre uses the problems of navigating the labyrinthine landscape of the destroyed city as a metaphor for the moral disorientation of the people—as soon as the inhabitants roll up their sleeves and turn the rubble back into a city, they will also regain the courage for a fresh start. Here, . . . *und über uns der Himmel* cleverly contrasts the memory that Hans' blind son has of the pre-war city—using documentary footage—with images from the bombed-out ruins, in addition giving Hans' son the ability to see the moral deficiencies of his father. The long, metonymic dolly-shot from left to right, parallel with the walking hero, therefore shows not just a character who has finally seen the errors of his ways, but also places him into a new and newly manageable space. Most importantly, the brave and determined look of the character named Hans is metaphorically displaced by the image of Hans Albers displaying here his signature look, a hawkish stare, thus inviting an identification from the spectator who has also lived through the war with the fictional Hans, via the phallic star power of Hans Albers, Nazi-cinema's biggest star.

Haneke edited Hans' walk through the rubble in order to underline the juxtaposition of the images and point to the repressed physical and spiritual wounds and the uninterrupted continuation of the career of Hans Albers.[10] As was mentioned above, Johanna's Hans is neither the star of *Münchhausen*, nor the hero from . . . *und über uns der Himmel*, all images at which she repeatedly looks with longing, but a broken man who fails to fill the roles of husband and father. Here, Haneke contrasts the phallic power that carried over from Nazi-cinema to the impotence of Hans. After Hans' request to see her, Johanna pulls her nightgown over her head and exposes her naked body: a bird's eye view from the ceiling shows the marital bed as a split image of impotence and castration. The image of the female body—instead of provoking fetishistic desire—seems to paralyze Hans.

We can now better determine the difference between Fassbinder's and Haneke's uses of intertextuality, and intertextuality in films such as *Scream*. Films like *Scream* parody but do not subvert the genre, instead establishing a chain of references via quotations, thereby addressing the spectator as "movie buff" who masters this chain, which is, in turn, safely anchored in the mythical past of the "Golden Fifties" or the "Cool Seventies." Enticing the spectator to recognize references to prior images as "past" is not only the strategy of Hollywood film and the genre of the *Heimatfilm*, but also that of Nazi cinema, with its apotheosis of past glory—certainly all antonyms of the New German Cinema. On the other hand, although all of Fassbinder's and Haneke's films refer to the syntactic elements of genre and to other films and media, those quotes and references are—unlike quotes and references in Hollywood film—located in a strange gap between original and quotation, constantly oscillating between old and new context. These films open a dialogue by shifting and undermining the positions of author and spectator and by stressing the double articulation performed by a quote. While postmodern films never actually surmount their genres, Fassbinder's and Haneke's films surpass the frame of their genre in order to critically question its presumptions, be they generic, ethical, or political. Furthermore, because of their actualization of the past, Fassbinder's and Haneke's quotes are caught in a political gap, one that is smoothed over and safely avoided by *Scream* and films similar to it.

Quoting from Collective Memory

Having discussed the quotes from and references to other genres and films, it is important to point out another emblematic construction of (mis-)quoting in *Maria Braun* and *Fraulein*. For lack of a better word, this labor could be called a work of intermediality, or maybe even "intermodality" in Haneke, since the filmic text emphasizes here that the image to which the reference is made has to be reconstructed first.

As was briefly mentioned, *Fraulein* appears to be primarily a period picture, as it evokes a specific milieu in a specific time, but like *The Marriage of Maria Braun*, the film does not reconstruct a period, but rather pointedly refers to images from the identity-building collective memory. "Collective memory," as Maurice Halbwachs explains,

> provides the group with a self-portrait that unfolds through time, since it is an image of the past, and allows the group to recognize itself throughout the total succession of images. The collective memory is a record of resemblances and, naturally, convinces that the group remains the same because it focuses attention on the group, whereas what has changed are the group's relation or contacts with other groups. (Halbwachs 1980: 86)

Implicit in this mechanism of projection and self-recognition is the differentiation of self and other. Only somebody who "belongs" can understand the cultural significance and emotive power of this "self-portrait," that, like a genre, is permanently remade from specific semantic elements. For example, "*Die schlechte Zeit*," as the hard years immediately after the end of the Second World War are euphemistically known in Germany, was a time when people often had nothing to eat but sugar on dry bread. There is also the black market, with its currency of American cigarettes, the "Ami" lover who supplied nylons and food for the whole family . . . All of these are specific images that come with a German background and need a specific cultural code for their understanding.[11] These images, as Halbwachs stresses, are a reconstruction,[12] a dangerous reconstruction, to be precise, as they uncritically provide a simple sense of belonging to a group shaped by shared positive values and virtues, a characteristic exploited by the Nazi's genius-film as well as the post-war *Trümmerfilm*.

Analyzing *The Marriage of Maria Braun* and *Fraulein* from the perspective of the ideologically problematic genre of the period picture, with its trove of images from collective memory, it is rewarding to compare them to a film that uses similar images differently. Twenty-five years after Fassbinder literally blows up the "Miracle of Bern" in *The Marriage of Maria Braun*, the German director Söhnke Wortmann dedicates an entire film to the German victory of the 1954 world soccer championship. In *Das Wunder von Bern* (*The Miracle of Bern*, 2003), Wortmann shows "*die schlechte Zeit*" and the newfound feeling of pride supposedly objectively and apolitically because seen from the perspective of a child. Like the father in *Fraulein*, the father in *Das Wunder von Bern* is a so-called "*Spätheimkehrer*," a POW who returns from Soviet captivity long after the end of the war. For a German audience this image of an emaciated, gaunt man who missed the first years of the "*Wiederaufbau*," the reconstruction of West Germany, implies that "he has suffered enough," still a common sentiment. In contrast to the cinema of Fassbinder and Haneke, these images are not shown as images but as an authentic reconstruction of a certain historical place in time, remembered in collective memory, indeed, a space to which only the spectator "in the know" is privy.

The problem of postmodernity—and here we need to recall the question whether Fassbinder and Haneke are postmodernists—has often been described as a loss of memory. While memory could still be reconstructed as "authentic experience" in modernity, this rootedness is not possible today. Because the past is no longer bound to a historical subject or a time, this past can no longer be lived as a collective experience. Instead, as Frederic Jameson explains in his definitive book *The Cultural Logic of Late Capitalism*, a nostalgic momentum of space replaces the past. A period film like Wortmann's *Das Wunder von Bern*, a perfect example of a film that creates a nostalgic momentum, makes a reactionary argument with its "that's how it was" perspective that claims to give an authentic insight.[13] Wortmann's film can certainly not be accused of excusing a historic crime, but it does arrest any discussion of a present political responsibility as it is again the nostalgic look into this carefully reconstructed space and not the past itself that is implicated. Indeed, by sealing the events of the past off in the realm of "historical" events that have no bearing on the political present, the director of *Das Wunder von Bern* does away with history by giving it an exhaustive interpretation in the form of an authentic experience.

At this point, we can begin to see the political implications of a specific deadlock that is also the central question that *The Marriage of Maria Braun* and *Fraulein*—in Haneke's case, his entire oeuvre—pose: when the past is just a nostalgic image and the future provides only a few vague possibilities, what can prevent the nihilism of a cynical "anything goes" in the political present? In an attempt to answer this question, we need to look closely at the complex way Fassbinder and Haneke quote from collective memory.

In *The Marriage of Maria Braun*, the report from the final game of the 1954 Soccer World Championship is so loud as to seem to originate as much from an intradiegetic source as from the extradiegetic space. Shortly before Maria's villa blows up, we see a close-up of a radio, clearly the source of the sound. However, even after the explosion the transmission of the enthusiastic announcer continues. This emblematic image, the (anti-)climactic explosion, is the result of the convergence of two syntagmatic threads, consisting of a quotation—an original soundtrack triggering images from collective memory—and a series of exchanges, embodied by the cigarette that causes the explosion. The first thread is bound to the medium of the radio. As the primary medium of the late forties and the fifties in Germany, it is heard on several occasions on the soundtrack—authentic recordings of public service announcements, an AFN report on the Morgenthau Plan and two Adenauer speeches.[14] But here, during the famous report from the final game of the 1954 Soccer World Championship against Hungary, for the first time somebody is seen listening attentively. The German victory, as well as the hysterical enthusiasm of Herbert Zimmermann, the announcer, has a firm place in Germany's collective memory, signaling a new-found pride: "*Wir sind wieder wer!*" This almost untranslatable statement expresses the sentiment of a new beginning and the end of the shame for crimes committed by Germans—we are "somebody" again. "The Miracle of Bern," as this event was soon dubbed, signals the height of the "economic miracle."

The second converging thread that Fassbinder inserts—the line of capital and exchange value—undermines the other. While the syntagma of quotation has firm referents in extra-textual, that is, historical reality (translatable as "the 'Miracle of Bern' is an event with a specific significance for the post-war German collective memory and this is the historic radio report from July 7, 1954"), the other series is bound to the constructed image of the cigarette. It is worth looking at this *motif* in *The Marriage of Maria Braun* in detail, especially as a similar visual *motif*—a close-up on the exchange of goods for money—can be found for the first time in *Fraulein*, and then in practically all of Haneke's films thereafter.

In the scene following the credit-sequence (the marriage), we see, inside the station restaurant, a group of German men fighting over something. The camera shows this struggle with a medium long-shot from a position a few inches above the floor, through the legs of tables and chairs. Only a few seconds later do we realize that the men are fighting for the cigarette-ends a group of American soldiers flick away. Significantly, the Americans are shown in fragments, their faces obscured by shadow: A short, extreme close-up of the horn-rimmed glasses of one, for example, and several rapid cuts that leave barely an impression, only some identifying features. The refusal to show the Americans in an establishing shot as is customary conjures up images from the collective memory of the first Americans as they appeared: their uniforms, their strange manners. Even their speech is muffled to convey their strangeness. Subsequently, when Maria begins to learn English, this does not happen again. Maria is insulted by this group of GIs. When Maria complains to the group of men in German, she receives as reparation two packages of cigarettes. Again, we only see a close-up of the hand putting the packages on the table. Maria acknowledges this exchange with a girlish giggle, and the men in turn seal the deal with roaring laughter. Thus, the cigarettes gain a symbolic value insofar as the transaction establishes a link between the sexist remark, which Maria does not even understand, and the reparation. Considering Maria's "amoral" behavior later, there is no moral dimension to this exchange, only a clear separation of exchange value and use value: With these cigarettes, she buys a brooch from her mother, which she exchanges for an evening dress that helps her find a job, where she meets Bill, and so forth.

Shortly afterwards—the time is still around 1945—we see a long and extreme close-up of these cigarettes. The cigarettes are Camels and clearly display the label "Made in Germany." That Camels, especially German-made ones, appeared much later should alert us to time being out of joint here. Indeed, this is the only thing out of place in this painstakingly constructed period picture. What Fassbinder does with this insertion of a wrong image into the place of an "authentic" image is a fascinating paradox: He shows the *absence* of an image. The image from German collective memory appears exactly where it was constructed, in the viewer himself, for we cannot help but replace the camels with "Lucky Strikes," the brand that fits the context. Had Fassbinder shown an authentic-looking pack of "Lucky Strikes," the brand of choice in 1945, the film would be nothing but a period picture, undifferentiated and nostalgic. Instead, this impossible memory-image that is not shown but only constructed gains an existence of its own, thus opening up a mode of questioning: Who is "Lucky"? Certainly not Maria, since the last strike to light her cigarette kills her. Maria, who thought she had mastered the game of exchange to the point where she sells her own body, must in the end realize that she was the object of a bargain. We could say that the only element that resists complete reification is the marriage-contract, precisely because it is only a marriage in name, a purely symbolic act that means nothing but signifies the one point that has no symbolic equivalence, since it has no value. This is why Maria insists on being married, even though she has many lovers. Hermann returns from Canada a self-made man with a fortune, and their partnership could be considered one of equals. For Maria, however, the contract is void because she recognizes now that she is nothing but an object.

This short-circuit of an absent image links past and future, film and reality, fact and fiction. The cigarettes and Maria become the phenomenal form of capital. In the final sequence, the last words of the reporter, whose diction and choice of words are reminiscent of Nazi announcers, gain a whole new meaning: "Aus, aus aus—Deutschland ist Weltmeister!" (a literal translation would be "Over, over, over—Germany is master of the world!"). The game is not only over for Maria; the crimes committed by Germans are forgotten, safely sealed off in the past, while capital is now master of the world. It is here, in the quotation of an absent image, that the "inter" of intertextuality opens up a space to subvert the theater of representation. Whereas films that follow the model of Hollywood Cinema, especially Nazi Cinema, provide a nostalgic narration of identity, here the emblematic images from Germany's past come with a clear index of their artificiality: "This is a reconstruction of the past." Maintaining the heterogeneity of discourse in the film, Fassbinder's emblematic underwriting subverts the ideological connotation of the images produced therein.

Considering the emotive power of images from collective memory, it is maybe not surprising that a general audience overlooked the sudden shifts in perspective, the constant framing and reframing, of Fassbinder's film in order to indulge in nostalgia, making it his commercially most successful work. In light of Haneke's above-quoted negative statement regarding Fassbinder's German trilogy, however, it is striking that *Fraulein* features for the first time not only the above-mentioned close-up on the exchange of goods for money, but also the permanent medial framing and reframing that would become the most important stylistic device in Haneke's oeuvre.

As was pointed out above, every quotation in *Fraulein* except the turn to color is retroactively framed. Even the puzzling appearance of *Münchhausen* dubbed in French is motivated, that is, framed, by the still black and white TV-screen. And it is absolutely plausible that the version broadcast on French television omitted the present-day framing story and shortened this German film considerably. However, the turning to color of *Münchhausen* and of the entire ending of *Fraulein* is now even more disturbing as it is impossible that a color TV should have stood in a bar in the mid-1950s. The only explanation appears to be that we are watching Johanna's (mad) vision of a happy ending. And this means we are not watching something that somebody else is watching—as this operation has been introduced and rehearsed before—but rather *with* somebody. Here, Haneke does not misquote an image from collective memory in order to alert the spectator that something is out of joint but instead misquotes, or rather, re-frames the medial *dispositif* itself, resulting in an aesthetic shock.

In his next film, *Der siebente Kontinent/The Seventh Continent* (1989), his debut as a director for the big screen, Haneke uses this type of intermedial quotation, to render unclear the ontological status of the images of the beach and the images that are intercut in the last scene of the film, as they might be located in the memory of the dying man or somewhere in the medial *dispositif*. However, Haneke repeats the reference to the medial *dispositif* famously in *Benny's Video* and then perfects it in *Code inconnu: Récit incomplet de divers voyages/ Code Unknown* (2000) and *Caché*. *Benny's Video* aligns the gazes of camera, camera operator, and spectator as it begins with images from a shaky, hand-held video-camera, filming the slaughter of a pig, thus immediately establishing a plane of a nonfictional real, as it is clear that this is not a filmic trick: a real animal is being killed. This realization is enhanced by the use of the hand-held video, evoking a documentary-style *verité*. Suddenly, however, the video stops, rewinds, then replays in slow motion, instantly adding the dimension of time to the positions in the filmic text, signaling that we are watching recorded footage of a past event that somebody else is watching. The manipulation of the video introduces an aesthetic split, turning the death of an animal into a fascinating spectacle, where the instant of death is now accompanied by what sounds like rolling thunder, drawing attention to the image as image that is, revealing the authentic slaughter as an object of the spectator's contemplation.

Caché, which is filmed on digital video, folds the difference between film- and video-footage back into the film, when an unremarkable shot of a house suddenly turns out to be a surveillance video that we are watching with the owners of the house under surveillance. *Caché* is also Haneke's only other film that directly references collective memory. Here, Haneke insists that the collective memory is very selective as images from the massacre of Algerians by the French police in 1961 seem to have been repressed and must be reconstructed in the mind of the main character.

From this perspective, yet another affinity of Fassbinder and Haneke appears, insofar as their proclivity for complex variations of genre and style is primarily the result of a program that runs behind the scenes, a thinking in images in order to solve a given problem. In the case of Michael Haneke's cinema, a problem that already poses itself in *Lemmings I* and *II*—how to undermine the media-saturated society's tendency to see the past as a series of miraculous events—finds a first solution in *Fraulein* and is then continued in *The Seventh Continent*, which features images that might or might not be located in the gaze of a dead man. In *Caché*, however, it is clear that the images from the past are not nostalgic flashbacks, but are solely actualized in Georges' memory. The last shot in *Caché*, just as in the very end of *Maria Braun*, is hidden (*caché*) behind the credits, and famously brings the film full-circle by repeating the basic set-up of the static surveillance shot at the beginning of the film, undermining any firm interpretation of a film that at first seemed to belong to the classic genre of the "whodunit."

The subtle difference between *Maria Braun* and *Fraulein* can be grasped in narrative terms. The insertion of original radio recordings and especially the quotation of the false image should still be considered a classic *mise en abyme*, insofar as these narrative devices refer to the reality outside the narrated fiction and draw attention to the level of *discours*. Here, the prominent display of TV-news that appear in practically all of Haneke's films after *Fraulein*—and that we also find, for example, in Fassbinder's *In a Year of Thirteen Moons*—would still fit into this category. However, the switch between ontological frames of reference that happens in *Fraulein, Benny's Video, Funny Games, Code inconnu,* and *Caché* is clearly a metalepsis in the sense that Genette (2005) speaks of it, insofar as it is aimed at exploring the implicit rules of representation itself (see here the previous chapter). Indeed, it is the retroactive readjustment of the frame of reference that is crucial here, because this metatextual move does not point to the banal fact *that* we are dealing with a fiction, but rather *how* we are normally dealing with representation.

With their technique of quoting, Fassbinder and Haneke destroy the unity of commercial cinema, where remembered images are always sublated in the whole of the narration. Instead, in *The Marriage of Maria Braun* and *Fraulein*, the filmic quotes develop their own textuality by breaking away from their "pre-texts" and thus constitute a commentary on these images. The resulting confusion—should we trust the images, the narration or the commenting authorial instance—plays again on the "inter" of intermediality. The contrasting of images from collective memory with those that appear in the film that we find in Fassbinder questions the film's epistemology and ontology, but maybe not as profoundly as Haneke, who recognizes that collective memory is now firmly anchored in the media. Both strategies unleash a chain of interpretations and make a permanently assignable meaning to the films' images impossible, drawing attention to the images of the past that are just as artificial.

It appears that Haneke indeed recognized the intention behind Fassbinder's visual rhetoric, saw the potential for overlooking these crucial and complex operations and solved the problem by transposing the juxtaposition of real and film into the contrast of the more unmediated images from video (the real slaughter of a pig, real clips from TV-news) and the completely mediated, that is, aestheticized images of the film, thereby drawing attention to the difference between safely "looking at" and the "watching with" that puts us in claustrophobic proximity with someone else. In doing so, he has brought forth the question of ethics in starkly defined terms: if indeed, rather than just "looking at" an innocuous representation, we are "watching with," our watching brings responsibility as well raising the question of the partner in watching. Rather than simply posing the question, Haneke addresses the question of complicit watching to the viewer who must then also extrapolate this mode of questioning to the sphere of politics that is not only an underlying theme for Haneke.

Virtual Decisions

While we are now able to determine the affinities and differences between Haneke and Fassbinder from the perspective of their use of quotations and references to other texts, genres, media and images, some questions that arise seem to be unanswered and point to the "other" of Hollywood that both *auteurs* claim to despise, even though both seem to play by the rules of Classic Hollywood Cinema in so far as their films follow continuity, have a story with a *dénouement*, realistic acting, etc. Here, it is important to remind ourselves that both directors have a background in theater and bring a decidedly different concept of space to filming. The theatrical space—at least in modern theater—is foremost an immanent space, insofar as the modulations of this space constitute the text and not vice versa. The performance, for example, of a classic play or an adaptation of a famous literary text might not appear that different from a more traditional *mise-en-scene*. However, the immanence of the theatrical space makes it impossible to take an overarching, atemporal perspective since the whole is never given, but can only be described as the result of permanently changing relations, including the relation with the audience.

As was mentioned in the first chapter (Frame I), Gilles Deleuze, at the beginning of his second cinema-book, credits the neorealist movement with developing a new aesthetic that gives the spectator not just an image with moving elements, but a true movement. Cinematic space, constructed by the montage of shots, now also includes the dimension of time while paradoxically retaining the theatrical aspect. Consequently, Deleuze claims that the scene is the basic cinematographic unit and not the shot (Deleuze 1989: 84). In order to conceptualize this different attitude towards space and time in post-war cinema, Deleuze introduces the pair virtual-actual which he sets against the pair possible-real. Thinking in the latter, is, to paraphrase Deleuze, dangerously easy, as the real is imagined to be just one possible outcome of many. However, the image thus produced is always "retroactively fabricated," a reconstruction that implies an omniscient perspective. In a virtual space, instead, characters do not follow possible trajectories (even though a realistic psychological motivation might be provided), but move according to the different concepts that are expressed through them (Deleuze 1994: 212). Again, we can find an affinity with Brecht who famously demands that actors keep a distance from the characters they are portraying and pay special attention to characteristic gestures. Translated into filmic terms, this means that these gestures—Maria lighting a cigarette, Johanna watching a film or a publicity shot—*are* the characters as they are determined by this exteriorization and not just a routine activity captured on film. In other words, there is no psychological "depth" to a character, some kind of inner kernel to which the spectator has no access, but it is solely the act that determines a person. It is important to note that the women's gestures actualize their virtual. Maria's lighting of a cigarette leads to her death, while Johanna who keeps looking at images finds happiness in a mad image, the fusion of her lover with Baron Münchhausen.

In his discussion of Deleuze, Alain Badiou correctly insists that pairs like the virtual/actual are only nominally opposed. Instead of an opposition, we need to think "the actual as the actualization of the virtual, on the one hand, and the virtual as the process of production of the actual, on the other" (Badiou 2000: 49). We already observed such a process in Haneke: when Benny's video stops, rewinds, then replays in slow motion, the dimension of time is added, distorting the image in the process. To put it in Deleuzian terms, Haneke is turning the movement image into a time image. Here, Haneke's virtual images seem to be stressing the processual character of the actualization, while Fassbinder's production of a virtual image of the packet of cigarettes evokes a frozen moment, a time out of joint. It could be said, also, that Fassbinder and Haneke need the foil of Hollywood cinema and its generic frame in order to build, or rather, think these virtual images.

Thus, another way in which Fassbinder and Haneke invite their audience to think politically is by creating virtual images which can only be understood if we think in a Deleuzian manner that does not fall prey to a possible/real opposition. Indeed to the same interest can be said to have as a kind of initiation into a new way of thinking about historical events that retain its political and ethical edge: political because the recalling or actualizing in the political present a choice made in the past; ethical because implicating the viewer in the question of the other.

This different conception of space also concerns the move from one medium to the other: to put a play on stage or to adapt a literary text for the cinema means to translate the concepts at stake into the immanent space of the other medium. In one of his rare examples, Deleuze illustrates the progression from virtual to actual with the way an organ, for example an eye, represents the actual solution to a virtual problem (Deleuze 1994: 211). Both problem and solution are determined and real. However they bear no resemblance to each other. Considered from this perspective, it makes sense that both Fassbinder and Haneke seem to be driven to adapt literary works that appear to be "unfilmable": in the case of Haneke, there is his only adaptation for the big screen so far, *La Pianiste/ The Piano Teacher* (2001) based on the eponymous novel by Elfriede Jelinek, which he transforms into a series that actualizes the virtually private and obscene components of public and private spaces, respectively, that are normally thought to be dialectically opposed. For television, there are Haneke's adaptations of *Das Schloß/ The Castle* (1997), *Die Rebellion/ The Rebellion* (1993), *Wer war Edgar Allan?/ Who was Edgar Allan?* (1984) and the early Bachmann-adaptation *Drei Pfade zum See/ Three Paths to the Lake* (1976), all of which seem, on the surface, to be unfaithful to the literary original, but which translate, or, as we might say with Deleuze, actualize, the complexity of the virtual problems.

The political impetus behind the creation of virtual images in Fassbinder and Haneke will not be clear if we insist on the impossibility of alternatives, that is, if we see the past as a series of miraculous events. The problem with which both Fassbinder and Haneke are occupied is one of choice: an alternative in the actual results in the typical notion of an outside power forcing somebody to act a certain way. Following Kierkegaard and Pascal, Deleuze points out that the crucial difference between a virtual choice and this pseudo-choice by force is the consciousness of the choice. Since the virtual is not opposed to the possible, this virtual choice can be remembered. Even if out of duty, extenuating circumstances or some other motive one chooses the wrong path, the other way still virtually exists. According to Deleuze, we can choose the "mode of existence"[15] of somebody who prefers not to know whether there are alternatives or not, or, as we might put it, we can choose the virtuous mode of somebody who actively chooses. This "choice of choosing" is an important motif in most Fassbinder movies,[16] and can already be found in Haneke's TV-films *Lemmings* and *Variation* (1983), where all characters seem to be unwilling to actively make decisions, as well as in his later films, especially in *Code inconnu* and *Caché*. As Deleuze explains, only someone who recognizes the choice between choosing and not choosing actively makes the decision between what amounts to the mode of existence of being driven by the opposition Possible/Real (the often repeated "we-couldn't-help-it" of post-war Germany), and the mode of existence of deciding (under moral pressure or out of a sense of duty) for one alternative, and in retrospect being able to remember this decision. In short, Fassbinder and Haneke present a Germany that refused its choice.

A brief analysis of the two above-mentioned speeches by Adenauer in *Maria Braun*—where Adenauer first swears that Germany will never carry arms again while in the second he argues strongly for re-armament—can elucidate these politically and ethically charged images of virtual modes of existence, which we can also find in Haneke's repeated insertion of original TV-news into his films. In two scenes in *Maria Braun*, the camera shows parties where the characters completely disregard a radio playing these speeches. If the two speeches had been only a background noise in a scene, the whole film would indeed be a self-reflexive reconstruction of a nostalgically removed past ("back then there might have been an alternative, but we just wanted to get on with our lives . . ."). The camera follows the embarrassing party, but with a distance, and the original recordings, equivalent to a citation, are too loud to be only intradiegetic. Because of their volume, the recordings move from being simply atmosphere to being self-reflexive, the comment being that Germans refused to actively choose between pacifism and rearmament, but rather passively allowed themselves to be swept along by circumstance. They chose not to choose. Clearly, Haneke follows Fassbinder's idea by inserting into *Fraulein* footage from a newsreel that also deals with rearmament.

This problem of the virtual choice is clearly linked in Deleuze, Fassbinder and Haneke with ethics. We have to decide between a resentful moral judgment (for example, "rearmament is evil") and the ethical judgment: "It was bad to refuse a choice for the benefit of the economic miracle." Indeed, it appears that Fassbinder mainly focuses on ethical heroes who stubbornly follow a chosen path even though it is "impossible"—*Faustrecht der Freiheit/Fox and His Friends* (1975), *Händler der vier Jahreszeiten/The Merchant of Four Seasons* (1972), *In einem Jahr mit 13 Monden/In a Year with 13 Moons* (1978), to name a few—while Haneke's main characters remain ignorant of their unethical refusal to act for which their children have to pay: the parents in the glaciation of feelings trilogy come to mind, Georges in *Caché* who does not recognize that it is his responsibility to remember the past, or Anne in *Code inconnu*, who does not intervene when the girl next door is killed.

In conclusion, it could be said that neither Fassbinder nor Haneke show a "true" unmasked Germany, and certainly not a better, utopian Germany, as, for example, Wim Wenders does in his films. Instead, Fassbinder and Haneke show virtual "Germanies." *Fraulein*, Haneke's intertextual debate with Fassbinder's *Maria Braun*, can be considered a crucial point in Haneke's career, insofar as some motifs that already occur in preceding films find a clear focus ("the perils of not-choosing") while some devices that appear in *Fraulein* for the first time and that are perfected later can already be found in *Maria Braun*: the quotes from collective memory, the medial dispositif, in short the virtual.

While the quotes and references in *Maria Braun* and *Fraulein* use their intertextual status to subvert the ideology of Hollywood-cinema, the ingenious machinery of those two films constructs with their help a space of virtuality. The ephemeral nature of this labor—referred to above as a work of intermediality, even "intermodality"—needs the paradoxical interplay of all possible aspects: form and content, original and quotation, the genuine and the forged, the actual and the virtual. The text refers here to its own textuality; it is the choice between modes of existence that is portrayed here. The seemingly paradoxical conditions—*auteur* film *and* Hollywood film, intradiegetic *and* extradiegetic, original *and* copy, a free Germany *and* a Germany where the later development is always already there—open up a critical interstitial of intermediality.

Frame IV

THINKING THE EVENT—THE VIRTUAL IN MICHAEL HANEKE

Critics generally understand Michael Haneke's films as a trenchant critique of our society and its postmodern relativism. One motive in particular that has earned Haneke the reputation of being "the last moralist of cinema": in practically all of Haneke's films since *Fraulein* the images of civil wars that happen in other parts of the globe appear flashing on TV-screens, apparently unnoticed by the characters. This instant mediatization of any event into a medial double, generally seen as simulacrum, here instantiates a "virtual reality" that takes over the real world, thus eroding all moral boundaries. Critics who seek to preserve certain moral values perceive this as a clear sign of Haneke's lamenting the erosion of the values they hold so dear. While it might be true that Haneke's critique pertains to the erosion of the sense of the real, his stance—especially as far as the role of the virtual is concerned—is more subtle and complex and deserves a closer look.

All of Haneke's films are also self-referential, ranging from frame-within-the-frame-shots—the video monitor on which we barely see the horrible action in *Benny's Video* comes to mind—to the direct address of the spectator in *Funny Games*. However, the most openly authorial and authoritarian gesture is not the alienation effect of breaking the fourth wall, but the shock of realizing that we are not gazing *at* something, but *with* something that Haneke used first in *Fraulein* and that was introduced above as the shifting of a frame of reference. The most prominent example is, of course, the beginning of *Caché* (2005), where a perfectly innocent shot of a tranquil urban neighborhood is suddenly revealed to be a surveillance video by a fast forwarding of the tape and by voices that comment on what can be seen on the tape. Here the gazes of audience, surveillance- and film camera, characters and unknown agent find themselves suddenly aligned—except that, of course, each of them sees something different. This difference is significant and, as I argue, it takes place on the level of the virtual, allowing us paradoxically to see what did *not* happen. As I show in this chapter, Haneke's cinema does not seek to represent the "truth of events," such as that which is commonly proffered by the media. Instead, it thinks events as *aporias*, as paradoxical and irreducible to one point-of-view, that is, one explanation. It thinks them as fragmented, multiple accretions of different perspectives with a temporality of their own, rather than as unitary, eternally fixed facts in a sequence. Seeing events as aporetic effects, a confrontation with them on the level of ethics that does not simply relegate them to the past, but *actualizes* them in the present, ethical consequences and all. Indeed, the films of Michael Haneke make a similar attempt with aesthetic means as the philosophy of Gilles Deleuze does through concepts to sensitize us to our relationship to the past, be it recent or historical. This attempt can be described as the thinking of a possible alternative to the global culture of so-called postmodernity where the past is increasingly obliterated by the eternal present of pervasive mediatization, apathy of the polis and general deracination.

Let us for a moment return to Haneke's purported defense of values in the mode of a critique of ideology. As was pointed out above, there is certainly a substantial amount of critique of ideology in Haneke's cinema. Certain moments in his early films—the ubiquitous television images in the "glaciation of feelings trilogy" and in the thematically related *Code inconnu*—appear to be perfect illustrations of Guy Debord's now-classic theses on the *Society of the Spectacle*. An often-repeated stylistic device in Haneke's trilogy, the extreme close-up on objects at the moment of their exchange—the hands of the choir boys in *Benny's Video* handing over money come to mind—suggests that the image of the limitless exchange of commodities has already become the phenomenal form of capital, and that life and image are one and the same. In short, it could be said that these close-ups perfectly illustrate the scathing analysis of thesis 49:

> The spectacle is the flip side of money. It, too, is an abstract general equivalent of all commodities. But whereas money has dominated society as the representation of universal equivalence—the exchangeability of different goods whose uses remain uncomparable—the spectacle is the modern complement of money: a representation of the commodity world as a whole which serves as a general equivalent for what the entire society can be and can do. The spectacle is money one can only look at, because in it all use has already been exchanged for the

totality of abstract representation. The spectacle is not just a servant of pseudo-use, it is already in itself a pseudo-use of life. (Debord 2002)

The "pseudo-use of life" also explains why the potlatch in *The Seventh Continent* must be suicidal. Once all moveable goods have been converted back into money, the paper money as material form of capital has been treated as excrement and every remaining object of use value has been destroyed, the life that remains after this subtraction must necessarily also be voided, because it is already void of any substance. The film ends with the nightmarish image of the dead eyes of the family staring at the nonimage of the television's white noise, their life-as-spectacle come to an end.

Another prime example of a society where the spectacle has mediated all social interaction into a spectacular "virtual reality" can be found in the guise of the seemingly-average bourgeois family in *Benny's Video*. Benny himself lives a monadic life, where even the view from his window is replaced by the live video-capture of the busy intersection. His family seems to have internalized bourgeois values completely, and like all the bourgeois families in Haneke's cinema, Benny's seems cold and sterile to the point of being dysfunctional, communicating only by notes or sarcastic, i.e., coded, remarks. As human beings, they are bankrupt consumers who have completely bought into capitalism. Such is the conclusion reached by many critics. And it is exactly the conclusion that Brigitte Peucker, Gail K. Hart, and Maximilian Le Cain draw in their readings of Haneke's cinema, finding an implied conservative message that weakens or even belies the critical import of Haneke's films. However, we must consider whether Haneke does not rather show us human beings who have become not only willingly dehumanized points in the exchange of capital, but also thoroughly mediated—or "spectacularized" to use Debord's language—members of a society with no promise of a return to wholeness ever held out by Haneke. If Haneke is said to ultimately fail because he leaves a backdoor in the form of a "return-to"—a return to values, substance, meaningful communication, in one word, wholeness—then we must pose the question of whether Haneke does not attempt a critique subtly different from the one observed by his critics, one that successfully avoids precisely the position these critics attribute to him. His critique of a thoroughly mediated society of postmodernity is not simply relayed as a moralizing message, but rather is produced by means of sophisticated cinematic techniques and filmic forms in careful relation to one another that have yet to be examined and explicated. As I show later in this chapter, Gilles Deleuze echoes Haneke's critique of the simplistic distinction between the real and mediatized "virtual reality" by contrasting the pairs of the real and the possible and the virtual and the actual. To do so, we must first engage Haneke's critics more closely on their terrain.

Looking at the dysfunctional families in the glaciation-trilogy, Peucker observes rightfully that form and content mirror each other, i.e., that the characters' attempts to cope with their fragmented lives is itself narrated in a fragmented style. From this, Peucker deducts that the family serves as emblem for the society as a whole, summing up the film's underlying message as: "The wholeness of the bourgeois family as a guarantee for the wholeness of society." Peucker concludes that "Haneke's films are multiply-anchored in notions of organicism after all" (Peucker 2007: 187). Comparing *Funny Games* to *Natural Born Killers*, Hart recognizes that in the Hollywood version of the senseless killings the perpetrators' actions "are mired in the muck of explanation" while Haneke's film refuses any explanation of what motivates these two natural born killers by constantly shifting their identities. Referring to Michael Haneke's own statements regarding the intention behind his project, Hart then compares this refusal convincingly to Schiller's and Brecht's program for an aesthetic education. This stance expresses for Hart the typical disdain and arrogance of "old European high culture" for less sophisticated forms of entertainment (Hart 2006: 70). In the final paragraphs of his article Hart basically accuses Haneke of beating a dead horse since the audience can very well distinguish between fact and fiction and no scientific evidence exists that violent films cause violence. Le Cain, in his overview of Haneke's films, arrives at similar conclusions. While he generally praises the visual sophistication of these films, which according to his reading serve to "re-humanize" the fragmented parts of society, Le Cain counts *Funny Games* as Haneke's only failure. With *Funny Games*, Haneke's intentions—"doubtlessly honourably moralistic," as Le Cain puts it—were to create a film that pits "heroic, beleaguered family battling for their lives and property against an unspeakable, child-killing other."[1] The film by Le Cain's account suffers from a reductive and caricatural representation and, again, defense of bourgeois values.

What is interesting here is that these critics, after a thorough analysis of the aesthetic devices used, see the strengths of Haneke's project, but arrive at a troubling conclusion, namely, that Haneke is a renegade "organicist" who appears to seek to bring us back to the fold of sound bourgeois values, only to hold them out as unattainable for us. Even Robin Wood's highly personal, enthusiastic and, at times, even gushing praise of *Code inconnu* ends with a note of puzzlement about an ending that suggests that "communication is impossible, the 'unknown code' that might save us will never be found" (Wood 2003: 48). Indeed, these readings must necessarily arrive at this conclusion because of their underlying assumption that Haneke pursues a basic humanism, with a message in the mode of the above-mentioned 'return-to,' or at least a recollection of, values that will help to heal—make 'whole'—the broken society at its very core, the basic family unit.

There are, of course, good reasons to take Michael Haneke as a "physician of culture," what Gilles Deleuze calls a "clinician of civilization, somebody who diagnoses the disease in society" (Deleuze 2001: 237), a point to which I return below in the next chapter. While Haneke certainly provides a diagnosis, however, he is far from suggesting a cure that works only within the limits of the already-moribund system. Furthermore, his diagnoses do not hold out the hope-against-hope that life and spectacle could ever be separated again, as some critics mistakenly conclude. They are already and indissociably one. In this Haneke concurs with Debord, who states in thesis 6 that the spectacle "is not a mere decoration added to the real world. It is the very heart of this real society's unreality. In all of its particular manifestations—news, propaganda, advertising, entertainment—the spectacle represents the dominant model of life." To assume that Haneke propagates humanistic values is tantamount to holding out a hope that Haneke has long abandoned.

Looking closely at Haneke's cinematic techniques and film style in the "Flight into Egypt"-sequence in *Benny's Video* in relation to theories of the point-of-view shot can provide some clues as to what is at stake in the insistence upon Haneke's critique being more subtle than critics' readings of it. The week that mother and son spend in a holiday resort in Egypt is important because the audience must retroactively locate Benny's change of mind in this short vacation that primarily serves to give the father enough time to accomplish the gruesome task of cutting up the victim's body into small enough pieces to flush them down the toilet. The obvious irony here is, of course, that the Biblical holy family flees into Egypt to avoid Herod's murdering troops, while Benny's "Flight into Egypt"' happens after an innocent has been massacred and appears to trigger Benny's flight from his "un-holy'" family.

The roughly 20 minutes of screen-time are filled with a repetition of all stylistic devices that we encounter in this film and, indeed, in all other films by Haneke. Rather than the extreme close-up on hands exchanging goods for money, Haneke's signature shot here is the video-image framed by a monitor or a television set, as well as people framed by doors and windows.[2] The significance of these frames, sometimes overlapping, warrants a short taxonomy: the basic distinction in *Benny's Video* is of course that between video and film. The video image is also the object of the film camera and appears sometimes framed by a TV-set and sometimes unmediated, but narrowed by the film's aspect ratio of 1:1.66. In either case, it is clear that only the grainy video image can render a moment from the past. For example, the moment when Benny literally flies and cries out "Mama, I am flying!" is shown on the small TV-screen in the hotel room. However, this scene is preceded by a shot of Benny filming another tourist who has just opened his parachute. Due to the abrupt transition and the grainy image, the audience must assume in the first seconds of the video that it is this tourist that they are seeing on the screen. Only the ecstatic cry identifies the flying figure as Benny and his mother as the camera operator. This transition is mirrored a short time later in the "Flight in(to) Egypt" sequence, once, when the intradiegetic sound, a Bach organ concerto on TV, becomes extradiegetic by being carried over into the next video, then again when the shaky, handheld video that Benny shoots is replaced by a calm pan across the landscape. Again, Benny wearing a cap and sunglasses is difficult to recognize, only his and his mother's voices identify him as the person in the picture and her as camera operator.

This crucial sequence functions on four distinctive levels. Firstly, it repeats the basic distinction of *Benny's Video* between video and film image, thereby stressing the importance of the basic cinematic distinction

FIGURE 14 Flight in/to Egypt (from *Benny's Video*)

between the *hors champs*—e.g., what happens outside of the field of vision of Benny's video camera—and the *hors cadre*, pointing to the image the director allows us to see and its constructedness. Drawing attention to the materiality of the film reveals the image as image in its manipulative power.[3] Secondly, only the video provides the functional equivalent of flashbacks—something that happens throughout the film but might have passed unnoticed by most viewers; this points to the paradox that the video capture of the present instantly passes into the past, thus creating difference in itself, the present's nonidentity with itself. Thirdly, the different film styles underline that Benny is, at first, not interested in a future audience. As opposed to the more touristy pictures his mother takes, Benny treats his video camera up to then solely as a device to capture and mediate reality. Even his video-diary on the hotel terrace seems to be more an externalization of his own thoughts and doubts than a message to another person. Not only does he expose his naked chest in a narcissistic gesture but he is also wearing a t-shirt with a picture of his own face on it. Significantly, it shows him with his full-length hair, i.e., before he became a murderer. Fourthly, Benny for the first time uses the implicit threat of sharing with others his video as a means to an end. In a short scene, he films his mother, who sits down on the toilet with the bathroom door open. Benny would probably not show this video to anybody, but makes the point that he is emancipated and not a child anymore.

Most importantly, however, this sequence works on a meta-level, combining all other functions to foreshadow the major mise en abyme of the film where all these levels or frames, if we want to extend the metaphor of the frame to the multiple frames of reference, are realigned. The repetition of a prior scene the audience witnessed earlier brings up the memory of the original circumstance. The recognition, then, that the director did not show Benny taping his parents and that Benny is now screening this segment for the authorities happens in a flash. Sharing his video with the police will, of course, emancipate Benny completely, cutting all ties to his family but also making him a director who makes images *for* somebody. This shock of realization, an abrupt adjustment of the frame of reference, was already rehearsed in the above-mentioned video of Benny's parachuting and, before, in the repetition of the girl's killing that Benny shows to his parents. The construction of these devices can serve as perfect examples of what Michel Chion famously calls an "acousmêtre," a person who is not visible but whose voice is heard, "a kind of acting and talking shadow," as Chion puts it (Chion 1999: 21). The voice of the young man who assaults Anne in *Code inconnu*, for example, is even more threatening and powerful when it suddenly comes from the *hors champs*. But maybe even more important for the cinema of Haneke than the "acousmatic voice," the voice whose source is not seen on screen but which is implied, is the opposite operation, when the audience has to assign an on-screen body to the voice they are hearing, as in Benny's ecstatic cry, mentioned above. Chion calls this "a voice that seeks a body" (see Chion 1999: 127–136). In any case, a voice without a body or a voice that seeks a body, the shock of recognition, when voice and body are associated, could be described as a reframing: the frame of reference that assured the spectator of a stable meaning is suddenly revoked. Indeed, the last sequence of *Benny's Video* features two instances of acousmatic reframing: at first, the audience needs to remember the key sentences of the cover-up ("The pieces must be small or they'll block the drains") concerning the disposal of the corpse and recognize the parents' voices in order to understand that they are witnessing a recording of something that they experienced from another perspective. Then, while the screen still shows the bedroom door, an unknown male voice from the *hors champs* asks Benny a question, and, after a cut, a hand handling a video-recorder is shown in close-up. Again, the shock of recognition stems from the necessary reframing—voice and hand must belong to a police officer, whose face the audience never gets to see. Instead, the video-monitor shows a glimpse of Benny ready to take off with his parachute, again demanding a remembering of the first reframing, but also pointing to the possibility that Benny handed over the incriminating video because of this flight in(to) Egypt.

Before drawing conclusions from Haneke's multiple frames and their alignment, let us consider Haneke's use of the point of view shot. Indeed, critics have noticed the curious incidence of the traditional point-of-view shot in Haneke's oeuvre. Insofar as these point-of-view shots are used sparingly, they are either reserved for the rare instances when we should identify with a character, for example for Eva in *The Seventh Continent* who will be murdered by her parents (see Bingham 2004), for the young boy in both versions of *Funny Games* (1997 and 2007), or for a direct reference to the conventions of Hollywood cinema. In *Code inconnu*, an action sequence—a child is falling from a roof—is later revealed to be a clip from a film in which one of the main characters has a role (see Wood 2003: 42). In any case, if a point-of-view shot occurs, it is already framed in multiple ways. The point-of-view shot of Eva looking at the boat, is, as Jörg Metelmann recognizes, an intertext to Antonioni's *Il Deserto Rosso/Red Desert* (1964) where a ship appears in a similar shot and where the reality of the vision is equally enigmatic: it could be a real ship but the shot also gains a metaphoric quality in relation to the journey on which the parents will later take Eva. As Metelmann points out, this is one of the few instances where Haneke uses extradiegetic music, in this case, Alban Berg's violin concerto "To the memory of an angel," in order to contrast the poverty of the parent's life with Eva's vision (Metelmann 2003: 76–78). The obvious irony in this choice is of course counterbalanced, or rather countered, by the mournfulness of the music itself and, again, disturbs the spatial and temporal continuum by foreshadowing Eva's death. The surprising action sequence in *Code inconnu* is also framed, drawing the viewer in with typical means—action, fast cuts, point-of-view shots—even though Anne's sudden change from struggling actress to member of an upper-class couple should alert the audience that this cannot be part of the diegetic reality. Significantly, we find again acousmatic voices at work, insofar as the action sequence is just being dubbed by the actors. Here, a new frame of reference retroactively discloses the prior sequence as fake, or rather, fictional in the framework of the diegetic reality. Haneke's point of view shot thus becomes something else, no longer a simple point of view shot but a multilayered frame of intertextual references.

Just how Haneke's point of view shot differs from the traditional point-of-view shot can best be shown by looking again at *Benny's Video* and *Caché*, thereby also showing that the sudden ontological adjustment effected by Haneke's use of point-of-view shots emphasizes the artificial character of the film itself in a complex form of self-referentiality. The aesthetic shock in *Benny's Video* of a shot that is suddenly revealed to be surveillance video clearly anticipates the above-mentioned beginning of *Caché*. There, as here, the bodiless acousmatic voices commenting on the events the audience witnesses abruptly adjust the frame of reference. In *Caché*, we find again the manipulation of the tape that we encounter in the sequence that begins *Benny's Video*, the slaughter of the pig. In the latter, the rewinding and slowing down immediately introduces the device of adjusting the frames of reference: we are watching Benny's video in a film called *Benny's Video*. As was pointed out above, all possible gazes overlap in moments like this—audience, characters, unknown agent, surveillance- and film camera all look at the same images. The crucial difference from a traditional point-of-view shot becomes immediately clear. In the traditional point-of-view shot "the camera assumes the spatial of a character in order to show us what the character sees, the camera lens, so to speak, becomes the eye of the character (hence also the metaphor 'camera eye'), with the result that our sensory perception is restricted to that of the character" (Branigan 1984: 6). However, in Haneke's films and here especially in the surveillance sequence in *Caché*, the shot rendered in a seemingly impersonal point-of-view that happens in the '"past" to the diegetic present and is taped in a locale different from that diegetic present suddenly is revealed as not only not impersonal, but as "part" of the diegetic present, that is, as surveillance. It is not only that the point of view of the surveillance causes the diegetic fictional reality to be split from within by a threatening element, whose provenance is unknown—the spatial and temporal continuum in the surveillance sequence as such is always already split. This amounts to an ontological and epistemological split that can not be overcome by any kind of "return" to a stable identification of subject and object of the gaze, not being predicated on such easy distinctions but instead calling them radically into question.

Having considered Haneke's nuanced use of the point of view shot, we can finally pinpoint the difference in Haneke's aesthetic. I would argue that Haneke deliberately transforms the classic point-of-view subsequence into these framed shots of and through another medium—an intertext under the guise of video or a Hollywood-style action film—in order to draw attention to the mediality and the temporality of all images. Indeed, every image in these films—the news specials on the war in Bosnia, the minor daily news ("a tramway accident in Stockholm"), the slaughter of the pig, the film itself—is always mediated, that is, framed. In a more traditional film that follows the convention of classic realist Hollywood cinema, a point-of-view shot is nothing but a supplement to a recording of events that is supposed to be basically objective. However, as several film theorists have pointed out, the shot/counter-shot mechanism of Hollywood cinema, with its classic realist narration, "sutures" the viewer with the filmic text. According to this model, the viewer interprets the glance of the "absent" person as source of a first shot and in a second step reads the counter-shot as the look of a diegetic person, shot one becomes signified for the signifier "l'absent." The second shot is in its turn defined by the point of view of the first shot—the "other field" as Dayan calls it—and is therefore the signified of the first shot. It is exactly through this tautological short-circuit, this displacement of meaning from one shot to the other, that the subject of enunciation shifts or inserts itself into the fiction. The image is taken as a "true" representation: "By means of the suture, the film-discourse presents itself as a product without a producer, a discourse without an origin" (Dayan 1976: 451). The position of the subject of enunciation is, however, a phallic and therefore impossible position. The permanently threatening castration stems from the real inability of the viewing subject to influence the picture, and this threat is sublated through a fetishistic disavowal, as Kaja Silverman formulates following Laura Mulvey (Silverman 1988: 30–31). Such sublation, however, is not the goal of Haneke's cinema. The ontological and epistemological split that develops in Haneke's films through his own use of point of view technique cannot in the end be sublated or sutured into an organic whole in the manner allowed by the traditional point of view shot of Hollywood cinema.

In his book on Kieślowski, Slavoj Žižek mentions two ways of refusing a suture with simple cinematic means: one is to set up a point-of-view shot, only to reveal the character through whose eyes we are supposed to see as located within the frame; the other option is to include the face of another person as a reflection in a window within the same shot. Žižek describes this as "the shift from the objective 'God's-view shot' into its uncanny subjectivisation" (Žižek 2001b: 38). In the early Haneke, this threat of castration is anticipated and underlined by the insertion of black film, a strategy that he later abandoned. Bert Rebhandl describes the effect of these inserts as destruction of the "conventional knowledge of the sequencing in storytelling and narrative causality" (Rebhandl 2005: 80–81). Beginning with *Benny's Video*, Haneke opts for the mediatized point-of-view shot discussed above, the uncanny subjectivization of the video-image with its threatening castration in the form of the disturbed space–time continuum.

Let us return to the question of how we might interpret Haneke's multiple frames and their alignment. In trying to assess the different devices used by Haneke, we can see not only a systematic and radical refusal of any closure, either in form or content, but, indeed, the systematic destruction of any possibility for a reconciliation of these fragments on any level. No frame, to stay with the metaphor, is entirely closed: the rules of the genre are established, then suddenly broken, images change their ontological status, suture is promised, then permanently refused, etc. It is important to recognize the temporal aspect behind this strategy, whereby a possible closure is announced, but then destroyed. The most infamous example here is, of course, the rewinding of the film *Funny Games* itself by one of the young killers, just after the audience has had a brief moment of hope for a narrative closure in the form of the genre-typical catharsis. This punitive impetus might be misunderstood as moralistic, as some critics have done, but the very possibility of a position on which to ground a moral judgment is also denied. What prevents Haneke's cinema from falling into nihilism, is, then, the insistence on the difference that is already in the image and the repetition that forces the audience to remember and readjust the frame of reference for this image. This readjustment, as I will argue below, can only be understood as an actualization in the sense that Deleuze uses this concept.[4]

In the case of *Caché*, Haneke finally formulates in a pure form the *aporia* that is already implicit in all of his films by concentrating all devices that were mentioned above—the overlapping gaze, the frame in frame, the acousmatic voice that reframes the image, the refusal of suture—in one sequence. As was pointed out above, this ontological and epistemological split can not be overcome by any kind of a stabilizing—hence reassuring—attribution to a subject and an object of this gaze. Indeed, this split is the very expression of this crisis. As was mentioned before, the film is shot on digital video, thus also *folding* the difference of film and video into one image. Here, we need to remind ourselves that, according to Deleuze, folding and unfolding should not be understood as oppositional movements (see here the introductory chapter). Haneke folds in this difference in order to ex*pli*citly point out the different ontological frames that cinema normally allots.[5] Consequently, the tracking lines of the video appear from an outside, the impossible realm of the *hors cadre*, the space where the surveillance camera also seems to be located—George would have found it otherwise, since he walks towards it in one scene, and the curious viewer will in vain rewind the film and freeze the frame in order to search for the video-camera in the bookshelf of Majid's apartment.[6]

The first sequence sets the stage for an exploration into the nature of surveillance by showing surveillance at work. The act of surveillance, in a continuous arc, becomes both an event and a staged performance—a surveillance is taking place whose only object or purpose is indeed the surveillance that took place. The implied audience of this circle is split into the audience in the cinema looking at this spectacle which is, in the diegetic frame of reference, "real," yet, in extradiegetic terms, staged entirely in order to point to its own mediality, and the audience's point of reference, the fictional addressees of the tape. As has been addressed in the previous chapter, this dizzying circle of self-referentiality could be seen as signs of a Brechtian program, as Metelmann has done (2003: 151–179), but the truly new dimension of filming that Haneke's *aporia* opens up is that the camera, as agent of the mediality, actually *performs* the difference in the repetition. Thus, by repeating the frame, the difference emerges as a kind of performance. It could be said that surveillance paradoxically happens and is impossible at the same time. However, it is only impossible when we refuse to acknowledge that the opposition is not between reality and virtual reality, but between the pairs possible/real and virtual/actual, that is, if we stay within the metaphysical view of a timeline where certain possible outcomes become reality.

It is at this point that the projects of Haneke and Deleuze overlap. Indeed, the nature of the difference that appears in the repetition should not be confused with the "virtual reality" that seems to provide such an easily-identifiable target for Haneke's filmic critique. While the instant mediatization of any event is certainly a prevailing theme in the cinema of Michael Haneke, it mirrors Deleuze's scheme by differentiating the pairs of the real and the possible and the virtual and the actual. For Deleuze the virtual is linked to memory, or "pure recollection": "What Bergson calls 'pure recollection' has no psychological existence. This is why it is called *virtual* [. . .]" (Deleuze 1988: 55). Instead of being a point on the chronological timeline, the present must paradoxically be grasped as coexisting with and independent from the past, which we have to actualize in order to have access to it, but should be careful not to think of as a subjective memory *in us*, but on the contrary as radically exterior: "Only the present is 'psychological,' but the past is pure ontology; pure recollection has only ontological significance" (Deleuze 1988: 56). Ontological here means precisely not psychological, internalized and subjective—a thinking that would be grounded in a model that imagines the future event as a realization of one of many possible outcomes. Instead, the virtual is as real as the actualized present.

At the moment of a perception, time "splits," as Deleuze puts it, and the actual perception-image gains its virtual image (Deleuze 1989: 81). It is precisely from this point of view that Deleuze can claim that the present is a function of the past, a contraction of the past. From this perspective, it is the psychological present that "passes," while what is normally understood as the past has an existence of its own that is independent from the chronological time-line and where everything is preserved more or less contracted, but without hierarchy: "The whole of our past is played, restarts, repeats itself, *at the same time*, on all the levels that is sketches out" (Deleuze 1988: 61, italics Deleuze). In *Caché*, the video images of the surveillance camera provide this virtual archive, while the images of the young Majid are always marked

FIGURE 15 Actualized Memory

as dream- and memory-images which are presently actualized in George's mind. Notably, the scenes when the young Majid kills the chicken and when he is forcibly removed by the authorities are clearly focused by and through the narrative presence of Georges. They are filmed from a low angel that suggest the point-of-view of "Georges-as-a-little-boy" and exaggerate the menacing appearance of the young Algerian boy.

Since the virtual has its own existence, the act of recollection asks for nothing less than a leap of faith: "The appeal to recollection is this jump by which I place myself in the virtual, in the past, in a particular region of the past, at a particular level of contraction" (Deleuze 1988: 63). This is exactly the jump required by the audience when an acousmatic voice requires the actualization of a prior image, i.e., transposes it to the present of the mind. An act of recollection can thus be compared to remembering the original circumstance of the frame. Again, it should be underlined that this is not a step back in time, but rather a search in a virtual archive for places where this text also appears. The past, as Deleuze explains, "is the virtual element into which we penetrate to look for the 'pure recollection' which will become actual in a 'recollection image'" (Deleuze 1989: 98). Arguably, these are images that are not visible on the screen, because this recollection-image appears in the mind of the spectator.

Underlying the couple virtual-actual is the distinction between possible and real, as commonsensical as it is dangerous. The reconstruction of a "possible" is deceptively easy, since it is made in the resemblance of the real. Deleuze writes in *Difference and Repetition*: "Such is the defect of the possible: a defect which serves to condemn it as produced after the fact, as retroactively fabricated in the image of what resembles it. [. . .] Actualization breaks with resemblance as a process no less than it does with identity as a principle theater" (Deleuze 1994: 212). In the case of Haneke's project, this means a "return to" older values is not only not possible, but the attempt is outright dangerous, since it introduces a teleology. Instead, Haneke's films as well as Deleuze's philosophy ask for a completely different concept of history that seems to be inspired by Walter Benjamin. In Thesis VI of the *Theses on the Philosophy of History*, Benjamin famously warns about the reconstruction of history and instead postulates an alternative to this historicism:

> To articulate the past historically [. . .] means to seize hold of a memory as it flashes up at a moment of danger. [. . .] The danger affects both the content of the tradition and its receivers. [. . .] Only that historian will have the gift of fanning the spark of hope in the past who is firmly convinced that *even the dead* will not be safe from the enemy if he wins. (Benjamin 2003: 392)

Written under the fascist threat of a teleological rewriting of history by appropriating the dead as "martyrs for the cause," Benjamin's messianic strategy instead retains this "moment of danger"—the moment when events took the wrong path—as a virtual image. The seizing of this moment means that we should remember what did *not* happen, or, in Deleuzian terms, actualize the virtual. Looking at Haneke's films, we can see that his entire oeuvre—and this include his work for television—demands from the spectator this act of recalling what did not happen, instead of harking on what should have happened.

With the actualization of the virtual, a virtual event comes into existence because the act of remembering is, in the words of Deleuze, always a "genuine creation (Deleuze 1994: 212)." The virtual is therefore something that will always be new and does not resemble the real at all, while the possible is only a reconstruction, a mere virtual reality. Whence the importance of the "pyramid scheme" in *Benny's Video*, a perfect illustration of acting in bad faith as opposed to the leap of faith required by Benny at the end of the film. This "virtual reality" of capitalism imagines time as a forking tree and the observers of the possible outcome—everybody's wealth will grow exponentially—as watching from an ahistorical, omniscient point-of-view. However, it can, of course, be proven mathematically that only the initial "players" will become rich (Valentine 1998). Significantly, the video-taped scenes from the two pyramid-parties show fights in the back-ground, stressing that the virtual reality of the game is already coming apart at the seams.

It is important to be precise about Haneke's and Deleuze's diagnosis: the characters in Haneke's films do not confuse the virtual and reality, i.e., succumb to a false consciousness, but rather are cut off from the past in the form of the virtual and can therefore not remember what did *not* happen, instead, projecting a possible virtual reality into the past and the future.[7] To stay with the example of *Caché*, we can quickly see that the traumatic event of the massacre of Algerians by the French police could have been dealt with in the typical form of a virtual reality based "on a true story," which, in turn, can easily be judged in terms of how "well" it represents the past (like, for example, *Nuit noire, 17 octobre 1961* by Alain Tasma, incidentally released in the same year as *Caché*).[8] However, Haneke introduces the event of the massacre of Algerians only indirectly, almost as an original sin that reverberates through the life of the characters, thus preventing a historicist appropriation. We should not forget that the main character of *Caché* can not possibly be found guilty since he was 6 years old at the time of the event and not able to foresee the consequences of his jealous actions. And he certainly had no influence on the abuse the Algerian victim possibly received in a French orphanage. If anybody is to blame, it is the parents who all too readily believed their son and didn't inquire about the disappearance of Majid's parents. However, it seems strange that Georges barely reacts to *the* traumatic event of the film, the sudden suicide of Majid. In the scene immediately preceding Majid's suicide, we see Georges acting in bad faith, manipulating images, in a shot that mirrors the surveillance shot at the beginning of the film. But instead of recognizing that he had failed to help the grown-up Majid, Georges afterwards still acts on his main fear, namely that of losing his public image, something that connects him to Benny's father, who also immediately thinks about the possible loss of his status. Even though shaken by the event he witnessed, Georges' primary concern seems to be whether his wife kept up appearances when she sent their friends away. And the next day, he assures Majid's son that he does not feel guilty at all. Indeed, Debord's sixth thesis, quoted above, holds true for Georges: "the spectacle represents the dominant model of life."

Deprived of any identification with the main character, we find here again the systematic and radical refusal of any closure that was addressed above. The *topos* of self-aggression that pervades Haneke's oeuvre, for example the murder-suicides in *Der siebente Kontinent* and *71 Fragmente*, the attempted self-sacrifice of the young boy in *Le temps du loup* or Erika's self-mutilation in *La Pianiste*, is remarkable insofar as none of these gestures carry any meaning. The destruction of any possibility for a reconciliation of the fragments exposes suicide and self-mutilation as completely nihilistic gestures that have no redemptive value. I return to this topic below in Frame V.

There is, however, one more perspective that can help us to seize a moment and remember what did not happen: in most of Haneke's films—as was pointed out above—a TV set displays news from an armed conflict around the world. In *Caché*, for example, the TV-set, which is ironically built into the bookshelves, is clearly centered in the frame, while Georges and Anne talk in the foreground, not paying attention to the routine display of violence. Indeed, the suffering person on the news is virtually always already all other victims. Again, we can formulate an affinity to Debord, who points out in his thesis 61: "The agent of the spectacle who is put on stage as a star is the opposite of an individual; he is as clearly the enemy of his own individuality as of the individuality of others." It is this individuality that needs to be seized, and this through the act of actualization of a virtual. We could say, then, that Haneke's cinema combines the radicality of a Debordian take on the mediatization of events with the Deleuzian response to postmodern condition.

In other words, to actualize the virtual means to think each event as aporetic and not as a metaphysical example for the nature of man and the typical horrors of war. Every actualization carries therefore an ethical demand, in this case, to actualize the virtual of the victim. When we remember Benny's enthusiastic response to his flight as the only time he shows any emotion, for example, we need to resist the temptation to read a "deeper," i.e., psychological meaning into this event, but should instead attempt to seize the purely ethical dimension of his action. The famous last scene in *Caché*—Majid's son talks to Georges' son while they might even be under the gaze of the surveillance camera, an event the allows several, mutually exclusive readings—is so not only the consequent refusal of closure, but also the actualization of the virtual of the entire film.

Frame V

A NEW ORDER: THE METHOD OF MADNESS

In a relatively short period of time, Michael Haneke's oeuvre developed from critically acclaimed films with a small distribution, co-produced by Austrian and German television, to works of French cinema, becoming almost synonymous with European art house cinema. It should be added that Haneke himself is quite media-savvy, insisting in interviews and in the short-documentary features that accompany the DVD-editions of his films that he, as the filmmaker, can only give one of many possible interpretations of the films he wrote and directed, adding to the image of himself as the heir to the European tradition of the socially critical *auteur*.[1] Like other European directors who previously took this spot in the imagination of the *feuilletons* (e.g., Peter Greenaway and Theo Angelopoulos), Haneke is addressing topics considered difficult measured by the standards of commercial cinema: the traumatic effects of violence, racism, sexism, and alienation. Considering his well-documented contempt for television and Hollywood cinema with its generic system (see Sharrett 2003; Cieutat and Rouyer 2005; Grabner 2005), which by critics and scholars alike are seen as postmodern excesses lacking in substance, it is not surprising that Michael Haneke has been labeled a modernist.

This reputation in turn clearly dictates the reception of Haneke's films, which are judged by their ability to take a readily identifiable stance against phenomena perceived as "typically postmodern," i.e., the reifying effects of consumer capitalism and the role of mass-media in it. One critic, representative of such a judgment, attests to "Haneke's perverse modernist desire to punish us for our collusion with the commodified—and thus, for Haneke at least, mendacious—narrative certainties of dominant cinema."[2] While there are certainly signature shots typical of Haneke (a close-up on the exchange of goods and money), typical scenarios (an oedipal triangle, often sharing the same names—Anna/Anne, Georg/Georges, and Ben), and recurring motifs (the droning of television and/or reference to current events such as the war in Bosnia) that warrant such a reading, I would argue that these surface phenomena are merely symptoms, and that it would be more fruitful to concentrate on madness, the one *topos* that appears in one form or another in all of Haneke's films. Therefore, instead of expecting a critique of our culture that we can apply when needed, we should accept, with regard to Haneke, Nietzsche's famous insight that philosophers and artists are "physicians of culture," an insight with which Haneke, who studied psychology and philosophy at the University of Vienna, is certainly familiar. In other words, instead of the normative demand for a cure, we should first accept the *auteur*'s ability to diagnose a disease in our culture by reading the symptoms.

With this shift in perspective in mind, we can readily see that there are two forms of madness in Haneke's films that need to be held apart: the everyday craziness of life in our fragmented, postmodern world and the madness of a criminal act, often linked to a violent, traumatic event that cuts all social bonds. Haneke seems to play here on the two German words for being mad: *wahnsinnig* (meaning "insane"), whose more commonly encountered noun form, *Wahnsinn*, could be translated literally as "delusional sense"—with the same double meaning of "sense" as in English—and the more colloquially used adjective *verrückt*, crazy, literally "out of joint." It is in this latter sense that madness in film is generally depicted: as a character's state of un-reason (*Ver-rücktheit*). It is important to point out that this craziness which befalls the evil stock character of virtually all action films is never motivated psychologically—the prototypical "bad guy" of Hollywood action films is evil incarnate in himself—but instead provides the hero's motivation for violence in the form of a morally justified revenge. In Haneke's cinema, however, madness becomes a new order that provides a new *sense*: we can locate this new sense, for example, in the form of a new code in the everyday craziness of racism in, for example, *Code inconnu: Récit incomplet de divers voyages*. When the civil order breaks down in *Le temps du loup* only actions of madness still make sense. And, cynically, the new order of madness provides perverse rules of the game in the *Familienroman*, the Freudian family romance of the tortured family in *Funny Games*. This chapter will look at the instances of this "new-order" madness in the cinema of cruelty that Michael Haneke unfolds and explore its subversive uses, especially as concerns not only Haneke's cultural analyses, but—on another and less understood level—his very stance concerning cinema spectatorship and the pedagogical role cinema plays for the viewer.

What is remarkable here is the affinity that Haneke's conceptual framework shows to philosophers like Michel Foucault, Jean Baudrillard, Jacques Derrida, Gilles Deleuze, Shoshana Felman, or Alain Badiou, who have been dismissed with the label "postmodern." Badiou, for example, calls for an "ethics of truths," while Felman reflects on the pedagogical use of trauma.[3] This does not mean that Haneke's films can be explained by reading these philosophers and "applying" their thought to his films; instead, it should be stressed that these films make a similar attempt with aesthetic means as does the philosophy of the above-mentioned thinkers. This attempt can be described as the thinking of a possible alternative to the global culture of so-called postmodernity.[4]

The basis for Haneke's unique take on madness can be found already in his first three films, the trilogy about alienation which he baptized "glaciation of feelings" ("*Vergletscherung der Gefühle*"): *Der siebente Kontinent* (1989), *Benny's Video* (1992), and *71 Fragmente einer Chronologie des Zufalls* (1994), as well as in *Funny Games* (1997), the last German language film Haneke wrote and directed until the recent *Das weiße Band*.[5] Noticeably, the family's murder/suicide in *The Seventh Continent*—apparently inspired by a real event—as well as the shooting spree and suicide in *71 Fragmente* indeed *do not make sense*. *Der siebente Kontinent*'s nuclear family is socially on the rise, with a long-awaited and hard-earned promotion for the father adding to their economic security, a well-established daily routine and, apparently, a comfortable life in their house. When the couple destroys all their goods and flushes the money down the toilet before killing their young daughter and committing suicide, their motives cannot be explained. Likewise, Max's humiliation at the bank at the hands of an aggressive customer in *71 Fragmente* certainly does not justify his taking out his aggression on innocent bystanders. However, if we take Michael Haneke as a "physician of culture," what Gilles Deleuze calls a "clinician of civilization" (1990: 237), we can establish a point of view from which this clinical picture does make sense. In short, we need to identify this new disease by carefully analyzing its symptoms.

The clinician of civilization, as Daniel W. Smith explains in his excellent introduction to Deleuze's *Essays Critical and Clinical*, "distinguishes cases that had hitherto been confused by dissociating symptoms that were previously grouped together, and by juxtaposing them with others that were previously dissociated. In this way, the doctor constructs an original clinical concept for the disease [...]" (1997: xvi). In the following, I bring out the most important of Michael Haneke's clinical concepts, still prevalent in his French-language films, by concentrating on the different forms of madness in his first four cinematic feature films. I focus on two concepts: trauma, which always results from a failed integration into the symbolic framework, and symbolic exchange, an objectifying (market) force that expresses itself in the infinite substitutability of object for object and object for money. As I argue, these concepts do not provide a cure, or a single identifiable cause for the disease, but rather introduce a pedagogy of the image, where the viewer is led away from seeking a transcendent, true image, or Truth, and instead is initiated into the (painful) taking of perspectives that yields unexpected, plural truths. The clinical concepts of exchange and trauma are only the first steps in the process of finding a possible cure, providing not a punctual event constituting a radical shift, but rather the bringing on of a different mode of thinking and praxis.

In his films, Haneke attempts what Deleuze calls a pedagogy, educating the viewer to more complex ways of reading, thus enabling the diagnostic work performed by the image: "There is a pedagogy of the image, especially with Godard, when the function is made explicit, when the frame serves as an opaque surface of information, sometimes blurred by saturation, sometimes reduced to the empty set, to the white or black screen" (1986: 13).[6] This pedagogy of the image appears in Haneke's films in the insertion of black film, but also in the painfully long sequences of the table-tennis player and the old man's phone conversation in *71 Fragmente*. In *Benny's Video*, it appears as the repeated slaughter of the pig (which we must assume is real, not "all Ketchup," as Benny calls cinematic bloodshed) and as the fictive slaughter of the girl, which we simultaneously see and do not see, being out of the field of vision of Benny's video camera, in turn the object of the film camera. This space that is not shown but that nevertheless exists in the fiction is known as *hors champ* ("out of field") in cinematic terms. In all these cases of video-in-film, the image is revealed *as* image with its manipulative power, thus drawing attention to the materiality of the *hors cadre*, the outside of the cinematic frame itself, the space of enunciation: What is it the director does not allow us to see? Do we really want to see it?

In the framework of clinical diagnoses, it is not surprising that in *Der siebente Kontinent* we do not partake in the couple's planning of the suicide and no psychological motive is ever given, while only the letters to Georg's parents are heard as voice-over. Benny, in *Benny's Video*, pressured to give an explanation for the slaughter of a young girl he encountered by chance, can only say that he "wanted to know how it is." Instead, Haneke's camera—which has often been compared to a diagnostic instrument (Seeßlen 2005: 52)—dissociates and isolates the protagonist's daily routines in order to facilitate the diagnoses. These routines—with some significant exceptions—are symbolic exchanges: buying and consuming food, leaving a note with some lunch money, renting videos, exchanging money for drugs, etc. In each instance, the camera focuses on the object of exchange, sometimes in extreme close-up. As an example, repeated scenes of shopping come to mind, or the long chain of hands in *Benny's Video*, passing on the goods and the money from one choirboy to the next.

The isolating focus on the object of exchange has the curious effect that the object as the actual agent seems to stand still, while the world revolves around it. Here, Haneke shows another kinship with Jean-Luc Godard insofar as a careful differentiation needs to be upheld between what Godard famously calls "*juste une image*" ("just/only an image") and "*une image juste*" ("a just/true image"). While the "just image" attempts to find a perfect expression for a concept, the images Godard and Haneke construct are "only images" that do not point to a transcendent point of view, but rather question it.[7] This differentiation in turn allows two different but not mutually exclusive readings or, rather, perspectives. One perspective that establishes itself in the foreground— and here the images certainly provide a "just" illustration—concerns the lack of meaning in this routine, stressing, as Adam Bingham aptly puts it, the "emotional vacuity of modern life":

> By showing only shots of hands turning off alarm clocks, hands preparing food, etc., the film very effectively states just how mechanically such tasks, the everyday tasks that make up these characters' lives, are performed. And thus just how empty their lives really are. (2004)

This perspective, however, provides the foil for a second perspective, which, since it is an abstract concept, cannot be shown, but is constructed by the constant repetition and insertion of a black screen that syncopates *Der siebente Kontinent* and *71 Fragmente*: the exchange of commodities. More akin to Eisenstein's famous plan to adapt Marx's *Capital* for the screen, Haneke crosses over in these moments to the genre of essay-film, effectively filming the paradoxical impossibility of showing the concept of exchange.

Michael Haneke's educated viewer, enabled to "see" the concept of exchange at work, must now be equally capable of seeing the exceptional.

That this network of symbolic exchange is firmly grounded in consumer capitalism and that words are used sparingly and entirely for the purpose of basic communication is not remarkable in itself. But the notable exception to this circulation of goods, seemingly a rupture of exchange, is the family's murder/suicide in *Der siebente Kontinent*, which takes the form of a suicidal potlatch with a carefully planned exchange of all moveable goods for money, withdrawal of cash and a final feast, followed by a methodical destruction of all furniture and the flushing of the cash down the toilet. This absolute annulment of the family's economic existence, however, is already foreshadowed by some breaks in the otherwise smooth symbolic exchange. When the brother-in-law's inability to get over their mother's death manifests itself at the dinner table, the couple responds to his emotional breakdown with an embarrassed silence. More telling, when the young daughter, Eva, feigns blindness at school, her mother promises Eva that she will go unpunished if she admits her guilt. Ignoring her promise as well as the daughter's obvious attempt to get attention—we see a newspaper with the headline "Girl: blind, but never lonely"—the mother slaps her in the face.

This violation of a symbolic debt finds its most disturbing manifestation in the rationalization that we witness in the suicide note that is left for the parents. Here, the couple explains that they pondered whether they should "take Eva with them" or not. After asking their daughter whether she is afraid of death, and obtaining her response in the negative, they decide that killing her would be in her best interest. A visual illustration of this decision is provided by the fish, whose agonizing death is shown in extreme close-up. At this point, Eva begins to understand her imminent death and resists when she is forced to drink the poisonous cocktail of sleeping pills. Eva as the child, however, is exactly that which escapes the symbolic exchange in the paradoxical form of the gift. As Jacques Derrida points out in *Given Time*, there can be no gift since every gift introduces its receiver into a vicious circle of gift and counter-gift, in short, an economic exchange which denies the very definition of gift as something that is given freely, without ulterior motive. Following Marcel Mauss's play on the etymology of gift, leading to the different meanings that the word gained in English, where it refers to something that is given, and German, where *Gift* means poison, Derrida states:

> In order to be gift, not only must the donor or donee not perceive or receive the gift as such, have no consciousness of it, no memory, no recognition; he or she must also forget it right away [*à l'instant*] and moreover this forgetting must be so radical that it exceeds even the psychoanalytic categoriality of forgetting. (1992: 18)

The only gift—and Haneke clearly points to it in the final sequence of *Der siebente Kontinent*—is therefore the impossible gift of existence that Eva as the child cannot perceive or recognize, but which in turn puts her parents into debt. Contrary to this debt—what we might call an ethical debt—the parents, by giving poison to their child, act on Eva as if she were a commodity in their possession, like the furniture or the fish, not something that is indeed given in the other, radical sense. Thus, the viewer realizes that, in fact, the family murder/suicide is not a rupture in the chain of exchange, but rather a radical form of it, radical because it takes the logic of exchange to a new, undeniably "logical" end, and radical because, as image, it calls attention to that very logic of exchange that the couple fails to overcome.

With this perversion of the gift in mind, we can now better determine Michael Haneke's clinical concept of the exchange. The repeated focus on the exchange of goods shows that the objects of exchange not only provide meaning, but that the protagonists in this circle also fully identify with this logic of exchange, thereby defining themselves as goods—a true perversion in the sense of Lacan's pun of the *père-version*, the father's version, where the subject denies its own excessive sexual enjoyment, its *jouissance*, and instead makes itself into an instrument of the Other's *jouissance*. The perverse logic of the parents' actions becomes apparent here: since the Other as the site of absolute alterity does not exist and cannot be appropriated by identification, serving as an instrument of the Other's *jouissance* means serving a pure projection of an inhuman logic. Characteristically, the (self) destruction is carried out without any apparent emotional involvement. Indeed, instead of seeing the potlatch as an alternative to the capitalist exchange of goods, one that replaces the utilitarian economy of lack with one of excess, as Georges Bataille famously suggests in *The Accursed Share*, the parents in *Der siebente Kontinent* fully identify with the exchange. Any forms of excess, be they emotional or other, have no place in this logic. The reaction to the brother's breakdown and the slap in the face that the spouse receives after declaring her love to her husband in *71 Fragments* also bear witness to this. And the cool reaction of the father in *Benny's Video* is telling. He sarcastically remarks: "*Nicht gerade die ideale Imagepflege!* (Not especially ideal for our public image!)" The problem is one of dealing with the excess, the nonexchangeable—or, as Bataille calls it, expenditure—which threatens the family's symbolic capital. Hence, the body of the victim in *Benny's Video* is entirely perceived as a problem of waste-disposal: "The pieces have to be small enough so that they don't clog the drain."

The audience, by virtue of Haneke's clinical camera, is pushed into the role of Polonius, who has to admit: "Though this be madness, yet there is method in it." Or, as the father at the beginning of the suicidal potlatch perceives: "We can only do this if we approach it methodically!" Only from this limited perspective—from the point of view of the exchange—does it make sense, *Wahnsinn*, to define the family entirely as a closed and dispensable economic circle that can be taken off the circuit without hurting the overall exchange. The sense of delusion stems from the logic of exchange, not a rupture with it, thus making "delusional sense."

This inability to deal with excess and the subsequent identification with the logic of exchange leading to a perversion points to a traumatic, i.e., failed, integration into the psyche's conceptual framework, a failure that Freud famously linked to the death drive. Here, we encounter a second recurring clinical concept, that of trauma, which in Haneke's oeuvre is already discernible in *71 Fragments* but is developed later in his French films, especially *Caché* (2005). According to Laplanche and Pontalis, trauma is "[a]n event in the subject's life, defined by its intensity, by the subject's incapacity to respond adequately to it and by the upheaval and long-lasting effects that it brings about in the psychical organization" (1967: 465). These traumas which appear in all of Haneke's films and are always linked to a violent crime, however, should not be confused with the trauma of the typical traumatized character that we encounter in many Hollywood films and whose trauma is usually eliminated or "solved" by the violent annihilation of the trauma's cause.[8] *Caché*, for example, goes to great lengths to establish George's innocence, who, as a 6 year old, out of jealousy contributed to the removal of an Algerian boy, Majid, to an orphanage, but who was of course too young at that point to understand the effects of his actions. In their concise introduction to the notion of trauma, Baranger et al. point out that in Freud's definition the traumatic should not be confused with the pathogenic. The trauma is instead an event that needs to be "historicized," that is, explained in the form of a history. However, as Baranger et al. stress, the resulting history is only valid from a very limited point of view: "This does not mean that historization is an arbitrary process. As analysts, we cannot propose to anyone any history that is not his own" (1988: 124). The historization that happens in Haneke's cinema is also not arbitrary but belongs to the mad point of view, the only point of view that provides a meaning. Much like an analyst, the audience of a Haneke film has to accept and identify with the mad point of view in order to avoid an arbitrary, i.e., relativistic, reading.

In *Caché* the actual traumata, always resulting from a failed integration into the symbolic framework, appear on three levels. The trigger for the events depicted in the film is the real trauma brought about by the brutal murder of up to 200 Algerians and the subsequent cover-up by French police in Paris on October 17, 1961. On a second, extradiegetic level, the audience can only imagine the abuse Majid must have received as a young Algerian boy, recently orphaned because of a massacre that was committed and covered up by the authorities. Majid's incapacity to deal with the traumatic loss of his parents and the abuse at the orphanage results in an apparently arrested development and his blaming Georges for his misery. The third type of trauma, finally, is the one to which Majid subjects Georges—and by extension the viewer—by his shocking and bloody suicide.

To take another example of Haneke's depiction of trauma, *Le temps du loup* puts this depiction of the violent event that traumatizes the viewer right at the beginning of the film when the father, a figure of calm and sincere authority, is suddenly shot down by a squatter, an event which we witness only through the sound of the gunshot, the blood on the mother's face, and her vomiting in reaction to the slaughter of her husband. The camera carefully avoids a shot of the body. The unknown event that caused the civil order to break down is never explained and, as in the case of Majid's imagined past, stays outside the frame of events unfolding on the screen, always present (we see burning livestock) but unexplained.

Another example of this extradiegetic trauma is certainly the incredible hardship and abuse the young fugitive in *71 Fragmente* must have suffered and to which he alludes in an interview he is giving on television. Again, it is an imagined trauma, requiring an act of imagination on the part of the audience. Apparently unfazed by his ordeals or the interview situation, the fugitive talks about his past. However, if a girl his age already works regularly as a prostitute, how desolate must his own life be? Likewise, the trauma of real historical event is, of course, omnipresent in Haneke's oeuvre in the form of news about violent conflicts that play unobserved in the background in, for example, Benny's room in *Benny's Video*, or the Laurents' living room in *Caché*. As in Godard's films—*Notre musique/Our Music* (2004) and *For Ever Mozart* (1996) come to mind—the war in Bosnia and the Gulf War are omnipresent here. And like Godard and other leading intellectuals, Haneke seems to suggest that the West has not dealt adequately with these traumatic events, that is, has failed to integrate them in its symbolic framework by appropriately historicizing them.[9]

A New Order

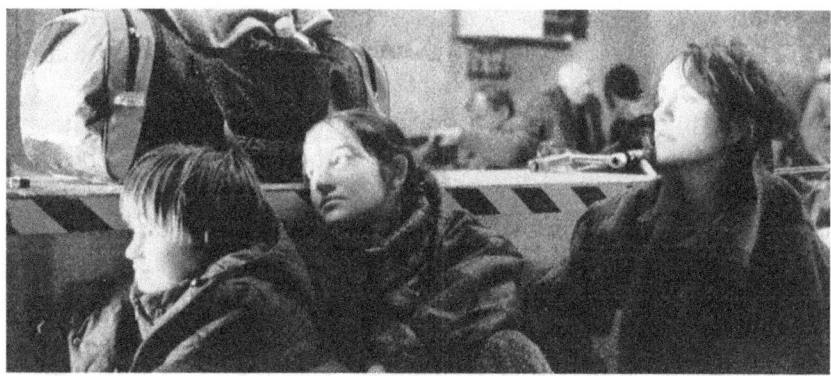

FIGURE 16 Traumatized – the fugitives in *Le temps du loup*

One could object, of course, that establishing trauma as the limit of representation is not exactly a new idea, especially in light of the paradoxes involved in representing the unimaginable of the Holocaust. What Haneke avoids with his complex strategy is the creation of a third, overarching position, one that embraces relativism in order to pursue a meta-truth. This relativism would indeed provide the closure that Haneke's films regularly deny. Again, Deleuze provides a theoretical rationale for this shift which he calls "perspectivism" and which he finds in the Baroque. As Deleuze puts it:

> [P]erspectivism amounts to a relativism, but not the relativism we take for granted. It is not a variation of truth according to the subject, but the condition in which the truth of a variation appears to the subject. This is the very idea of Baroque perspective. (1993: 20)

Instead of the omniscient perspective of traditional narrative cinema, Haneke's films create conditions in which a truth appears to the viewer, as uncomfortable as this truth might be. The truth espoused by this position is not "capital t" Truth, but a plural truth that appears, sometimes briefly, in a given perspective and that is not subjective: just images, and definitely not a just image. Avoiding an image that somehow "captures" a transcendent truth is key here. The clichéd "life is crazy," for example, is inverted and appears as a life that suddenly makes sense when the viewer is forced to take the perspective of the senseless event.

As is the case especially in *71 Fragmente* and *Code inconnu*, the events unfolding on the screen make sense only from the paradoxical point of view of the traumatic event—the *Wahnsinn*—that provides the only link for the different storylines. While in *71 Fragmente* the characters are finally connected by the rampage and the contingency of being in the wrong place at the wrong time, *Code inconnu* adds another dimension by linking different kinds of racism: the thoughtless cruelty of Jean's action and the policemen who automatically take Jean's side, but also the sexism and projected racism of the young Arab who attacks Anne. This perspective that is forced on the viewer is puzzling for many critics who seem to resist what Haneke's pedagogy of the image effectively demands, a thinking from the mad perspective of the traumatic event.[10] Here again we need to acknowledge that Georges and Anne in their different incarnations are objectively innocent. From the point of view of the event, however, their inability to work through or "historicize" the traumas makes them guilty. In this sense *Crash*, by Paul Haggis (2004), could be considered the exact opposite of Haneke's *71 Fragmente* and *Code Inconnu*, with which it shares some structural similarities. *Crash* attempts to find "just images" in order to purvey a strong message, while Haneke's films question the entire concept of the "just," overarching image.

That the appearance of trauma in different forms in Haneke's films can easily be mapped onto Lacan's well-known topology of the Borromean knot, which illustrates the formation of the subject using the entwined circles of Real/Imaginary/Symbolic, underlines the importance of this concept, enabling us to see even better the significance of the perspectival shifts in Haneke's films.[11] If we take the filmic text as a form of the Symbolic and the unseen traumas as the Imaginary, the Real appears mostly in the form of a historic event that is mediated by television. There is, however, another image that Haneke carefully constructs in his films, with the notable exception of the *Le temps du loup* and *La Pianiste* (2001). This pedagogical image appears *just* briefly with the shock of realizing that we are not gazing *at* something but *with* something, thereby traumatizing the viewer with an abrupt shift in perspective.

At the beginning of *Caché*, as I pointed out before, a perfectly innocent shot of a tranquil urban neighborhood is suddenly revealed to be a surveillance video by a fast-forwarding of the tape and voices that comment on what can be seen on it. Here the gazes of spectator, surveillance- and film camera, characters, and unknown agent find themselves suddenly aligned—except that, of course, each of them sees something different. A similar moment appears twice in *Benny's Video*, first when the video of the killing is shown to the parents, and then when Benny shows a video of his parents to the police. And in *Code inconnu* we must realize that a puzzling scene showing Anne frolicking in a pool with another man and a dramatic last-minute rescue of a little boy is only a film in which she stars. The function of this shift is pedagogical in that it educates the viewer about trauma, giving him or her a wake-up call, a taste of trauma first-hand. It short-circuits viewer identification by suddenly putting the viewer in the subjective position of first-person narrative. This is doubly traumatizing because he or she never expected to occupy this position, and because it is also occupied by the unknown agent. The viewer is thus made to bear and confront a troubled ethical position with which he or she must identify at that moment.

However, the most pronounced instance of this traumatizing shift in perspective appears in *Funny Games*, certainly Haneke's most controversial film so far, shocking audiences and critics since its release.[12] While it might be possible for an audience to take a distanced stance towards the violent events depicted in *Le temps du loup* and *La Pianiste*, *Funny Games* refuses any relieving perspective. Again, this refusal of closure works on several levels, the most surprising being the mastery on the intradiegetic level over the diegesis that one of the sadistic killers suddenly deploys. When the mother can grab the shotgun and at least partially avenge the slaughter of her son, the other killer frantically looks for the remote control. He then proceeds to rewind the scene until the crucial moment and thus prevents the mother from reaching the gun in the rerun. This, along with the other self-referential moments, not only destroys the phantasm of an imagined, possible happy-ending, but also the spectator's mastery over the text.

In his perceptive reading of *Funny Games*, Brian Price recognizes that the theme of mastery is established already in the first game of *Funny Games*, the family's classical music guessing-game: "The satisfaction the couple takes in correctly matching name to sound, sign to signifier, is both an expression of cultural mastery and an expression of confidence in an essential bond between the word and sound, speech and authentic self" (26). This bond relates also to the mastery of the spectator, who expects a bond between the text and self, authentication of self by the filmic text. This expectation is mocked by the killers' discussion about the reality of fiction, which "is as real as the reality that you see likewise," right after they throw the mother overboard.

Read on a superficial level, the smug superiority of Peter and Paul, the killers, combined with the film's self-referentiality, would point to a "fallacious allegory," as an enraged reviewer has remarked.

Tellingly, it is especially Haneke's refusal to show the acts of violence, focusing only on the effects, that angers this critic: "It is an immoral procedure and a lie to show the victim's bodies as the sole place of violence" (1998: 39). Price is correct here in insisting that *Funny Games* is not about violence but about the unrepresentability of pain. As he explains, pain that is linked to a cathartic effect in the end serves an ideology: "Instead, pain here mobilizes thought, but ironically does so by its refusal to find a word or image identical to it" (2006: 29). A traditional moralist perspective would seek to provide a meaning, a transcendent point of view, while *Funny Games* insists that the body of the victim is indeed the only space where the image of violence can be found. The conscience of the perpetrator certainly stays clean. Hence the repeated instances of paradoxically innocent guilty persons, like Georges in *Caché*. The young black man in *Code inconnu* who berates Jean for his insulting gesture unwittingly condemns the woman whose dignity he wanted to protect to being deported. And even Benny's deed, as horrible as it is, would not count as premeditated murder, while the parents' careful planning of their criminal act is perfectly rationalized by the reference to a higher order.

It seems, then, that the two clinical concepts that Haneke diagnoses—and that are here called "exchange" and "trauma"—are related in *Funny Games* insofar as there is a class conflict carrying the events. Interestingly enough, this class conflict relates to the audience, not the killers. Not only are the two killers familiar with their victims' way of life, easily able to turn the gated community into a prison camp, but, as their knowledge of golf and sailing shows, they are not impostors but clearly part of the upper-middle-class that they are murdering. Ultimately, the audience's envy of the life of the rich is punished by the traumatizing events we are forced to see, or, what is worse, the spectacle of which we are denied. Again, the killers' actions do not make sense unless we accept the point of view of the exchange fully. Indeed, the only difference between killer and victim seems to be that Peter and Paul do not buy into the values of high culture and morality but fully identify with completely free-floating, fully exchangeable rules of the game that they change at will, even breaking the basic rule of fiction when they break "the fourth wall" by addressing the spectator and changing the diegetic reality. To come back to the viewer of Haneke's films in general, he or she is thus forced to follow the logic of exchange to its end and to confront it in all its traumatic "fullness," thus gaining insight into his or her own implication in this exchange. Or, to follow through the metaphor of the physician of culture, the viewer gains a bill of (ill) health regarding his or her stance on—and in—exchange.

What Haneke shows might be summarized thus: it is not so much that late capitalist culture is characterized by the disease of madness as regards the logic of exchange, but rather that the logic of exchange proceeds prosaically, sanely to its end. Furthermore, to invoke the task of the physician of culture introduced at the beginning, through the concept of trauma newly associated to that of exchange, the viewer is given a unique perspective or view, a brief but true image of that madness and his or her position, both ethical and structural, in it such that the "perspectivality" of the perspective—its constructedness, the manner of its production—is itself briefly visible. The view is thus also a view into the production of this (produced) perspective.

Inevitably, what follows Haneke's clinical diagnosis is the demand for a cure. However, here we need to resist again the temptation to find a cure in the form of a transcendent perspective. As was shown above, by reading the symptoms, Haneke's cinema proceeds in two related steps necessary to diagnose the disease in our culture, whereby the filmic text appears as a form of the Symbolic and the unseen traumas to which the characters are subjected as the Imaginary, while the Real appears mostly in the form of a historic violent event mediated by television. First, Haneke's cinema forces the spectator to accept the only perspective that makes sense, the mad perspective of the *Wahnsinn*. Second, it employs a pedagogy of the image that teaches its audience new ways of seeing in order to avoid the construction of a finalizing—that is, true and just—perspective instead showing "just images."

However, the formulation "just images" should not be understood as irrelevant images or images that convey a relativistic truth that, in the end, is as good as any other truth. As already stated, perspectival truth, while not the same as metaphysical Truth, does have a truth-value appearing in the perspective. To put it in other words, the value of the "cure" lies in the viewer's renewed critical stance that arises from the pedagogical initiation of Haneke's films. These mad—*wahnsinnige*—images demand that the spectator situate him- or herself vis-à-vis the new order that they create. The pedagogical initiation through these images is thus such that the viewer is made to look critically not only at the filmic images, but at his or her own extradiegetic reality implicated by the diegetic madness.

Frame VI

SELF/AGGRESSION:
VIOLENCE IN FILMS BY MICHAEL HANEKE

While it is a commonplace to note that the films of Michael Haneke deal with situations of violence, film criticism as well as the rapidly growing scholarship on Haneke have neglected to remark that the *topos* of self-aggression also pervades his oeuvre. Already his early works for German and Austrian television feature suicides and murder-suicides. We find, for example, the suicide and murder-suicide in *Lemminge, Teil 1 Arkadien/ Lemmings, Part 1, Arcadia* (1979) and *Lemminge, Teil 2 Verletzungen/ Lemmings, Part 2, Injuries* (1979), respectively, and the complete refusal of the father to live and the suicide of the rebellious son in *Fraulein* (1986). Two early films that put Haneke on the critical map as an *auteur*, *Der siebente Kontinent* (1989) and *71 Fragmente einer Chronologie des Zufalls* (1994), feature murder-suicides. When looking at more recent films by Haneke, the farmer who hangs himself in *Das weiße Band: Eine deutsche Kindergeschichte/ The White Ribbon* (2009), the shocking suicide of Majid in *Caché* (2005), and the attempted self-sacrifice of the young boy in *Le temps du loup* (2003) come to mind. One could conclude that a life is not worth much in a film by Haneke. And, indeed, the 2007 shot-by-shot English language remake of his own *Funny Games* (1997) made in collaboration with a large Hollywood studio, drew the ire of the critics because it showcases the torture of the nuclear family, while at the same time systematically refusing any form of meaning: that the parents' offer to throw their own lives into the wager in order to save their child's is, of course, futile when the killers are already in complete control.

As I see it, what the critical discussion of Haneke notably leaves out is twofold: When considering whether Haneke is indeed a political filmmaker and then dismissing him as, at worst, a conservative, or, at best, a filmmaker who manages to effect an ethical engagement on the personal level, that of the individual viewer, critics ignore Haneke's mode of ontological filmmaking. It is the very ontological levels of his films—shifts between which are signaled by different media, the extradiegetic space, narrative devices, genre markers—and the manipulation or perturbation of the latter and, by extension, of the different ontological levels through montage that play a role in the analysis of other, also extradiegetic ontologies, among them political ontology (not to be confused with the approaches of political science). Secondly, as we might expect from an *auteur* like Haneke, when posing questions about politics in this mode, be it in the German or French context, this discussion takes place on the plane of violence in representation itself, that is, his films focus not only on the representation of violence (*how* is it represented?), but also the violence that is done *by* representation.

After comparing suicide in films by Haneke to the way suicide is often functionalized in films, my essay will first establish a link between Haneke's critique of our society and Michel Foucault's description of modern politics as biopolitics by briefly introducing the concepts of two philosophers who build on Foucault's concepts but take them in slightly different directions: Giorgio Agamben's notion of life that is stripped of any political dimension and thus reduced to "bare life" and Gilles Deleuze's description of the society of control. This chapter will then show how aggression in Haneke is routed into auto-aggression, in psychoanalytical terms a *passage à l'acte* where the subject is reduced to an object. I will argue that Haneke shows situations where life is reduced to bare life, and where the already weakened link between bare-life-self and society collapses into itself. In the third, and final, part of this chapter, I will discuss the question of the *mise-en-scene* of suicide and other acts of auto-aggression, specifically, the problem of the witness.

Suicide and Politics

The violence in Haneke's films is always focused on the educated urban middle class, which is clearly his prime audience. As many reviewers have pointed out, Haneke's audience needs a masochistic streak to allow itself to experience the demonstration of unmotivated and unrequited violence. David Sorfa clarifies that "it is particularly the self-satisfied liberal consumer of Art House films that is perhaps the most discomfited by the experience" (Sorfa 2006: 96; see also

Cousins 2007: 224–225). The violence, Sorfa states, renders the domestic space truly *unheimlich*. Violence, something that is not supposed to happen in the bourgeois household other than as a spectacle on the television screen, is shown as being merely suppressed. Indeed, the claim could be made that violence in Haneke is bound to the class of his prime audience, something to which European reviewers seem to be more attuned than their American counterparts.

Fatima Naqvi convincingly argues that Haneke targets the bourgeois self-image as a victim of circumstance. In his first films, he targets the Austrian bourgeoisie in particular, with its often-repeated claim that Austria was Nazi-Germany's first victim. Then, in his later films, it is the middle class in general that is subjected to his critique.[1] In considering this, we should not forget that Haneke's films are also extremely self-reflexive, dealing with the hidden rules of representation. In other words, the question is not in which form violence appears, but rather, *how* can violence mean something at all when it is represented? In this context, Brigitte Peucker's sophisticated arguments that consider violence in films by Haneke in the light of genre are worth reviewing. As she shows in a close reading of Haneke's feature films and his adaptation of Kafka's *Das Schloß*, these "films are composed against the generic backdrop of the bourgeois melodrama" (Peucker 2007: 155). Following Peter Szondi's influential discussion of the bourgeois melodrama, Peucker argues that whereas in the bourgeois melodrama climactic scenes condense emotions in a static tableau in order to elicit empathy from the spectator and sublimate the lack of political action, Haneke breaks with this tradition and shows violence in a cold and fragmented, as Peucker calls it on several occasions, "modernist" style. However, as Peucker concludes towards the end of the chapter, this violence does not introduce the political into the genre: "Acts of violence in Haneke's films are often directed against the self or otherwise remain in some sense familial. Insofar as a political agenda is expressed in Haneke's films, it may very well lie in demonstrating the inefficacy of such acts." The spectator is thus refused "an outlet for the affective tension" thus created and, constantly reminded of the filmic apparatus, instead becomes personally engaged (Peucker 2007: 156). There is, however, more to be said about the political, as I will show later.

While the absence of a critical interest in the topic of suicide in Haneke's oeuvre is in itself interesting, it is maybe more fruitful to trace another remarkable—but unremarked—absence: none of these gestures of aggression and auto-aggression carry an ascribable meaning, that is, none of the other characters "learns a lesson," nor does the spectator feel especially elevated by, for example, witnessing the tragic end to a long suffering. If we take a look at films about suicide—and there are not that many—we can quickly see that Haneke's lack of ascribable meaning is unusual. Let us consider a famous example: *Leaving Las Vegas* (Mike Figgis 1995), a film that Roger Ebert assures us is "operatic in its passion and tragedy" (1995). What Ebert refers to is of course the prototypical melodramatic dynamic that brings about the spectator's catharsis via the leading character, who, in the *dénouement*, sees the error of his ways and breaks down over the dead body of the woman. In opera circles this is known as the "Madame Butterfly effect." And indeed, by the end of *Leaving Las Vegas*, in a reversal of genre-typical gender roles, Ben Sanderson, the character played by Nicholas Cage in his Oscar-winning performance, has taught "the hooker with the heart of gold" what love is and dies with her in his arms.

However, as Terry Eagleton is quick to point out, a wronged lover does not throw away a worthless life when he or she commits suicide. On the contrary: "Sacrifice is not a matter of relinquishing what you find worthless, but of freely surrendering what you esteem for the benefit of others. It is this which marks the difference between the suicide and the martyr" (2003: 35). Even though the unfortunate woman of a typical melodrama piece might have suffered a fate "worse than death," or decided that this life is not worth living without the one she loves, her life paradoxically obtains value after she has surrendered it. It is not surprising, then, that the self-sacrifice for the so-called "greater good" is standard fare in propaganda films. What this type of sacrifice and the woman of melodrama share is the "earned" status of martyrdom in which there occurs an exchange of life for meaning. What the martyr gains in the exchange of life for meaning has two dimensions. Not only does his or her life regain value after the suicide, but this exchange also proves to the others—in a completely tautological gesture—that the Big Other, the cause or movement without whom the martyr cannot live, actually exists: "I give my life for the cause, therefore the cause is worthy and does exist!"

What stays unsaid in this morbid deal is important for the understanding of the functioning of violence and suicide in Haneke's films: for the meaning of the tragic self-sacrifice to emerge, this spectacle has to appear under the implied gaze of others, often later generations, a mechanism that present-day producers of the so-called "martyr-videos" understand all too well. The well-known obsession with ocular metaphors in fascist propaganda makes sense once we realize that it is concerned with the implicit gaze of future generations: "looking back at the martyrs of the movement," "future generations will look back at us," etc. Watching the performance of such a self-sacrifice puts the spectator in turn under a questioning gaze demanding to know whether the spectator will be judged worthy of this sacrifice.[2]

It is in the treatment of violence that Haneke's films show a clear awareness of the politics of Nazi Germany, of which Haneke's own native Austria was a part. Indeed, looking at Haneke's oeuvre, it becomes clear that it does not escape him that the nation that saw itself under the gaze of later generations is also the nation that trained its gaze not to see an enemy but a purely logistical problem. Just to mention a few filmic examples of this efficiency in Haneke's oeuvre, for Benny's father in *Benny's Video* (1992), the body of the girl his son just slaughtered is purely a waste disposal problem, while the suicidal parents in *Der siebente Kontinent* treat their daughter as their property and not as a person to whom they are indebted.

A STATE OF EXCEPTION

All that this reductive gaze sees is what the Italian philosopher Giorgio Agamben, following Walter Benjamin, calls, in his book *Homo Sacer,* "bare life." "Bare life" designates the "incremental remainder" that is left over when somebody's political rights, what we might call their very "humanity," are completely stripped away. In a forceful reading of Carl Schmitt, Michel Foucault, Hannah Arendt and especially Walter Benjamin,[3] Agamben comes to the conclusion that the same foundational momentum that creates any sovereign state (the simple performative speech act: "We lawfully declare our sovereignty by giving ourselves a law!") must *necessarily* create the conflation of politics and life. Laws can be suspended in times of crisis, be it a civil war, a catastrophe, illegal immigration, or any other crises that threatens the sovereignty of a nation. The decision to exceptionally declare such a state of emergency paradoxically takes exception to the exception itself, thus establishing a grey zone that is at the same time inside *and* outside of the law. A person in such a state of emergency could *de facto* be kept in legal limbo, even killed, since this *homo sacer*—Agamben evokes here what he himself calls "an obscure figure of archaic Roman law"—is without any political rights (8). In these zones—Agamben calls them "thresholds" or "zones of indistinction"—we do not find prisoners who, although separated from the community, still are subject to the penal code, but rather inmates who have nothing but their "bare life" (20).

The explanatory power of Agamben's model stems from his insight that states, totalitarian and democratic alike, do not proclaim "enemies of the state" in the mode of a simple "us/them" distinction. "Them" would imply a true outside to the state. As Deleuze and Guattari point out[4]—and Agamben would seem to be in general agreement about this—the modern state is like a machine that works to abolish the outside just as it produces the conditions under which people can be reduced to a "bare life." In his seminal article "The Cultural Logic of Late Capitalism," Frederic Jameson arrives at a similar conclusion. In postmodernity, as he explains, the past is no longer bound to a historical subject or a time and cannot be lived anymore as a collective experience, and instead a nostalgic momentum of space is evoked. Consequently, the decisive distinction of public and private space is eroded. In other words, private space is now fully encoded by capitalism in terms of value, while public space becomes a succession of privately owned anonymous malls and transitory spaces. In *71 Fragmente*, for example, Haneke focuses on typical "non-places,"[5] often showing the Romanian boy in long shots in shopping malls and subway stations where he can easily hide in plain sight as he is not even worth a look.

In this regard, the so-called *glaciation of feelings*-trilogy—*Der siebente Kontinent, Benny's Video* and *71 Fragmente einer Chronologie des Zufalls*—describes the same phenomenon. The nuclear family in the earliest film, *Der siebente Kontinent,* is from the beginning reduced to its economic (inter-)actions by a focus on acts of consumption and exchange—here, objects are handled by hands in close up and bodily needs are taken care of in a timely fashion.[6] The family's space might still be considered private, but the members of the family are entirely identified in terms of value, as they and their possessions can easily be taken out of the calculation in a zero-sum equation: an implosion of value. From this perspective, the young man who runs amok at the end of *71 Fragmente* is, indeed, a double of the families from *Der siebente Kontinent* and *Benny's Video* and not their opposite. The public murder-suicide at the end of *71 Fragmente* is simply an inversion of the "suicide-murder" that happens in the seclusion of the family home in *Der siebente Kontinent,* as both are threshold spaces where humanity is already completely stripped away.

The implosion of value central to Haneke's films should not be confused with an abdication of typical *civic* values, as many critics have done. Indeed, Michael Haneke's diagnosis of the crisis of Western civilization might appear extreme—at no time does he suggest that we could gain access to a space that is not yet colonized by capital or that could somehow be returned to a prior condition. The camera in *Der siebente Kontinent* and *Benny's Video* often frames hands in extreme close-up as they exchange goods for money in fast-food restaurants or supermarkets. The domestic space in the *glaciation of feelings*-trilogy, in turn, appears as anonymous as those malls. It is significant that the young man in *71 Fragmente* snaps in a bank over a minor altercation that ensues when he is refused money. What appears as an explosion that connects the victims in a random event of violence is only another implosion as the killer realizes that he has no symbolic value other than his monetary value. His private space is already conflated with public space. Consequently, this sudden act of aggression can instantly become another event in the news. In other words, contingency and contiguity become one, just as public and private space are mapped onto each other and everybody becomes a *homo sacer*.

When we invoke the polite, white-gloved killers in both versions of *Funny Games* who transform the in-between space of the gated community into a camp and install their own "law of the threshold" in the form of rigged "bets" and "wagers," it should be clear by now that we are not dealing with the murderous excess of some lawless perverts, but with a reenactment of the modern state's conflation of law and politics: there is no law but that of their enjoyment of torture. This conflation makes it possible for the state to regulate not only the everyday life, but the *biological* life of its citizens, and also to exclude certain people from the body of its citizenry, and in turn to regulate their biological life. That does not mean that the guards in Abu Ghraib, a concentration camp, or Peter and Paul in *Funny Games* do not enjoy their games of torture; on the contrary, they visibly enjoy themselves. What happens is that the conflation of law and politics creates a situation where somebody's sadistic impulse becomes the law of the moment. The very existence of pictures from Abu Ghraib clearly shows that the guards had no sense of wrongdoing or of committing an offense.

Before returning to the main topic of this essay, it is crucial to point out how important this political concept of bare life is for Haneke. His films abound with threshold situations that lead to sudden acts of aggression. In *Le temps du loup*, an unknown apocalyptic event has reduced the entire country to a state of exception and at the beginning of the film, the father of the family is shot point-blank in the face by a squatter in his own house while he is attempting to negotiate a solution in the classical liberal mode of discussion and negotiation.

Again, this and other crimes stay unpunished because nobody is in a position to declare a deed unlawful—a point that the film stresses. But the definite proof of Haneke's political intent is indeed the virtually identical remake of his own film, *Funny Games*, made 10 years after the first version and specifically for the American market, precisely because it is a repetition of images. As many critics pointed out, after 9/11, Guantanamo Bay and the Abu Ghraib-scandal, scenes of torture do not appear as far-fetched and divorced from reality as they used to, which provides an insight into the motivation to remake his own film for the US. And indeed, while they understand what motivates the conspiratorial look into the camera, the direct address of the spectator and, especially, the rewinding of the film itself by Paul, these self-referential devices still riled the critics who ultimately dismissed them as nothing but cheap jokes. However, to quote Kubrick's Dr. Strangelove yet again, "it is not only possible, it is essential!" to have a self-referential dimension built in if one wants to make a political film: a film can only be truly political if it refuses a relativizing, overarching point-of-view such as the established ontological difference between text and spectator that a Hollywood-film and a Nazi propaganda film normally provide, and the dimension of self-referentiality is crucial in this undertaking. Classic realist texts like the latter provide a transcendent point of view that more or less openly guides the viewer to a reading that subsumes everything under a more or less complex explanation; in other words, this type of text provides a closure. An apt example, mentioned already before, would be *Schindler's List* (Spielberg 1993), which keeps its humanist perspective. For a filmmaker like Haneke—and also Godard, who famously hates *Schindler's List*—any such explanation constitutes an attempt to make sense out of and close off the haunting question of how human beings can be so cruel to other human beings in the first place. In *Funny Games*, the torturers tauntingly provide the list of possible pseudo-psychological answers themselves: the killers had a difficult childhood, they were abused as children, etc. These answers are ultimately rejected by Haneke. When Paul, the sadistic mastermind, finally reveals his absolute mastery not only over his captives but also over the text itself by rewinding the film, he cuts down the possibility of easy answers to just two perspectives, thereby incriminating the spectator: the perspective of those inside/in power (the killers) and those not-inside (the victims). In Haneke's view, the only answer to the "why?" question is not an answer, but a refusal to play along with the enterprise of explanations in this mode. Our interrogation should rather turn to what makes us so sure that we possess an essential human quality differentiating us from the cold-blooded killers. The question should be "What if Paul is just like us?" The answer might of course disappoint humanists who tend to look for reasoned explanations. As Slavoj Žižek bluntly states apropos of a search for humanist explanations, "what they are actually afraid of is that they will find *nothing*" (Žižek 2001a: 65, italics by Žižek, see also 65–68). To read a cause in Hitler and the Holocaust covers up the possibility that there is no sense in that mass killing, only a responsibility for the future.

It is here that Michael Haneke's affinity with the German New Wave and its preoccupation with the political appears most clearly. Like Fassbinder, Wenders, or Herzog, Haneke does not leave the framework of narrative cinema, but rather subverts narrative cinema by its own means, "destroying" it and its explanations from within. As in Fassbinder's intertextual portrayal of German history, Herzog's inquiries into imperialism, or even Wenders' sometimes-metaphysical ruminations on German identity, we find in Haneke the haunting presence of the German past. In his films, with their singularly obsessive inquiry into acts of aggression that arise out of threshold situations, the haunting presence of the German past with the value it places on self-sacrifice gets translated thus: in a situation where life is stripped of what is known as the political in the traditional sense and reduced to bare life—a remainder perceived as worthless and irredeemable—self-sacrifice has no value, and therefore no meaning.

The question that consequently arises—and that seems to puzzle many critics—is: "Does Haneke promote a return to values in order to make life worth living again?" This question, and his penchant for stylistic austerity, has brought Haneke the ambiguous label of being a modernist. Ambiguous because this implies, at best, a hidden conservatism that claims that values actually existed before we lost them, and, at worst, that Haneke is just a fraud whose modernism amounts to a fascination with violence, and using images of violence to sell films purportedly *against* violence.

Here, we need to look again at the working concept of the political in Haneke in order to see that he is not a modernist filmmaker, but rather a critic of modern politics. His concept of the political—and this is also how Agamben understands politics—is clearly a Foucauldian model of "biopolitics." For Michel Foucault the emergence of biopolitics is linked to modernity: "For the first time in history [. . .] biological existence was reflected in political existence; the fact of living was no longer an inaccessible substrate that only emerged from time to time, amid the randomness of death and its fatality; part of it passed into knowledge's field of control and power's sphere of intervention."[7] In the following, I return to the problematic of suicide in Haneke by first considering it from the perspective of this Foucauldian "knowledge" before turning my attention to the filmic devices and techniques of mise-en-scene that give Haneke's representations of acts of auto-aggression their discomforting, uniquely *political* force.

Auto-Aggression

Suicide came into knowledge's field of vision early on with Emile Durkheim's sociological study, *Suicide*, from 1897. Here, Durkheim famously differentiates between four types of suicide: (1) "Egoistic suicide" occurs when the bond between the individual and society is so weak, when "the loss of cohesion" (169) is so great, that social ties cannot prevent a person from taking his or her life. (2) "Altruistic suicide," its opposite, is something a propaganda film would show, a "sacrifice that is imposed by society for social ends" (220). (3) "Anomic suicide" happens in times of sudden and dramatic changes in social norms, as in "the case of economic disasters" (252). Here, the individual feels in opposition with those new norms to which adjustment seems impossible. And (4) "fatalistic suicide," happens when the opposite of anomy is the case, when a society is too strict and regulating, so that the only escape seems to be death (276).

The four types of suicide defined by Durkheim gave sociologists at the time a theoretical handle on the topic, and they can also serve the argument here. It is interesting to see that altruistic suicide and fatalistic suicide apparently make good material for Hollywood melodramas, but, for reasons pointed out above, can be disregarded here: neither the martyr-suicide, as was pointed out above, nor the tragic Romeo-and-Juliet-plot have a place in Haneke's universe. However, the suicides in Haneke seem to fit the categories of egoistic and anomic suicide. The modern society he depicts is a society in a permanent state of anomy, where all social bonds have been reduced to economic transactions. As mentioned before, in *Benny's Video*, but also in most other films, we find the recurring motif of hands in close-up exchanging money for goods. The existence of the family in *Der siebente Kontinent* is reduced to the motions of their daily routine; that is, they do not exist as a social entity but, like capital, entirely as the performance of changes and exchanges, and this, notably, even includes the exactly-timed exchange of bodily fluids. Therefore it is crucial to understand how precise and consistent Haneke is in his depiction of the classic institutions of modernity—family, school, army—, which he finds to be permanently in crisis. The most prominent examples can be found in Haneke's German-language TV-films and movies: the title of the two-part *Lemminge* already points to an entire generation that lost its bearings, where neither family, nor school, nor army can provide any support. The second part ends with one of the main characters, a captain in the German Army, unleashing his pent-up frustration on some unsuspecting recruits after he alone survived crashing his car into a tree in order to kill himself and his wife. And the glaciation of feelings-trilogy portrays families that seem to function with only perfunctory communication and schools that are at best a storage facility: the especially drab and joyless physical education class and the run-down school in *Der siebente Kontinent* come to mind, and, in *71 Fragmente*, the gun that makes the shooting-spree possible has been stolen from the army.

In an extrapolation of Foucault's theses, Gilles Deleuze, in a short essay, calls the type of society that Haneke depicts a "society of control": "We are in a generalized crisis in relation to all the environments of enclosure—prison, hospital, factory, school, family. The family is an 'interior,' in crisis like all other interiors—scholarly, professional, etc., where there is no longer an outside to the system" (Deleuze 1986; see also Hardt and Negri 2000: 22–23). As Michael Hardt explains in his reading of Deleuze, the dialectics between inside and outside regulated the entire system of the modern nation-state. Here, the private space of the family was clearly separated from the public space of politics. With the gradual waning of this distinction, the difference between us and them, nature and culture, public and private collapses into a system where the outside is basically abolished, where everything is interiorized: the others now have "only" a different culture, nature needs our protection, and what used to be public space is privately owned and operated (see Hardt 1998: 141). The way shopping-malls, fast-food chains and video-stores appear in Haneke's films as cultural wasteland provides a perfect illustration indeed for Deleuze's concept of the society of control.

Deleuze's concept also provides a fascinating insight into postmodern racism. And here, we find of course several examples in Haneke's films. As Hardt explains, elaborating partially on Etienne Balibar's theories of "differentialist racism," in postmodern racism the ontological difference of race is now also interiorized, that is historicized, insofar as only cultural differences exist. While this sounds like a version of the now-familiar and classic liberal stance—"there are no biological differences between the races"—in reality, this relativism becomes an argument for cultural segregation after the fact, by judging how each culture performs in the market place. Hardt states here that ". . . racial supremacy and subordination is not a theoretical question, but arises through free competition, a kind of market meritocracy of culture" (Hardt 1998: 146). Again, in Haneke, this postmodern racism seems to coalesce in what used to be public spaces and leads to immediate and unmediated aggression. Among many examples, we can cite here primarily Haneke's two Paris films, *Code inconnu* and *Caché*. In the former, there is Amadou's valiant gesture of defending the honor of Maria, the Romanian beggar, which leads to his arrest and her deportation. And in *Caché*, the police acts solely on the suspicion of Georges, the upper-middle-class TV-personality, arresting Majid and his son without proof. In all these cases, racism appears not as a direct discrimination based on race, but as a more diffuse and institutionalized racism that cannot not be fought by anti-discriminatory legislature.

What happens, then, at these points of encounter—be they contingent, racist, ritualized—marked by immediate aggression is a perfect example of a *passage à l'acte*. Such a "passage to the act," as the *Dictionary of Lacanian Psychoanalysis* explains, is "an exit from the symbolic network, a dissolution of the social bond." The subject acting out should not be seen as psychotic, but the *passage à l'acte* "does entail a dissolution of the subject; for a moment, the subject becomes a pure object" (Evans 1996: 137). In other words, the acting out not only negates the link to society, but also to oneself. Significantly, in Žižek's account, the *passage à l'acte* even entails a suicidal dimension. Using *Taxi Driver* (Scorsese 1976) as an example, he explains:

> when Travis prepares for his attack he practices in front of the mirror the drawing of the gun; in what is the best-known scene of the film, he addresses his own image in the mirror with the aggressive-condescending "You talkin' to me?" In a textbook illustration of Lacan's notion of the "mirror stage," aggressivity is here clearly aimed at oneself, at one's own mirror-image. This suicidal dimension reemerges at the end of the slaughter scene when Travis, heavily wounded and leaning at the wall, mimics with the fore-finger of his right hand a gun aimed at his blood-stained forehead and mockingly triggers it, as if saying "The true aim of my outburst was myself." (2005)

In Haneke, the suicidal dimension of the aggressive *passage à l'acte* is related to the reduction of life to a devalued form of existence, where the devaluation takes on not only capitalist, but often also clearly racist overtones. In its purest form in Haneke, the murder-suicide of the family in *Der siebente Kontinent*, the *passage à l'acte* is remarkably calm in its execution and takes the form of a zero-sum situation—all liquid assets are transformed back into paper money, then systematically destroyed—so that the aggressive dimension appears as secondary, only as an effect on objects like furniture, animals, and children.

Before turning to the mise-en-scene in the final part of this essay, a preliminary summary of our discussion is appropriate. In Haneke's films, the—albeit temporary—dissolution of the subject in the *passage à l'acte* has a suicidal dimension and seems to be facilitated by the threshold situations that we find in our contemporary society of control, where no social bonds or rules prevent this short-circuiting of subject and object and where life is already reduced to a worthless "bare life." In contrast to the martyr-suicide that tautologically proves the value of an ideological construct, the mostly male characters negate in a definitive move the already-diminished nexus of self and society by destroying themselves and others.

Funny Games, which I take here as two parts of the same film, seems to be the odd one out, insofar as there is no apparent suicide in the film. However, it is important to understand the significance of the two killers belonging to the same class as their victims, as Peucker rightfully underlines (2007: 147)—they are cultured, well-spoken, versed in the right brand names, and know how to golf and sail. In the American version, we could imagine Paul and Peter to have met at an elite liberal arts college, maybe in a class taught by a well-meaning professor like Rupert Cadell (James Stewart) from Alfred Hitchcock's *Rope* (1948). In both films, the auto-aggressive momentum of the *passage à l'acte* is aimed at the aggressors' own class.

The Paradox of the Witness

As was pointed out above, for the meaning of the tragic self-sacrifice to emerge in propagandistic texts, the suicide has to appear under the implied gaze of others. Regardless of the above-cited reputation of Haneke's oeuvre as "violent," acts of aggression towards another person always happen off-screen and are only present to the viewer by the sounds and/or their aftermath: the camera stays outside the bank during the shooting spree in *71 Fragmente*, only to join the victims in a close-up as their blood seeps on the floor. Benny's slaughter of the girl can be seen neither in nor recorded on *Benny's Video*. And the cold-blooded killing of the father in *Le temps du loup* is mirrored by the mother's shocked face. Last, but not least, the infamous slaughter of the little boy in *Funny Games* happens while the spectator watches Paul preparing a sandwich, and the Hollywood-style revenge of the mother is undone by the rewinding of the film. In contrast to this off-screen violence, suicide in Haneke almost always happens in front of a witness who seems to be strangely unaffected by the horrible spectacle and not traumatized in any way. In *Lemminge, Teil 1*, the brother jumps to his death in front of his sister, who appears calm afterwards. On the other hand, the parents who do not witness this event but, as we are told, were injured at the end of the war protecting their children are instead devastated. In *Lemminge, Teil 2*, the major who killed his wife in a murder-suicide but who survived with injuries seems to be unchanged.[8] The mother in *Fraulein* appears just the same after she sees her husband wasting away by his own will, and even after her son, cornered by the police, blows himself up while she watches his hide-out. The piano-teacher in *La Pianiste*, of course, draws up a meticulous plan to make her lover a witness to and an accomplice in her torture, only to find out that he is not the least troubled or affected. Here, again, the spectator is witness to her self-mutilations, cutting her genitals in the bathroom and stabbing herself in the shoulder in the last scene. In *Caché*, it seems strange that Georges barely reacts to the traumatic event of the film, the sudden suicide of Majid. Instead of recognizing that he failed to help the grown-up Majid, Georges afterwards still acts on his main fear, namely that of tarnishing his public image.[9] Even though shaken by the event he witnessed, Georges' primary concern seems to be whether his wife kept up appearances when she sent their friends away on a pretext. And the next day, before falling into bed, he convincingly assures Majid's son that he does not feel guilty at all.

Although Haneke's exclusions (the spectator only sees the aftermath of violence) and inclusions (a witness to a suicide appears unfazed) seem unwarranted at first, we find underlying them, not coincidentally, a commentary on the standard demand of neo-fascist reactionaries regarding witnessing. At the beginning of his book, *The Differend*, Lyotard refers to just this neo-fascist demand and the paradox it implies: Bring me a single witness who can testify . . . As Lyotard explains, since by definition the only true witness—the one who experienced *everything*—is paradoxically the one who was killed, there *is* no witness at all. All *real* witnesses to an act of violence are either dead, or they are perpetrators and would therefore perjure themselves if they spoke. And, as we can deduct from this perversion of legal argumentation, this "reasoning" serves as a silencing device that insinuates that the person bringing forth the accusation is nothing but an impostor. In all brutality and simplicity the survivor is told: "S*ince you are not dead,* *you must be a liar; how else could you stand here and testify?!*' The inherent judgment denies the victim his or her existence as a victim by including the frame of reference of a statement (the reality so to say) into the argument itself. As Lyotard explains, this argument is not only circular, it is truly totalitarian: "If the requirement of establishing the reality of a phrase's referent according to the protocol of cognition is extended to any given phrase, especially to those phrases that refer to a whole, then this requirement is totalitarian in its principle" (Lyotard 1988: 5). Keeping in mind the rewinding of the film by the killer in *Funny Games*, we can imagine this argument being like a film that is spliced back into itself: the representation of reality is printed back onto itself like a Moebius-stripe and we make what should be the absolute and irreducible plane of our argumentation an object for our cognition.[10] This is Haneke's way of showing totalitarian gesture at work.

Here, we find the double-bind situation that vexes most of Haneke's critics. It would seem that Haneke is playing into this principle of exclusion, removing all witnesses because they are inauthentic. When Haneke violates his audience and forces it to agree to the draconic rules the filmmaker imposes, does he not claim an exception, however slim, for himself? There is, however, an often overlooked exception to the exception in Haneke's oeuvre: a child is a perfect witness for Haneke. Haneke's unsentimental portrayal of children is noteworthy here. He takes pains to avoid the impression that we could reclaim their worldview in any way or that children could be seen as "essentially innocent" in any way—they are driven by their desires like everyone else. However, children are innocent of the violence that they witness. Here, I would not contradict Christine Wheatley who claims, following Kant, that children in Haneke are in an ethical state of nature (2009: 164). However, although Haneke appears to be an extremely precise and analytical filmmaker, he always stresses movements and developments over structure. Significantly, children cannot just stay in a state of nature, but have to grow up. Benny in *Benny's Video*, overcomes his parents' obsession with their image in society and turns himself and them in to the police; and Ben in *Le temps du loup*, is able to give meaning to the community by his readiness to sacrifice himself for it, to bring up just a few examples. The real tragedy for Haneke, then, lies in a child to whom such a development is denied—the girl that is beaten to death at the house next door in *Code inconnu*, for example, or Eva in *Der siebente Kontinent* who is granted one of the few instances of nondiegetic music in Haneke, tellingly in the form of the haunting violin concerto, "To the Memory of an Angel" by Alban Berg, as was mentioned before.

I will focus in the last paragraphs of this chapter on Majid in *Caché*, the most spectacular suicide and certainly the emblematic figure for self-aggression in Haneke's oeuvre. To come back to what was pointed out above, Majid is not a martyr. His suicide under the eyes of the hidden camera and Georges does not lead to any cathartic moments, as we could imagine them in a mainstream film: shocked by Majid's anomic suicide, Georges uses his influence to produce a show decrying the long-repressed massacre of Algerians by the French police to counteract the tape's becoming public knowledge and leading to Georges' humiliation. Of course, nothing like that happens because Georges does not consider himself guilty and bound to act in any way. In the scene immediately preceding Majid's suicide, we see Georges acting in bad faith, manipulating images in a scene that mirrors the famous surveillance shot at the beginning of the film—first, we look at Georges' show, only to find out that we are looking with Georges who is editing the footage. Indeed, Georges lives in a world where the difference between public and private has finally been abolished—his dining room and his set in the TV-studio look alike—a world that is just image. In *Caché* itself, as the allegory of this very situation, there is no longer a difference between film and video.

Georges' memory reveals that he did indeed act maliciously and lied to his parents, but Georges was a child at the time and could certainly not be called guilty. However, his parents certainly could, and the adult Georges *is* guilty of not helping the distressed Majid, in the same way that France—indeed the First World in general—is guilty of, and has not accepted responsibilities for, and the effects of its past colonialist actions, as many critics remark (see Ezra and Sillars 2007: 219; Mecchia 2007: 134; Wheatley 2009: 164). After being forcefully removed from the farm, it is entirely left to the audience to imagine to what kind of abuse Majid was subjected in a French orphanage in the nineteen-sixties and seventies. There is no direct witness to the abuse that leads to the state of an arrested development clearly indicated by the childish drawings and Majid's behavior, just as there is no explanation for the arrested development of the title character of *La Pianiste*. All we have as a proof for the violence is Majid's body, the body of the immigrant who thus stands for the vanished bodies of the murdered that cannot be retrieved and whose disappearance ultimately cannot be witnessed.

On the other end of the spectrum, so to say, in strong opposition to the silenced witnesses of totalitarian politics, we find the perspective of Georges-as-child. It is crucial to note that the traumatic event of Majid's removal from the farm is shown from the point-of-view of Georges as child and not, as a more generic film would do, inserted as a flashback. All these scenes of involuntary memory are framed by Georges-as-child: Majid appears menacing and the camera is situated at the height of a 6 year old. Clearly, the point of view is bound to Georges in whose memory this scene takes place. Here, in the recapturing of the past in the present, we can begin to determine the meaning of Majid's suicide. While it is certainly a *passage à l'acte*, where the "worthless, non-productive immigrant" acts out societies' racist impulses, this suicide is primarily a gift to George, just as the tapes and the drawings are gifts. "I wanted you to be present!" Majid tells Georges who, of course, does not recognize what he is forced to witness as such. But the images from the past are actualized in his memory, just as we have to recognize that we were watching this shocking suicide *with* the surveillance camera.

It would seem, then, that the surveillance camera can thus be said to acquire the status of a witness, an impossible witness who nevertheless proclaims in no uncertain terms Haneke's refutation of the neo-fascists' manipulation of the paradox of the witness for their own, unethical ends. In denouncing this manipulative abuse of the paradox, Haneke not only insists on the full validity of the paradox, but also points to the role the medium of film plays in thinking it through critically. Inasmuch as film (and video, Haneke's other medium) can be used to manipulate events and represent them in a certain way, there is also the possibility of a responsible *medium* that constitutes an irrefutable witness that precludes total evasion of guilt even as it has no power to instill any sense of it. But, in the final analysis, perhaps Haneke is showing through filmic means that the necessary, irrefutable witness, too, is a fiction as it depends on the independence of the medium, more specifically the camera, itself. In a world where all distinctions have been conflated, where the difference between inside and outside no longer holds, the difference between medium and montage has suffered a similar fate. It is, after all, as a result of *montage* that we have the surveillance camera in place to record the suicide of Majid. Perhaps what Haneke is calling for is a mode of responsible montage, the only kind that can do justice to the paradox of witnessing by unfolding all its aspects, and yet without finding a solution to simply make it go away.

In other words, and to come back to Georges as witness, the child-witness is Haneke's way of not falling into the trap of a totalitarian mode of representation and its maintaining in bad faith a paradox, that of the bare-life witness, the *homo sacer*, whose sacredness it does not really espouse. Instead, through the attentive and subtle use of filmic montage, and because there is, in the end, no *real* distinction between our extradiegetic space and the virtual space of film, Haneke is able to lay at the door step of the attentive viewer the gift of violence done *by* representation. Violence is moved back to the present, is literally "re-presented."

Frame VII

THE MORAL OF THE LONG TAKE

The four films that the Austrian director Michael Haneke shot in France transformed him instantly, if not into a French, then into a European *auteur*. Judging by cast, topic, and style, these films—*Caché* (2005), *Le temps du loup* (2003), *La Pianiste* (2001), and *Code inconnu: Récit incomplet de divers voyages* (2000)—appear in the best tradition of a classic French *auteur*-cinema. Without doubt taking a pay cut, but achieving some of the best performances in their entire career, Juliette Binoche (*Caché* and *Code inconnu*), Daniel Auteuil (*Caché*), and Isabelle Huppert (*Le temps du loup* and *La Pianiste*) lend their reputations and screen presence to these films, which normally would have had trouble receiving financial backing, even in France. Based on the genres to which these films appear to belong, Haneke willfully embraces traditional *auteur*-genres. *Caché/Hidden*, probably the most successful film of the four, uses elements of the crime/mystery thriller—a genre evocative of Claude Chabrol's entire oeuvre, as was mentioned in Frame III—to deliver a scathing critique of French society's failure to come to terms with the past. The post-apocalyptic *Le temps du loup/The Time of the Wolf* stands firmly in the tradition of other French meditations on life after the collapse of society—Chris Marker's *La Jetée* (1962) comes to mind, as does *Malevil* (Christian de Chalonge 1981) and *Le Dernier Combat/The Last Combat* by Luc Besson (1983). *La Pianiste/The Piano Teacher*, on the other hand, could aptly be described as a daring adaption of a complex literary text that was generally considered "unfilmable"—certainly a genre in itself that generally invites fruitless discussions about the "fidelity to the source." *Code inconnu* with its multiple strands of narration reflecting the sometimes-chaotic life in a big city is also not unusual. In the same year as *Code inconnu*, for example, Laurent Firode released *Le Battement d'ailes du papillon/Happenstance*

(2000), a film that also deals with coincidental encounters and their serious consequences.

Looking at Michael Haneke's oeuvre, we can quickly see that the many references to genre-conventions remain on the meta-generic level, insofar as the generic markers mostly provide false leads. As I have already pointed out in this book, all of Haneke's films evoke one or several generic frames, only to disappoint viewers' expectations. The two versions of *Funny Games*, just to mention two Haneke films that enraged the critics, initially set the mood for a typical "horror/thriller," in this case the subgenre of the "home invasion thriller."[1] While the absence of the genre-typical denouement might not be too disturbing, the self-reflexive moment of giving the killers not only power over their captives, but also over the entire narration certainly inspired some of the most derisive reviews a film by a European *auteur* has ever received. A struggle for narrative hegemony is, of course nothing new; however, these struggles normally result in a paradoxical conflict only on a textual level, for example, when a voice-over narrator is killed later in the film, as in *Laura* from 1944 by the Austrian-born Hollywood director Otto Preminger, or in the neo-noir *Casino* (Scorsese 1995).

Turning our attention back to Michael Haneke's French films, it is crucial to remark that his references to the generic tradition are aesthetically motivated insofar as the stylistic tradition of French cinema is concerned. The stylistic tradition of French cinema and the theoretical debates that shaped it, as I will argue here, play an important intertextual role. Indeed, Haneke solves a problem in these films—and here Haneke appears quite Deleuzian as he thinks in images—that not only occupies Haneke's entire oeuvre but also that of the *nouvelle vague*, a problem that could be summarized quite succinctly as: "How can a film realistically depict violent events without falling into a voyeuristic celebration of violence that will further numb the audience?" However, in order to determine how Haneke solves this problem, we need to first map out the intertextual relations of this problem in French cinema.

The stylistic tradition from which Haneke's French films spring can be informative concerning above all the extended length of the takes, whose presence in the films is not surprising for a director who cites two films by Bresson as well as films by Tarkovsky, Antonioni, and Rossellini as his major influences in the 2002 *Sight & Sound* poll.[2] Here, we need to distinguish between the different forms such a long-lasting shot can take. There is, first, the long take in the form of a static camera, where the action happens in the fore- and/or the background. Second, there is the tracking shot where the camera accompanies, for example, a couple walking down the street, travelling parallel to the action, often on dolly-tracks. This shot is therefore also known as dolly-shot or, in French, as "*le travelling.*" A combination of the two would build a "*plan séquence,*" literally a sequence-shot, a scene comprised of a single long take, often with changes of focus and a moving camera. The most famous long take in cinema is probably the beginning of Orson Welles' *Touch of Evil*, where Welles, long before the invention of the steady cam, was able to create a shot that lasts over 4 minutes and comprises changes in depth of field, sophisticated tracking shots and crane movements. Haneke normally avoids over-complicated long shots but *Code Unknown*—on which I will concentrate here—features an incredible *plan sequence*, a parallel *travelling* up and down a busy Parisian street that begins with Binoche's character leaving her building and ends nine and a half minutes later with an arrest.

First, let us consider the long-shot vis-à-vis the French tradition. The long dolly-shot—the *travelling*—has a special significance for the *nouvelle vague*. In July 1959, during a spirited discussion of *Hiroshima, mon amour* (Alain Resnais 1959) held by some critics of the *Cahiers du Cinéma*, Jean-Luc Godard, only a few months before shooting his own first feature, utters the cryptic remark: "*Les travellings sont affaire de morale/ Tracking shots are a question of morality.*" The French *morale* has a slightly different meaning than the English word, and it works as either "ethic" or "moral doctrine", or as moral in the sense of "moral" or "lesson" of the story. The question Godard answers was actually aimed at Eric Rohmer, who had stated that he found that *Hiroshima, mon amour* still had "rather enervating moments." Asked whether he meant this "morally or esthetically," Godard cut in, saying, "It's the same thing. Tracking shots are a question of morality."[3] At the end of this part of the discussion, he adds another layer of meaning, albeit opaque, to this strange dictum by referring to another paragon for the nouvelle vague, Sacha Guitry, and crediting him with the solution of the "famous false problem of the text and the image" (Domarchi 1959: 6; Domarchi in Hillier 1985: 62). This, of course, begs the question of what this "false problem" actually is, but I will return to this later. It could be said that the moral of the French debate and of a Haneke film is essentially the same: an ethic or moral doctrine. For Haneke, this ethical doctrine amounts to an impetus to teach the viewer something about his ethical stance vis-à-vis what he is watching on the screen, both as medial production and depiction of historical event, with, again, no divide between form and content.

Before unraveling these related questions, let us look at another example of authorial outrage as it is instructive for a comprehension of Godard's remark. Less than two years after this discussion during which Jacques Rivette was also present, the latter critic and filmmaker delivers a scathing critique of *Kapò* (1959), a famous film at the time by Gillo Pontecorvo, who later made *La Battaglia di Algeri/ The Battle of Algiers* (1966). In *Kapò*, the director, in order to strengthen the emotional impact of an inmate's death, uses a forward dolly-shot to center the dead woman who threw herself against the electrified fence of a concentration camp, thus contrasting the aesthetics of the image with the cruel manner of her suicide. A director who does such a thing, Rivette exclaims, "only deserves the deepest contempt" (Rivette 1961: 54). Here, then, we find the irreducible positions in unadulterated form in two films that attempt to depict an event of absolute violence: On one side, in *Hiroshima, mon amour*, Resnais' complicated rendering of the traces the traumatic impact of World War II left in the memories of two survivors of, respectively, the bombing of Hiroshima and the war in Europe. On the other side, Pontecorvo's *Kapò*, aiming at a realistic depiction of the price of survival in a concentration camp, something that must necessarily fall short of the real horror of a camp, therefore causing Rivette to call his essay "*De l'abjection*," in English, "of abjectness."

To understand the irreducible positions taken by the directors of these films—the better ultimately to understand the irreducible stance of Haneke—it is important to follow the development of this discussion, whose later expression came with Serge Daney, who belonged to the second generation of critics at the *Cahiers du Cinéma*. Daney revisits the debate in a fascinating article in 1992. Indeed, he literally revisits the memories of his first encounter with the films covered in the aforementioned *Cahiers* articles, mainly Resnais' *Nuit et Brouillard/ Night and Fog* (1955) and *Hiroshima, mon amour*. Daney's basic move is to show that he has to be personal to define the "*abject*," which would translate as sickening or loathsome, but could also mean the obscene and absolute opposite of the self, if we want to retain Kristeva's definition of the abject (Kristeva 1982). The abject, as Daney sees it, is decidedly not only situated on the side of the spectator but really anchored in one's own personal reaction to a film. As Daney points out, a look at the obscene can never again be as innocent as that of the first American documentary crews just arriving at the concentration camps. Therefore, the "non-images" of Resnais are infinitely preferable to the abjectness of a more or less realistic recreation, an "aestheticization" after the fact, as Daney calls it, which only serves to ease our bad conscience (1992: 11). Perfect examples for a continuation of the type of aesthetic Rivette sees in *Kapò* can easily be found in films by Steven Spielberg. *Schindler's List* (1993) and *Amistad* (1997), for example, both realistically recreate scenes of extreme violence in order to engage the spectator and cause feelings of repugnance and moral indignation.

The next step in Daney's essay—his statement that the modern cinema is cruel—is more difficult to understand, as he presumes a thorough knowledge of Bazin. Referring to Bazin's penchant for long takes that include potentially dangerous encounters in the same frame (uniting, for example, a lion and a child), Daney states that the modern cinema—and here he includes the great European *auteur*-filmmakers, as well as the Japanese directors they admired—is cruel insofar as it hides nothing from the viewer, especially nothing unpleasant. This realism, as Daney reminds us, should also be seen as a reaction to the realism of propaganda films, a realism that could rather be called a "'réalistique'," as he states (Daney 1992: 14). What Daney does here, I think (apart from the obvious reference to a famous posthumous collection of Bazin-essays that the editor, François Truffaut, named *The Cinema of Cruelty*, see here Frame I), is cut through the Gordian knot of the problem of realism in Bazin.

At this point, a short excursus is necessary, especially since Michael Haneke addresses all of Bazin's notions of realism and since Haneke is certainly an especially cruel *auteur*. Directly after the complex *plan sequence* at the beginning of *Caché*, a series of pictures from the war in Bosnia is inserted. In the frame of the narration, these photographs of death and destruction are taken by Anne's, the main character's, boyfriend, a photo-journalist whose letter to her accompanies the slide-show as a voice-over. However, it is clear to the viewer that these snap-shots are not fictional, that is, recreated for the film, but are actual documents of the war. The frames of reference are therefore twofold: (1) intradiegetically, the photographs bring the war in Bosnia into a relation with the film's topics—miscommunication, racism, nationalism, the failure to render assistance and (2) extradiegetically, the real documents bring into relief the ontological but also the ethical questions *Code inconnue* addresses. Several times throughout the film, the viewer is tricked, again by playing on generic conventions, to engage emotionally with a situation, only to be shown that these inserts are "only fiction." For example, a dramatic scene, in the style of typical Hollywood-*mise-en-scene*, in which Anne fails to save a child from falling from the roof of a high-rise, is revealed to be a movie in which Anne is acting. Furthermore, the voices we hear are from the narrative present, as we see Anne and her co-star in a sound booth dubbing their voices.

Code Unknown contrasts the spectator's real emotions, which are easily triggered by a fairly conventional clip, with the lack of emotion towards the real atrocities that come to us via the constant newsfeed from television. For the filmmaker, the ethical question here is, of course, an inversion of the one Daney asks: should an artist use pictures of real atrocities in a fictional text?

Partially due to a translation into English that does not catch all the nuances of Bazin's metaphor-prone style, Bazin's passionate praise of long take and deep focus over montage has in the English-speaking criticism long been understood as a dogmatic judgment on the grounds that these devices come closer to our perception of reality than a montage of shots, and that Bazin indeed takes the relation between the object and its photographic image as indexical. Interestingly, as cinema is less and less dependent on light causing a chemical reaction on actual film stock and might soon reach a point where entire scenes are composed digitally, there has recently been a renewed interest in Bazin, defending him against simplistic interpretations and providing a more nuanced reading.

While Douglas Smith does not engage the canonical interpretations of Bazin directly, he points out some breaks in Bazin's dogmatic insistence on spatial and temporal unity, an "elasticity" as Smith puts it (2004: 94–95). As Smith shows with a close reading of some of Bazin's lesser known writings on documentary films, Bazin's realism is not based on an ontological presence, "but ultimately a realism of loss and absence, motivated by a self-defeating desire to preserve what cannot be preserved" (Smith 2004: 100–101). Here, we see not only a direct link with Bazin's article on "The Ontology of the Photographic Image," where Bazin famously traces the genesis of photography in the embalming of corpses in ancient Egypt, but also to a key statement on the relation of film to time:

> The photographic image is the object itself, the object freed from the conditions of time and space that govern it. No matter how fuzzy, distorted, or discolored, no matter how lacking in documentary value the image may be, it shares, by virtue of the very process of its becoming, the being of the model of which it is the reproduction; it *is* the model. (Bazin 14)

As Daniel Morgan points out in his illuminating analysis, it is important to carefully look at Bazin's wording—the image has the ontological status of the photographed object, but the depicted objects are now outside of time (Morgan 2006: 450–452). Morgan then concentrates on an important implication of Bazin's statement: if the viewer is free to take completely new perspectives on this new object freed from time, it also means that a shot is not faithful to reality but to an impression of reality—here Morgan refers to another of Bazin's canonical texts, the praise of Orson Welles' deep focus photography (Morgan 2006: 456). Realism, then, is not based on a similarity with the extradiegetic reality, but "an attitude the filmmaker takes toward reality itself," as Morgan concludes in a detailed study of several of Bazin's key texts (Morgan 2006: 463).

Jonathan Friday comes to a similar conclusion. He underlines that Bazin takes a decidedly psychological perspective on film, analyzing the "psychological effects of the photographic mode of representations" (Friday 2005: 344). Friday (2005: 342) points out a passage in Bazin that carefully distinguishes two forms of realism: "The quarrel over realism in art stems from a misunderstanding, from a confusion between the aesthetic and psychological; between true realism, the need that is to give significant expression to the world both concretely and its essence, and the pseudorealism content in other words with illusory appearances" (Bazin 1958: 13, 1967: 12). It is this "pseudorealism" that Daney refers to as "réalistique," a realism that is implicitly still wedded to a simple, direct equation of reality and photographic image.

As I mentioned above, Daney circumvents this long discussion by treating the problem, as in the Godard quote from above, as another "false problem of text and image," that is, stressing that a film must always be "read" not watched, as he points out (Daney 1992: 16). Hence, instead of looking for an indexical relation between film and reality, Daney asks whether there can still be "any index/sign (*indice*) for abjection." Or, to put it in slightly different terms, he asks whether the filmic text still has the power of posing such an interdiction, or whether the "lucky charm"—*grigri* as Daney calls it—of an abject travelling, which he himself never even saw and only knows from Rivette's article, has lost its power (Daney 1992: 14). Here, we could translate Daney's fetish according to the Freudian terms of a fetishistic disavowal. In the case of Daney, the disavowal concerns the difference between form and content of such a shot: a tracking shot *must* be a question of morality, as Godard has it, otherwise there would really just be a simple difference in degree rather than quality between realism and the *réalistique*.

We can now see in what sense Daney's position resonates with the more recent scholarly arguments briefly summed up above. Further, I think, we can now understand Daney's final statement regarding the abjectness of the tracking shot in *Kapò*—as he concludes: "This travelling was immoral for the good reason that it put us, him, the film-maker and me, the spectator there, where we were not. There, where I, in any case, could and would not want to be." (Daney 1992: 18–19). This statement begs the question of whether a film does not do exactly that by its filmic nature whereby spectators identify with depicted characters, or better, are interpolated into spectatorial positions that put them "there, where we were not." However, here we must again differentiate between the two types of realism. Recreating an image of past atrocities and using montage and shifting camera positions to strengthen the emotional impact on the spectator by way of this representation results in a pseudo-realism that puts the spectator in the position of a symbolic mastery over the text, also suggesting a mastery over reality. Spielberg's intentions in making the above-mentioned *Schindler's List* and *Amistad*, are, without doubt, honorable, but the striving for absolute authenticity in recreating these images, superseding even the ban on nudity in Hollywood Cinema, does amount to such a suggestion of mastery. As a result of the overarching will to authenticity to which aesthetic choices are subordinated, Spielberg makes the unfortunate choice to use a voyeuristic convention, and the key scenes that depict the utmost dehumanizing moment of mass murder are erotically charged as a result: in *Schindler's List*, the female prisoners are herded naked into a shower, expecting to be gassed, while the camera stays outside looking in through a peephole. In *Amistad*, on the other hand, dozens of slaves are horribly killed by drowning. As the naked men, women and children are drawn overboard one by one, the camera frames their writhing bodies in a medium close-up from above. The almost intolerable cruelty of the event thus stays on the side of the image. To invoke the concept of cruelty in cinema discussed in an earlier chapter, cruelty needs to be inflicted on the viewer and not simply conveyed in the image. When it stays on the side of the image, it is reduced to a theme or topic and loses the pedagogical thrust that Artaud believes cruelty should have.

Here, the case of Godard is instructive regarding Haneke. As Colin MacCabe explains in his biography of Godard:

> The filming of the camps has been at the centre of Godard's concerns from the very first. The failure to prevent or record the camps is one of the major, if not *the* major theme of the *Histoire(s)*. From very early on, Godard held that the only way to film the camps would be from the perspective of the home life of one of the guards. (2004: 328)

Asked, again, about his often voiced dislike of Spielberg, Godard states: "I don't know Spielberg personally, but I don't like how he transformed the gas chamber into a shower room" (Dupont 2001). It is precisely the "how," the aesthetic means chosen to depict an event, that concerns Godard and also Haneke for whom, as a critical German-speaking artist of his generation, a coming to terms with the Holocaust is practically mandatory.[4]

In contrast to the *réalistique* of Spielberg, the type of realism that Bazin, Rohmer and Daney have in mind (and that Haneke practices, as I show through examples) is one that takes a moral perspective on reality, formulating an interdiction in the vein of the biblical ban on exactly those cruel images shown by Spielberg, arriving instead at a true "cinema of cruelty." As noted in the introduction, Haneke never shows the act of violence but its effects. *Caché*, for example, follows Resnais' *Hiroshima, mon amour* aesthetically in that it shows the effect of a long forgotten violent event—the killing of Algerian protesters by French police in the sixties—on the psyche of people who were only children at the time. Avoiding pseudo-realism, *Caché* painstakingly frames images from the past in the mind of Georges, the main character. Like Resnais, Haneke also uses what could be called visual rhymes, especially in long takes. For example, one of the mysterious videos that is sent to Georges contains a moving point of view shot down a corridor, leaving clues for him to track down Majid, whose parents were killed in the massacre. The same long take is repeated, now with Georges in it, when he walks towards Majid's apartment.

A filmic recreation of the event, released in the same year as *Caché* (as mentioned above in Frame IV), can serve as a counter-example: *Nuit noire, 17 octobre 1961* by Alain Tasma, produced by the French TV channel Canal+, attempts a realistic rendering of the event, also introducing protagonists with whom the viewer can identify—a victim, a young police officer who gets caught up in the events. The climactic massacre uses all typical cinematic means- rapid cuts, handheld camera, close-ups- in order to draw in the spectator, culminating in a scene where the dead and the dying are thrown into the river. As gripping as this scene is, this putting us "where we were not," results in a strange catharsis that runs counter to the doubtless -honorable intentions of the film-maker. Instead of raising consciousness, the aestheticization after the fact that Daney decries results in a suppression of any question of morality. The event is safely located in the past and the guilt is clearly on the side of the perpetrators, thereby easing the bad conscience of the viewer.

It is, therefore, highly significant that Haneke shot *Caché* entirely in digital video, erasing the boundaries between the surveillance (i.e., the diegetic past) and present, an aesthetic choice which allows him to undermine any ontological certainty, thereby also stressing the untimeliness of the images. The realization that an image is from the surveillance tape always comes after the fact. The emotionally tense scene of Georges' first visit at Majid's apartment, for example, is filmed relatively conventionally, with changing camera angles. Then, after short interludes—Georges lying to Anne, and the Laurents at the pool—we see the last minute of Georges' visit again, from another angle. It ends with Georges leaving and Majid sitting at his table, sobbing. Suddenly, we hear Anne's voice "Here, that's all" and must realize that we watched the recording with Anne. After this sudden shift, Georges explains to Anne the historical background, the *nuit noire*, the black night of the massacre. The event is thus not reconstructed, but recalled, just as we had to recall the scene in order to recognize the repetition.

On the heels of the problem of representation that I have analyzed comes another problem, namely, that apart from extreme positions of ideological distortion nobody believes in the power of images anymore and therefore hardly anyone reacts with genuine feelings of disgust to violent events depicted with aesthetic means. The latter seem to amount to an anesthetization of violence. Haneke's insertion of TV-news is often misunderstood by critics as being just another call to arms, as a moralist's patronizing condemnation of our society's hypocrisy, not only regarding the purported power of images. Haneke indeed addresses the problem thematically in films like *Drei Wege zum See* and in *Code inconnu*, where the photo-journalists are asked whether their dangerous work actually serves any purpose other than adding to the problem. But nowhere does Haneke suggest that a return is possible, or that a time existed where an event conserved by film or photography brought on change. In this, Haneke seems to share the succinct political analysis that Daney delivers in his essay: Daney points out that the power of images is lost because images are now firmly on the side of power that is publicity (Daney 1992: 17). Here we come back to the above-mentioned "false problem" of image and text, because publicity practices a complete separation of form and content, insofar as any image can arbitrarily serve to sell any content. Famously, during the war in Bosnia, some pictures of atrocities were used for propaganda by both sides. The question, it seems, needs to be expanded, as it concerns not only the violent event and the aesthetic means of representing it, but also how images can be wrested from power. In the following, I will look at how Haneke answers this twofold question.

Michael Haneke frequently resorts to a static camera set-up in order to bring forth a mood of hopelessness in a situation. The use of this device goes back to his first cinematic feature, the critically acclaimed *Der siebente Kontinent/ The Seventh Continent* (1989). It then found a perfect expression in *71 Fragmente einer Chronologie des Zufalls/ 71 Fragments of a Chronology of Chance* (1994), where we witness the painfully inarticulate phone conversation of an old man and a long static shot of a man playing table tennis against a wall. These shots would certainly fit within the framework of Bazin's argument in favor of the long take, as discussed above. In order to explain his disdain for films like *Kapò* and other films that reconstruct the past, Daney briefly refers to Lacan's concept of *forclusion* (foreclosure), the French translation of Freud's *Verwerfung*: it is not a repression of guilt, but indeed a complete exclusion of the *non-du-père*, the no/name-of-the father from the unconscious, resulting in psychotic hallucinations. This difference is quite important because a repression results in a neurosis—according to Lacan's famous formula: "Neurosis is a question that being poses for the subject" (Lacan 1977: 168). And the question for the obsessional neurotic is precisely the one that Michael Haneke seems to tackle in *Code inconnu* and *71 Fragmente*, the question of the contingency of our existence.

We find ourselves now in yet another strange situation, because this question is the pseudo-philosophical question *par excellence*, the "why am I here?," the "what does it all mean?," a question that Tom Tykwer already spoofed in his *Lola rennt* and that films like the above-mentioned *Le Battement d'ailes du papillon* und *Crash* by Paul Haggis (2004) attempt to answer in earnest. These films, it needs hardly to be pointed out, with their clear message of humanism, are polar opposites of Haneke's films. Looking at Haneke from this perspective, Haneke does not suggest a repressed truth in any of his characters. Georges' mother clearly remembers the events and does not want to talk about them. Majid is completely traumatized and certainly recalls very well what happened. Georges, whose dreams haunt him until they reveal the past, does not seem to suffer from guilt, and although he might be ashamed of what he did as a 6 year old, he is not responsible and thus does not experience real guilt. Instead, in Haneke the *forclusion* is the refusal to integrate the reality of massacres, elsewhere or in our own past, into our ideological field. The result is not a return of the repressed but the above-mentioned psychotic hallucinations in the form of the *impossible* camera that cannot be integrated into the ontology of *Caché*.

What, then, is the political perspective that can be garnered from this state of affairs? To put it in slightly different terms, in what sense do the everyday psychotics depicted by Haneke reflect a political thrust in his films? Daney sums up the task of cinema in terms that grasp Haneke's program perfectly:

> since the filmmakers did not film the politics of Vichy in its time, their duty, fifty years later, is not to redeem themselves imaginarily, with the likes of *Au revoir les enfants* [by Louis Malle 1987], but to draw the portrait right now [*actuel*] of the good people of France who, from 1940 until 1942, the Vel' d'Hiv round-up included, did not protest. Cinema, being the art of the present, its qualms are without interest. (11)

This "right now" is the actualization that I mentioned in the first chapter, not a retroactive projection, the "this is how it was" of bad cinema, but the art of the present, the re-presentation as re-*presenting*, making *present* once again.

The difference between *Caché* and *Nuit noire, 17 octobre 1961* boils down to the "non-images" of the former that demand a discussion in the present and the abjectness of a more or less realistic recreation of the latter that depoliticizes the past event. In Haneke real events are never recreated and reality- that is, the instant mediatization of an event- enters via TV-news. This can only mean that there is no message that is conveyed and Haneke is no moralist. Instead, the moral is in the (long) take.

Frame VIII

THE FUNNY FRAME

While finishing this book in the summer of 2009, two uncanny coincidences opened up on the plane of immanence. The day after the much-publicized death of Michael Jackson on June 25, 2009, I watched, again, *71 Fragmente einer Chronologie des Zufalls*. Here, Haneke inserts twice the same clip about accusations of pederasty against Jackson, something I had completely forgotten since my previous viewing. The news about Jackson overshadowed every other event this summer, just as it did when Haneke made the film. The peculiar effect of this curious inclusion of pop-culture news made me realize that Haneke's insertion of TV news in general serves as a time stamp. The fascinating effect of including selected news footage is that it literally dates his films. Not only that—the films become better with time. Any event that is immediately mediatized can be said to be summarily sterilized and removed from its political context. Haneke's films recreate these contexts because every viewing automatically actualizes the news footage in the viewer's memory. That is, it reframes these insertions as images over and over again.

Another funny coincidence, a real "Haneke-moment," happened the day after I watched *Caché*. The news broke that Sergeant James M. Crowley, a white Cambridge police officer, had arrested Henry Louis Gates Jr., a black Professor at Harvard University, for disorderly conduct. The twist that no writer would have dared to put in a film script—and that some would call "ironic"—is, of course, that Gates is arguably the United States' most famous scholar of African American studies, while Crowley is himself an instructor, teaching racial sensitivity to his fellow officers. A fully cinematic dimension opened a few days later when President Obama, himself an emblem for a post-racial America, invited the opponents for a beer. This chance encounter directly resonates with the altercation of Georges and the bicyclist in *Caché* to which

I already referred above in Frame III in my short review of the film. The conflict is one of images, indeed a real anamorphic mirroring, as it is impossible not to see race and class in this picture. A perceptive article in the *New York Times* about the incident points to this:

> More than once on that afternoon, Professor Gates told Sergeant Crowley, "You don't know who you're messing with," according to the police report. But one of Sergeant Crowley's friends in Natick, Mass., where he lives with his wife and three children, said, "The professor didn't know who he was messing with." (Van Natta and Goodnough 2007)

There are possible explanations, and of course, there is even an objective recreation that the article indeed provides. The policeman, suspecting a break-in, had no idea who the scholar was and the jet-lagged professor was "weary from the 14-hour flight and nursing a bronchial infection" (Van Natta and Goodnough 2007). This recreation of "what really happened" began already and will certainly spawn a deluge of commentary. Reading with Haneke, the perspectival truth, the entire milieu (town/gown, rich/poor, black/white, power/powerless) is actualized here in this short paragraph that attempts to see both sides, not only because the immediate question arises whether the professor was represented correctly in this quote, which employs a colloquial expression. What is legible here and what Haneke points out in all of his films is exactly this: any representation is always already distorted by violence. And it clearly does not matter if this is a representation of the other or the self. Haneke unfolds this violence in the Deleuzian sense, not by undoing it (a utopian solution) or overdoing it (Peckinpah) but by redoing it, that is, repeating it in an eternal return.

In the light of these two, almost uncanny, coincidences, Haneke's *Das weiße Band* provides a fascinating occasion to reassess some of the issues raised in this book and certainly also to point to some that have only been implicitly addressed in this book. Seen from the right perspective, these incidences and coincidences are truly "funny" in a farcical way. The interrogation of Martin, the Pastor's son, by his father is a performance of a farce, as the outcome of this attempt to bring out the truth of the matter is already clear from the start. But it is almost funny to see how the father, a brilliant rhetorician, avoids calling the event by its proper name. The consequences are of equally brilliant simplicity: when Martin goes to bed, he has his hands tied to the frame of the bed.

Here, we have to acknowledge a final frame in Haneke, the Funny Frame. The bafflement resulting from the displacement of two completely mismatched frames onto each other is, at least for a short moment, *almost* funny, at least as comical as, for example, an especially inspired *bricolage*, a quick fix with the aid of mismatched and inappropriate materials. For the sake of argument, I will briefly construct a possible objective truth—exactly, of course, what Haneke avoids: Martin, like all 14-year-old boys, really masturbates; or, Martin, subject to religious indoctrination from early childhood on, constantly fights the temptation to masturbate. His father's move is, as he puts it, "to spare the confession" and, then, to spare Martin the temptation by tying down his son's hands. The Truth, then, is not the irrefutable proof of stained bed sheets, a real admission of guilt, or even a shot that actually shows Martin masturbating, but the "Truth" that amounts to nothing more or less than the Foucauldian knowledge that is externalized in the father's power.

This scene of the confession is connected by a hard cut to an equally "funny" scene that follows this interrogation and where the truth is now as bluntly formulated as it was skillfully obscured in the scene before: this scene opens immediately with the orgasm of the Doctor who had just mounted the Midwife from behind, both fully clothed. The Midwife then formulates an objectively true statement: "You did not miss me!" and, after his puzzled inquiry, adds "I say that because it is the truth." Their relationship is one defined by the objective truth. In a later scene, after an unsuccessful attempt by the Midwife to pleasure her lover, he tells her: "To tell the truth, you repulse me." The two then proceed to objectively formulate more statements of the truth: he molests his daughter, she smells bad, etc . . . culminating in the Doctor's statement of his true feelings for her at that very moment: "By god, why don't you just die?!" Here, the too-open truth hides the true perspective that the film allows us to see: the Doctor and the Midwife's relationship is driven by their respective self-hatred.

With *Das weiße Band*, it seems, we come back to issues raised before in the discussion of *Fraulein*. As I have mentioned above, in Frame II, at the beginning of *Das weiße Band* the narrator promises that his story will provide insight "into certain occurrences that happened in our country." The inevitable expectation that the film will somehow comment on the rise of fascism is ultimately disappointed. The viewer forced to reflect on this statement and provided with the 20/20 vision of historical hindsight cannot find an explanation: there is neither a German exception to be found, nor are the so-called "proto-" or "micro-fascisms" that raise their heads to be blamed. In Frame III, I discussed Haneke's *Fraulein* as an overcoming of Fassbinder, and it is crucial now not to misunderstand this new period picture as a sign of

Haneke's softening or of a more "viewer-friendly" turn. The painstakingly authentic creation of a past in his most recent film will, without doubt, again be interpreted by some critics as a call for a return to values because the promise of providing an insight into the rise of fascism erects a frame of reference that stirs the viewer's attention to the topics of uprootedness and loss of values caused by modernity, and these have generally been considered the appealing elements of National-Socialist propaganda. The community that Haneke constructs, however, seems to exist in a curious bubble—isolated (all means of transportation are owned by the estate), the villagers live in a strange hybrid of late feudalism and capitalism. Again, Haneke skillfully contrasts the "universal history" of the historic film—that I briefly describe above in the first Frame—with the perspectival truth offered by this film. When Gustav, the Pastor's younger son, asks his stern father in a memorable scene whether he can nurse an injured bird back to health, our perspective is Gustav's and we experience the love for the authority of those who "grew up in captivity," as the pastor aptly puts it. Therefore, the conclusion that the destruction of this community brought forth by the cataclysm of World War I caused the desire to recreate the community afterwards is certainly valid.

But here, before we come to a hasty conclusion, I need to come back to the probable perpetrators of most of the acts of terror, the children. Children, as I explained above in Frame VI, are perfect witnesses for Haneke, the exception to the exception. Haneke avoids the impression that children could be seen as "essentially innocent" especially in *Das weiße Band*: Klara, the Pastor's oldest daughter, rams scissors down the throat of her father's beloved parakeet in order to punish him. However, as in all other films, the children are innocent of the violence to which they are subjected. And the acts that they commit are a true perversion in the sense of Lacan's *père-version* that I address above in Frame V. When the children punish the Baron's son for his privilege and torture the Midwife's son for his condition, they make themselves into an instrument of the Other's *jouissance*, carrying out their society's secret wishes. The Stewart's son—who could get away unscathed—clearly wants to be punished when he provokes his father to carry out an especially violent beating. Indeed, this society's ideology is aptly conveyed by an image that the Baron evokes in his plea to the populace to help him fight the elements that threaten the peace of the community, the very paragon of a community that could live happily ever after, were it not for the outside element that threatens it. What the film shows, then, in its portrayal of the apparently cyclical and harmonic life is the material existence of the village's ideology that manifests itself in its recurring practices and routines that effectively constitute the subjects of this community who inevitably misrecognize themselves as the cause and origin of this ideology. The perverse logic of a recreation of such a community in the form of the shared experience of a *Volksgemeinschaft*, a pure people, becomes immediately apparent. However, as I stated above, the Other does not exist and cannot be appropriated by identification, creating a pure people in spectral form only. Serving as an instrument of the Other's *jouissance* means serving as a projection of an inhuman logic.

Now, in this final frame, a snapshot might be possible, if this metaphor is allowed here, that will allow us to briefly arrest Haneke's movement that carries us towards "the not-external outside and the not-internal inside" and formulate a cursory assessment of Haneke's project. If we follow the concepts that Haneke creates in *Das weiße Band* and all other films before that, it becomes clear that the diagnosis of this "physician of culture" is indeed that we have lost our connection with the past. But it is equally clear that a recreation of the past is not only counterproductive, but outright dangerous.

Haneke's cinematic concepts clearly show that we have lost the present and the image of the past has already disappeared. This past will now assault us in the form of the future: The conspiracy of Georges' and Majid's sons in *Caché* or the conspiracy of the children in *Das weiße Band* should then be seen as a paradoxical return of the repressed future. Libby Saxton is therefore absolutely right in pointing out that the images we see from Majid's and Georges' childhood are not flashbacks but memories,[1] because a flashback would mean that we could move back in time. With Haneke, there is only a forward movement possible, and this movement means nothing less than the loss of cherished forms of identity and identification. The impossible position of the camera in *Caché*, and the uncanny authorial presence throughout Haneke's oeuvre is, then, the position of Benjamin's angel of history. To quote again Walter Benjamin's "Fifth Thesis": "For it is an irretrievable image of the past which threatens to disappear in any present that does not recognize itself as intended in that image." We ought to remember that the disappearance is not a passive or inconsequential one, but rather an event of violent proportions in its own right.

With Benjamin, we could say that Haneke's cinema guides us towards "the core of the allegorical way of seeing, of the baroque, secular explanation of history as the Passion of the world—its importance resides solely in the stations of its decline." And, again, we return to the face that "is" the close-up:

> Everything about history that, from the very beginning, has been untimely, sorrowful, unsuccessful, is expressed in a face—or rather in a death's head. And although such a thing lacks all 'symbolic' freedom of expression, all classical proportion, all humanity—nevertheless, this is the form in which man's subjection to nature is most obvious and it significantly gives rise not only to the enigmatic question of the nature of human existence as such, but also of the biographical historicity of the individual. (Benjamin 1991: 343; 1998: 166)

In *Das weiße Band*, Haneke contrasts static long shots with a steadycam that closely follows the characters and frames their faces or their heads, creating the impression that the person is standing still while the world around them moves. These people, known only by their professions, are not to be seen as symbolic but, indeed, as allegorical.

As Deleuze underlines in *The Fold*, allegory in Benjamin—and we should add, in Haneke—should not be understood as the personification of an idea; instead, "allegory uncovers nature and history according to the order of time. It produces a history from nature and transforms history into nature in a world that no longer has its center" (1993: 125). Producing a history of nature is also that for which Bazin's realism aims. This realism, as was pointed out before in the chapter on the long take (Frame VII), asks from us that we resist the temptation of a symbolic reading in relation to the hero and instead participate in convoluted relationships, or, as Benjamin calls them, "constellations" (Benjamin 1998: 132). This close reading asks for a different sort of engagement with the text: "Whereas romanticism in the name of the infinite, intensified the perfected creation of form and idea in critical terms, at one stroke the deep gaze of allegory transforms things and works into stirring writing." In short, Haneke's films require a movement from inside the fold to the nonexternal outside, in other words, an allegorical gaze. Benjamin continues: "The image, in the field of allegorical intuition is fragment, rune. [. . .] The false appearance of totality goes out" (Benjamin 1991: 154, 1998: 176). The terms of the word play on the double meaning of *Schein* (shine, glow/appearance) should not be thought as opposites, but again as folds within one concept. This fold-asfoil of one order is needed to think the other. Haneke needs the fold of Hollywood-cinema as much as the Baroque drama needs Greek tragedy.

Throughout this book, I have repeatedly compared films by Haneke to some of those "shiny" mainstream films, especially those by Spielberg who personifies what is left of classic Hollywood-cinema. Spielberg, of course, is no longer the guarantor for box office success. This honor goes to Michael Bay whose *Transformers: Revenge of the Fallen* (2009) made at the time of this writing grossed far over 800 million dollars worldwide. Michael Bay, born in 1965, clearly belongs to another generation than Michael Haneke or Steven Spielberg, who is about four and a half years older than Haneke. And Bay's stroboscopic editing style is now the epitome of postmodern cinema. As Peter Bart writes, "some of the older film editors, among others, termed Bay's style 'frame-fucking,' referring to the fact that the beginning and the end of most scenes were eviscerated in an effort to speed the storytelling" (Bart 1999: 232; see also Bordwell 2006: 155). In contrast to assessments of Bay, Michael Haneke is quoted as saying: "I've been accused of 'raping' the audience in my films, and I admit to that freely—all movies assault the viewer in one way or another. What's different about my films is this: I'm trying to rape the viewer into independence" (Wray 2007).

I will end this book with a perspectival question—is it better to fuck the frame or to rape the viewer into independence?

Frame IX

PLOT REVIEWS

DREI WEGE ZUM SEE/THREE PATHS TO THE LAKE (1976, TV, 97 MINUTES)

This co-production of the German regional public television station Südwestfunk and the ORF, the Austrian state television, was written and directed by Michael Haneke, based on the eponymous short story by Ingeborg Bachmann, first published in Bachmann (1972: 130–233). A very unfaithful English translation has been published (Bachmann 1989: 117–212).

Drei Wege zum See follows Elisabeth Matrei (Ursula Schult), a successful photojournalist in her fifties, first on a visit to her ageing father (Guido Wieland) in the provincial Austrian town of Klagenfurt, then for one evening in Paris upon her return. During the film, an omniscient voice-over, mostly taken verbatim from the short story, gives information that is mostly doubled by what the camera shows. Later in the film, the voice-over gives an insight into the protagonist's inner life through the use of free indirect speech. With flashbacks that seem to be triggered by Elisabeth's memory, as well as the information that the voiceover provides, a picture slowly begins to emerge: as a teenager, Elisabeth felt extremely protective towards her brother Robert who was also very close to her. Apart from a short marriage to an American, she has never stayed in a long-term relationship. The visit to the father's house follows her brother's wedding in London. However, travelling from London to Austria in high-season turned out to be more difficult than Elisabeth expected and she has to wait for days in a London hotel frequented by Africans.

Additionally to the voice-over and the often confusing flashbacks, *Drei Wege zum See* also shows snapshots of Elisabeth at a younger age and of her work as a photo-journalist. The voice-over explains that she always had "Fernfieber," the travel bug, and dreamed of seeing the world. She did not attend university, but always had a knack for grasping things quickly, thus appearing more educated than she actually is. Her current profession, photojournalism, is also something that she picked up on the fly rather than through study. A protégé of a renowned French photographer, she began quickly to make a name for herself in the field, not only taking pictures of places all over the world but also of celebrities like Chagall and Hemingway. Also, a sub-plot emerges during Elisabeth's various attempts to reach the lake—futile because of the construction of a new highway that blocks the old paths: she realizes that Trotta (Walter Schmidinger), a cynical, deeply conflicted intellectual with whom she breaks up and about whose suicide she only finds out months after the fact, was indeed the love of her life. These news cause a crisis from which she escapes by throwing herself into a passionate affair with Manes (Udo Vioff), a man who, like Trotta, has no spiritual home. In the emotional climax of the film, Elisabeth throws herself into the arms of Manes, while brief flashbacks reveal how much she is thinking about Trotta.

After she returns from her last attempt to reach the lake, a conversation between her father and Elisabeth takes place, triggered by the modernization of the rural region, as well as a conversation between her and Trotta that took place years before on the subject of the decline of Austria, a discussion that points towards post-war Austria's self-stylization as "Nazi-Germany's first victim."

A chance meeting with a former classmate—a widowed storekeeper who is aged beyond her years—triggers another set of memories from schooldays and former relationships. After running from the store, Elisabeth calls her lover in Paris, telling him to send her a telegram with the words "Very urgent! Need to leave for work immediately!" Guilt ridden, she leaves her father, fearing that she will never see him again. At the Vienna airport, she runs into Trotta's cousin (Bernhard Wicki), whom she had met before and who was obviously in love with her. He tells her that he is now married and has a young child, hinting that he did this to forget her. The realization that this man loved her clearly upsets Elisabeth. Suddenly, the cousin returns, they silently hold each other's hands. At the gate, the cousin stuffs a note into her coat pocket and pushes her trough the door. Arriving in Paris, Elisabeth accidentally drops the note. After pondering if she should even pick it up, she opens it and finds, instead of an address, a note: "I love you—I have always loved you."

From a conversation with her much younger lover, Philippe (Yves Beneyton), in a taxi in Paris, it becomes clear that Philippe lives off Elisabeth's money and has a relationship with a girl his own age, something of which Elisabeth is aware. The girl is now pregnant and Philippe declares that he wants to marry her, in spite of the girl's "capitalist pig" father. Back at her stylish apartment, Elisabeth acts nonchalantly. She opens a telegram whose contents appear superimposed over the shot of Philippe reading it. Elisabeth is called to cover the new offensive by the Vietcong. Over Philippe's protests, she declares that she will take the job and asks him to leave.

In the final scene, while we see Elisabeth aimlessly wandering through her apartment and finally lying down, the voice-over informs us that she has not met the man who could be of a unique importance to her life. The last sentence, slightly changed from the final words of Bachmann's text, hints at a premonition of death:

> *She fell asleep, already at the edge of sleep hit by a dream, and touching her head and her heart because she didn't know where all the blood was coming from. Nevertheless, she was thinking: It's nothing, it's nothing, nothing else can happen to me now. Something might happen to me, but it doesn't have to happen to me.*

LEMMINGE, TEIL 1 ARKADIEN/LEMMINGS, PART 1 ARCADIA (1979, TV, 113 MINUTES) AND LEMMINGE, TEIL 2 VERLETZUNGEN/LEMMINGS, PART 2 INJURIES (1979, TV, 107 MINUTES)

This two-part film was directed by Haneke based on his original script and produced by Sender Freies Berlin (SFB) and the Österreichischer Rundfunk (ORF). Credits for the cinematography of Part 1 are shared by Walter Kindler, who also shot *Variation* for Haneke, and the famous Polish cameraman Jerzy Lipman, who shot *Kanal/Canal* (1957) for Andrzej Wajda and *Nóż w wodzie/Knife in the Water* (1962) for Roman Polanski. Lipman alone is credited for the cinematography of Part 2.

The first film, set in 1959 in a small town outside Vienna, follows five teenagers in their last year of high school. From different social backgrounds, all suffer from the oppressive atmosphere of the fifties. Fritz Naprawnik (Christian Spatzek), in spite of admiring his Latin teacher (Walter Schmidinger), has a relationship with the teacher's wife, Gisela (Elisabeth Orth). After the adulterous relationship becomes known and Gisela becomes pregnant and attempts to end the pregnancy, she returns to her husband. The shy and demure Evi Wasner (Regina Sattler) finally finds the courage to have sex with her high school sweetheart, Christian Beranek (Christian Ingomar), the Doctor's son. After this first, awkward and, for her, shameful experience leads to her pregnancy, Evi tries to electrocute herself in a botched suicide attempt. She has to leave school immediately and marry Christian.

While the aforementioned characters come from middle class families, the Leuwen family is decidedly upper class. Herr Leuwen (Bernhard Wicki), the handicapped family patriarch, rules the household with an iron fist, assisted by his bedridden wife (Gustl Halenke). Their children, Sigrid (Eva Linder) and Sigurd Leuwen (Paulus Manker), vent their frustrations in acts of vandalism against cars. When they are found out, Sigurd commits suicide in front of his sister's eyes by jumping from a ladder. Sigrid leaves for Vienna.

The title of the two-part film stems from a tirade by Herr Leuwen. After his son's suicide, and informed by Sigrid that she will immediately drop out of school and move to Vienna, he accuses his children's generation of being lemmings, "voles that wallow in their own filth," as he declares, "with the intention of croaking as soon as possible." Only towards the end of the first part do we learn that the parents were injured during the last days of the war protecting their children in an air raid.

Set in 1979, the second part of *Lemminge* begins—unusual for Haneke—with a flash-forward of a car crashing into a tree. During the first part of the film, the viewer has to reconstruct what happened in the 20 years since part 1, as the cast looks nothing like the young actors from the first part. While the first part appeared in parts as a family melodrama, with many scenes set in the Leuwen's dark mansion or at night, the second part features long scenes that show the characters moving around aimlessly in their homes or outside.

Christian Beranek (Rüdiger Hacker) is now an officer in the Austrian army, a job for which he seems ill-suited. Eva (Monica Bleibtreu), frustrated and depressed next to her emotionally distant husband, is having an affair. Pregnant and single, Sigrid Leuwen (Elfriede Irrall) returns to the family mansion that she has inherited. Collecting her father's belongings, including his death mask that the alcoholic minister (Norbert Kappen) accidently breaks, she meets Fritz Naprawnik (Wolfgang Hübsch) who is now a doctor and estranged from the hospital owner's daughter, Bettina (Vera Borek). A reunion of the classmates, to which Fritz brings the emotionally troubled Bettina, becomes the emotional center of the second part. Bettina accuses the four of hypocrisy and leaves. Sigrid remembers her father's accusations.

Christian states that he agrees with Bettina "that there is nothing of which we could be proud, that we can hold on to."

Eva, dropped by her lover over the phone, has a nervous breakdown. In the hospital, she sees Fritz. The two become lovers. Christian, recently diagnosed with stomach cancer, finds out about the affair and attempts to kill his wife and himself by deliberately crashing the car into a tree—the accident we see at the beginning of the film. He survives. The last images of the film show him in a freeze frame shouting at some recruits who failed to greet him.

Variation oder "Daß es Utopien gibt weiß ich selber!"/Variation or "Utopias exist, yes I know" (1983, TV, 98 minutes)

The cinematography for this film is, again, by Walter Kindler. It is written and directed by Michael Haneke for the SFB, Sender Freies Berlin, a public TV-station.

Georg (Hilmar Thate), a middle-aged art teacher at a high school, seems to be in a well-grounded relationship with his wife, Eva (Monica Bleibtreu). They share the house with Georg's sister Sigrid (Eva Linder), a musician who seems to have a history of mental illness. Returning from a performance of "Stella," Goethe's play about a man caught between two women, Georg opines that the threesome that the young Goethe had in mind as an ending is a lot more appealing than the double suicide that ends the later version, but he also admits that this tragic ending is a lot more realistic.

Georg's own life becomes a variation of "Stella," when he falls in love with Anna (Elfriede Irrall), a journalist who interviews him about his work. Anna lives in a relationship with the high-strung Kitty (Suzanne Geyer), a frustrated actress and alcoholic. Georg and Anna seem mostly concerned with their own emotions. All parties involved react to the realigned relationships according to their temperament: Georg is reluctant to commit or be honest, the emotional Kitty resorts to physical aggression, Anna seems stable and composed but has a nightmare about Kitty killing herself, Eva unsuccessfully attempts to seduce her cousin, while Sigrid seems to regress to childish behavior.

A few months after Georg and Anne move in together, we see how the life of the characters has evolved through letters to Georg and Anna that can be heard in voice-over. Both, Eva and Kitty, have found consolation in their careers. Eva suggests a meeting of all parties involved. Sigrid doesn't come and while the couple and Eva and Kitty exchange banalities, we see Sigrid's preparation for suicide. At the end of the awkward and unfruitful meeting, it appears that this was a flashback and that she survived. In the bar, Anna writes a letter to Georg and has the waiter deliver it. She declares that she loves him but needs time to think through everything. Georg reads the letter without betraying any emotion and goes to the movies to see *Der Stadneurotiker* (the "city-neurotic"), the title under which Woody Allen's *Annie Hall* (1977) was released in German.

WER WAR EDGAR ALLAN?/WHO WAS EDGAR ALLAN? (1984, TV, 83 MINUTES)

The script was written by Peter Rosei and Michael Haneke based on Peter Rosei's eponymous novel, published in 1977. Since Haneke changed Rosei's draft significantly, the credits list the pseudonym "Hans Brosciner" as writer. The cinematography is by Frank Brühne who also shot *Messer im Kopf/Knife in the Head* (1978) by Reinhard Hauff. The film is shot on location in Venice, Italy.

Drug and alcohol abuse make it difficult for an art student (Paulus Manker) to distinguish between fact and fantasy during his stay in Venice. A visit from the family's lawyer (Guido Wieland) informs him about his estranged father's death. The inheritance allows him to continue his life of aimless wandering and occasional drug binges. In the expensive café that he frequents as often as the cheap tavern where he drinks himself into oblivion, he meets the mysterious Edgar Allan (Rolf Hoppe). Independently wealthy, Edgar Allen seems to be connected to Venice's high-society as well as to a mysterious ring of drug dealers. The main character attempts to unveil Edgar Allan's secret, suspecting the latter of being the boss of the dealers and involved in high-profile murders. The ending suggests that Edgar Allan is a figment of the main character's imagination.

FRAULEIN: EIN DEUTSCHES MELODRAM/FRAULEIN (1985, TV, 113 MINUTES)

The script was written by Michael Haneke and Bernd Schröder. The cinematography is by Klaus Hohenberger and Walter Kindler. The film is shot in black and white, with the exception of the last 4 minutes.

Johanna (Angelica Domröse) runs a cinema that also screens American films in English for GIs in small town in West Germany in the mid-1950s. Her husband, Hans, is still in a POW camp in Russia and is believed to have died there. His brother (Heinz-Werner Kraehkamp) runs the successful family business, a building company that employs André (Lou Castel), a former POW from France who stayed in Germany after the end of the war and with whom Johanna has a passionate affair. Even though she is pressured by her family, Johanna refuses to have her husband declared dead. Her daughter (Mareile Geisler) is dating an American officer who drives around in a shiny Cadillac convertible, while Mike (Michael Klein), her rebellious son, looks up to André and is impressed by André's career as a show wrestler.

A letter from the association of war returnees causes the family to purge the house of André's trophies and his pictures just before Hans (Peter Franke) returns, bitter and depressed. He remains an outsider, overwhelmed by the hectic pace at the booming family business, and is unable to reconnect to his family. Hans withdraws to the basement, chain-smoking and building a cathedral out of matchsticks. Johanna carries on her affair. Reading Mike's diary, Hans finds out about his wife's affair and Mike's adoration for André. Broken up over this, the camera shows that he has urinated on himself.

For Christmas, Mike has organized hard-to-come-by consumer goods on the black market. Disappointed by his parents' rejection of the ill-gotten goods, Mike later burns his father's model cathedral. André suddenly returns to France. Mike, part of an organized German-American gang which burglarizes army barracks, is cornered by the police and barricades himself. Johanna, called to convince Mike to give himself up, arrives too late—a large explosion kills Mike and his gang. Her daughter leaves for the United States.

Hans is now completely bedridden. Johanna pulls the tube from the intravenous device, takes the Cadillac and sets out to search for André. She finds him in Brittany in France, where he is living with his family in a small village. André did not tell his wife about the affair, having also lied to his family who thinks that the Germans held him back after the war. While making love, Johanna tells the shocked André that she has killed Hans. She laughs hysterically.

Intercut with her confession to a German policeman, Johanna is shown at a hotel bar in France. Suddenly, a familiar fanfare makes Johann look up: on TV, the ending of *Baron Münchhausen* (Josef von Báky 1943), an important intertext in *Fraulein*, appears in color, dubbed in French. A countershot shows her now also in color. André arrives and tells her that, following suit, he has also killed his spouse, while the gesture of cutting somebody's throat is performed on screen by Baron Münchhausen. Johanna laughs and laughs over the last images, which show Münchhausen's miraculous escape.

DER SIEBENTE KONTINENT/THE SEVENTH CONTINENT (1989, 104 MINUTES)

Haneke wrote and directed his first feature film, a production of Wega Film, Vienna. The cinematography for this film, shot in an aspect ration of 1:1.85, is by Anton Peschke. *Der siebente Kontinent* is divided into three parts, the first part lasting about 35 minutes, the second only 15 minutes and the third part taking up the rest of the film, another 55 minutes. Each part covers a day in the family's life and is set in a consecutive year. The pattern established in the first part of the film—disorienting close-ups, voices from off-screen and the insertion of black film between scenes—is repeated throughout as we witness fragmented scenes from the family's daily life. The inserts vary in length according to the preceding fragment.

The film opens with a close-up on an Austrian license plate. The plate is suddenly sprayed with foam. After a cut, we see a close-up of a headlight being sprayed down. The next shot shows the inside of a car from the back seat, a man and a woman—barely visible in the darkness—are sitting silently in the front. The credits leave the view through the windshield unobstructed as the car is moved through a carwash. The camera follows the car, a small sedan. As it leaves, a little girl becomes visible sitting in the backseat from whose point of view the scene before was shot. While the car leaves the frame, the camera centers on a large billboard that shows an exotic beach with large stones in the foreground and the inscription, in large letters, "Welcome to Australia" and, smaller in the bottom left corner, "Australian travel Agency." This image—without the inscription but with the waves moving in an otherwise static image—will appear several times during the film. After 5 seconds of black film, a white title appears on a black background: "Part one: 1987."

A close-up on a radio alarm clock on a nightstand shows the time: 5:59. When the numbers roll over to 6:00, the news begin to play—the beginning of the first Gulf war—and continue to play through the obviously well-established morning routine that we witness entirely in close-ups: hands open and close doors, put toothpaste on the tooth brush, tie shoes, feed the fish, prepare coffee and tea, etc. The mother wakes the daughter. When the family sits down to have breakfast served by the mother, the shot is framed such that we only see the family's hands around the round table, but are able to reflect on the contents—obviously, the family is not rich, but keeps a certain standard, getting up early to eat together a traditional breakfast (eggs, orange juice, jam, and cold cuts) on nice plates.

The girl is dropped off under a damaged sign: "Primary and Vocational School for Boys and Girls." As Evi (Leni Tanzer) runs away from the car (and the camera), she appears to be about 7 or 8 years old. The mother, Anna Schober (Birgit Doll), is dropped off at an optician's shop. The father, Georg Schober (Dieter Berner), parks the car. As he walks away from the car, a voice-over is heard: the mother reads a letter to her in-laws that fills us in, in simple words, on the back story and the names: repeatedly praising their son: Georg has received a promotion but now has to suffer under an incompetent superior. Anna has recently lost her mother, leading to her brother's severe depression. Evi, "our problem child," suffers from asthma. While the letter is read, the camera follows Georg in long-shots as he walks through a chemical plant. Only now, about 11 minutes into the film, can we discern his face for the first time.

A teacher (Elisabeth Rath) carries Evi out of a room and sits her down. We see her face for the first time, in close-up. The increasingly impatient teacher tries to get Evi, who claims that she can't see anything, to open her eyes. It becomes clear that she was lying. Anna can be seen in close-up behind an optical machine, examining a client to whose anecdote about a classmate from long ago she is obviously barely paying attention. Anna and Georg are shopping. Again, only their hands can be seen. The food they buy is mostly shrink-wrapped or frozen and the pork chops looks unappetizing in the harsh light of the supermarket. The cashiers are shown in close-up. Highly concentrated on adding up, they do not look up or communicate in any way.

At home, Evi is doing her homework while the television plays commercials. Georg takes a shower. Anna puts the groceries away and begins to prepare dinner. A phone call from the teacher informs Anna about Evi feigned blindness. Anna confronts Evi: "Sag mal, spinnst du?!" ("Are you crazy?"). First, Evi denies the episode, and her mother tells her that she only wants to hear the truth, and that nothing will happen to her. Evi simply says "yes" and, after a brief hesitation, her mother slaps her in the face. The cut arrives with the sound of the slap.

Anna, upset, stares out of the window. We see the street from her point of view. Later that night, Anna's brother, Alexander (Udo Samel), has a nervous breakdown at the dinner table. While Anna comforts him, Evi and Georg watch silently. Cleaning up, Anna finds a newspaper with the headline "Blind—but never again lonely!" Later, she asks Evi whether she feels lonely, but Evi says no.

The second part is set in 1988. Again, Anna's letter to her in-laws, read in voice-over, fills in background information, telling proudly that Georg has finally been given the long-awaited promotion and that his boss has now accepted a dinner invitation. The man whom Georg replaced appears at work to collect his personal belongings. Georg, who had the items sent to the human resources office, is embarrassed. On the way home, the family passes the scene of an accident where a family had just been killed. In the carwash, Anna has trouble suppressing her tears. She reaches back to hold Evi's hands.

Part 3: 1989: After a return from a visit at Georg's parents in the countryside, Georg declares that they have to cancel the newspaper subscription. It is now Georg's voice-over that informs the parents that the family wants to "pull up stakes" and that he quit his job. At school, Evi complains about being itchy. Withdrawing all their money from the bank, Anna tells the clerk that they "will emigrate, to Australia."

The rest of the film is dedicated to the careful preparation and execution of the parents' suicide and the killing of their daughter with the sleeping tablets that the family had horded for some time. The realization that the Schobers do not plan to emigrate comes slowly. Only Georg's suicide note addressed to his parents—read in voiceover and briefly visible in close-up—informs the viewer that, after careful deliberation, they decided "to take Evi along," because she, "is not afraid of death." The morning after a festive dinner, the family sets out to methodically and silently make all their belongings unusable: clothes, photos, documents, furniture are carefully destroyed with the aid of scissors, hammers, an axe, and even a chainsaw, while the money is carefully torn up and flushed down the toilet. The destruction of the large fish tank, with the ensuing slow death of the fish shown in close-up, seems to be the only emotional moment for Evi.

Evi is the first one to die, followed by her mother. Georg notes day and time of his family's death on a wall and puts a question mark after his name. The last images of the film show brief glimpses from the film, including the exotic beach, intercut with the white noise of the TV-screen and a close-up of Georg's dead face. A title informs the audience that the "family S. was found on 2/17/89" (i.e., several weeks after their death) by authorities alerted by Anna's brother, and that Georg's parents did not believe that the Schobers committed suicide.

BENNY'S VIDEO (1992, 105 MINUTES)

Written and directed by Michael Haneke. This is Haneke's first collaboration with the Austrian cinematographer Christian Berger, who also shot *71 Fragmente einer Chronologie des Zufalls* (1994), *La pianiste* (2001), *Caché* (2005), and *Das weiße Band* (2007) for Haneke. The film is shot in an 1:1.66 aspect ratio.

The film begins with a shaky, hand-held video of the slaughter of a pig with a bolt gun. Benny (Arno Frisch), a teenager, shot the video during the family's visit at a farm. He is fascinated by the moment the bolt enters the pigs head and reverses and replays it in slow motion. We learn from another video clip that Benny's older sister, Evi (Stephanie Brehme), attempted to make money with a pyramid scheme. The game was interrupted by the Father (Ulrich Mühe).

Benny lives in a darkened room surrounded by the latest video and audio equipment. His Mother (Angela Winkler), a gallery owner, leaves him pocket money and a note in the morning. Benny seems to be a loner in school, with just one friend, Ricci. In the afternoon, he frequents a video store where he normally rents action and horror movies. On one of his outings to the store, he meets a young girl (Ingrid Stassner) roughly his age.

Unlike Benny, the only child of a well-to-do couple, the girl has four siblings and lives on the outskirts of town. While they are waiting for the pizza to cool off, Benny enacts a sadomasochistic joke. First, mimicking a man in the subway, then a dog at her feet, then, finally, painfully twisting the girl's arm, he declares that this is "a policeman in the subway." Benny shows the video of the slaughter. All the girl has to say is: "It's snowing." He tells her that when he was still little he did not want to look at his dead grandfather in his coffin.

Benny shows her the bolt gun used to kill the pig and which he stole. He loads it and tells her to pull the trigger. When the girl refuses, he tells her that she is a coward, to which she replies that he is one. Benny pulls the trigger and the girl falls on the floor, moaning and crying. Benny asks her to be quiet, but when she doesn't stop, he kills her with the gun. With the television on and rock music blaring, Benny finishes his homework. The body of the girl is still in the room, covered by a blanket. Afterwards, Benny undresses and cleans the blood on the floor. He slowly rubs his body with the blood, an action which he films. He also films the girl's body, which he carefully positions for the camera, and immediately watches the video.

During a sleepover at his friend Ricci's place, it seems as if Benny wants to confess, but then stops. His sister is not home when he tries to visit her. He aimlessly wanders through town, goes to the movies and finally enters a hairdresser's and has his head shaved. Back home, Benny remains silent while his father berates him about his "concentration camp look."

At school, during computer class, Benny attacks Ricci from whom he had borrowed the homework. He is sent to the principals' office, but goes home instead. At home, Benny's father joins the mother while Benny shows her the video tape of the killing. The father interrogates Benny: Did he know the girl? Did somebody see them together? Benny is sent to bed. His father rationally dissects the pros and cons of alerting the authorities. Then, after deciding against it, he lists the possible courses of action. He decides to cut up the body into small pieces and burn the girl's clothes.

The mother and Benny leave for a weeklong tour through Egypt, a vacation that is carefully documented on video. At one point, Benny goes paragliding, ecstatically crying out: "Look, Mom, I'm flying!" Towards the end of their stay, the mother bursts out crying. Benny watches her helplessly.

At home, everything seems back to normal, apart from some small changes. The father has removed the drapes from Benny's windows and the mother now takes the time to have breakfast with Benny. When his father asks him why he did it, Benny hesitantly answers that he, "wanted to know how it is, probably." The parents not only do not oppose their daughter's pyramid scheme, but actually host the event.

At the end of the film, Benny shows the tape of his parents planning the cover-up to the police. When he leaves the room, he runs into his parents who were just brought in for interrogation. After the three stare at each other, Benny says, "Sorry," and leaves.

Die Rebellion/Rebellion (1993, TV, 90 minutes)

Michael Haneke adapted this short novel by the Austrian journalist and writer Joseph Roth for the ORF, the Austrian state television.

Here and in his Kafka adaptation, Jirí Stibr, who mostly works for television, does the cinematography.

The omniscient narrator introduces the main character, Andreas Pum (Branko Samarovski), who "was content with things as they were. He had lost a leg and been given a medal. He believed in a just god. One who handed out amputations but also medals to the deserving" (Roth 1962: 7, 1999: 2). The narrator continues to provide background information and explains Pum's desires, often switching to free indirect speech. Andreas Pum has lost a leg while fighting for his fatherland in World War I and is recovering in a hospital. His dream of a secure postwar existence in the form of a small store or as attendant in a park or a museum—images that are shot in bright colors—is destroyed by political upheaval. He also does not receive a prosthetic leg, but, to his joy and relief, he is at least allowed to work as a licensed organ-grinder on street corners.

Andreas Pum rents a place with Willi (Thierry van Werveke), a small-time pimp. These scenes appear especially washed-out and drained of color. During one of his outings as an organ grinder, he attracts the attention of Kathi Blumich (Judit Pogány), a recently widowed woman who loses no time to signal her attraction. The love-smitten Pum courts her. Widow Blumich's little daughter Klara (Katharina Grabher) takes a liking to him. Slowly but noticeably, the film becomes more and more colorful. The acquisition of a donkey to carry the organ and Andreas' marriage seem to signal a happy ending.

The following sequence begins with sepia-toned historical footage of a large demonstration into which Haneke splices shots of the characters. As the narrator informs us, Andreas Pum, who is firmly on the side of the authorities and regards the protestors as "heathens," is so tired that he takes the tram home. Here, he notices a fellow passenger: "It was the first time in Andreas' life that he had taken a dislike to the face of a well-dressed gentleman. But the physical intactness of this particular gentleman now offended Andreas. It was as though he had only now discovered that he was a cripple and others were healthy." (52/61) Andreas overhears the gentleman complaining loudly about people who pretend to be handicapped. Andreas feels singled-out by this and, to his own surprise, yells loudly: "You fat belly, you!" (62/53). After the ensuing shouting-match, the conductor quickly takes the side of the gentleman and asks Andreas Pum to leave. He refuses and is dragged out by force, while the other passengers call him "Jew" and "Bolshevik." A policeman takes a dislike to Andreas after Andreas demands that he arrest his opponent. The policeman takes Pum's organ-grinding license and leaves without a word.

At home, Andreas does not find any understanding. On the contrary, Widow Blumich throws him out of the house and immediately finds solace in the arms of a neighbor. She sells the beloved donkey. Pum, now without means to support himself, confuses court orders and misses his trial. In absentia, he is condemned to spend time in jail. Even though the time appears to be short, he emerges from jail visibly aged.

In the meantime, Willi has made a fortune overseeing the hiring of attendants for the city's toilets. He gives Andreas a job in one of the many lavatories that he manages. While on duty, with a pet parrot as his only companion, Pum dies on the floor. His dying vision is the donkey with the organ, again filmed in color. The voice-over tells us that the judge asks Andreas whether he would like to go to a park or a museum to work. With his last breath, Andreas says: "In die Hölle (to hell)!" The jovial Willi is the only person at the funeral. He leaves to find a replacement for Andreas' old job.

71 Fragmente einer Chronologie des Zufalls/71 Fragments of a Chronology of Chance (1994, 96 minutes)

Written and directed by Michael Haneke. The cinematography is by Christian Berger. The third and last installment in Haneke's trilogy of "glaciations of feelings" begins with an insert, telling us matter-of-factly that "on December 23, 1993, the 19-year-old Maximilian B. shot 3 people in a bank and then himself." This title card is followed by a lengthy TV-news clip with a superimposed title that reads "12 Oct. 1993." The following 71 fragments of varying length follow the lives of several characters who will be at the bank during the rampage. The fragments are separated by sudden inserts of about 2 seconds of black film and interspersed with newsreel footage from the time in which the film is set.

A Romanian Boy (Gabriel Cosmin Urdes) enters Austria hidden in a truck that delivers washing machines. A gun is stolen by Bernie (Georg Friedrich) from an army barrack. Max (Lukas Miko) acquires the gun with the help of two middlemen. Max, a student of German studies who seems to react strongly to unfairness, is also a competitive table-tennis player. In a memorable shot that lasts almost 3 minutes, Max plays against a machine that relentlessly bombards him with balls.

Inge (Anne Bennent) and Paul Brunner (Udo Samel) plan to adopt Anni, a girl from an orphanage, but their advances to win her trust fail. Tomek (Otto Grünmandl), an old man, has a daughter from whom he seems to be estranged. She works as a teller at the bank to which Hans (Branko Samarovski) delivers money in an armored truck. The taciturn Hans tells his wife, Maria (Claudia Martini), over dinner that he loves her. Suspicious about his sudden declaration of love, she asks him why he said that. He slaps her. They continue eating until she tenderly puts her hand on his arm.

The Romanian boy, who had made a subway station his playground and home, is caught and appears on national television, telling matter-of-factly about his life on the streets in Bucharest and now in Austria, where people, as he puts it, "don't pay attention to their belongings." Paul is struck by the boy's detached demeanor: "He appears so unreal." The Brunners decide to adopt the boy instead of Anni.

Max is on his way to his mother's and needs to fill up his car. Running late, he has no cash to pay and runs across the street to the bank, only to find out that his debit card does not work. Annoyed by the long line, he attempts to jump the line and is attacked by a male customer. Max returns to his car, sits silently for a few seconds, then returns to the bank and shoots indiscriminately at the people in the bank. He returns to his car and kills himself. Outside, the Romanian boy is waiting for Inge Brunner to return from the bank.

The end of the film is a news reel that we saw before, now containing an additional segment about Max's killing spree. We do not know which of the characters was killed. This insert was shot by a professional news crew that Haneke hired to do this clip.

Funny Games (1997) and *Funny Games U.S.* (2007)

Written by Michael Haneke. The cinematography for the 1997 German language version of this film is by Jürgen Jürges, who used to work with Rainer Werner Fassbinder on some of his best films: *Satansbraten/ Satan's Brew* (1976); *Angst vor der Angst/Fear of Fear* (1975); *Fontane— Effi Briest* (1974) and *Angst essen Seele auf/Fear Eats the Soul* (1974). Next to Christian Berger, Jürges is the other director of photography with whom Haneke most frequently collaborates. He worked for Haneke on the 1-minute short film for *Lumière et compagnie/Lumière and Company* (1995), and also shot *Le temps du loup/The Time of the Wolf* (2003); *Code inconnu: Récit incomplet de divers voyages* (2000).

For *Funny Games U.S.* (2008), a shot-for-shot remake, Haneke chose Darius Khondji, who is responsible for the cinematography of *Alien: Resurrection* (1997), *La Cité des enfants perdus* (1995) and *Delicatessen* (1991), as well as *Panic Room* (2002), and *Se7en* (1995), among others.

Driving to their weekend retreat in a gated community on a lake, the Schober [Farber] family [Anna (Susanne Lothar)/Ann (Naomi Watts), Georg (Ulrich Mühe)/George (Tim Roth), and Schorschi (Stefan Clapczynski)/Georgie (Devon Gearhart)] pass their time with a musical guessing game. The classical music they choose for their game is suddenly interrupted by extradiegetic noise, a shrill cacophony of music and screams ("noise-punk" by the experimental musician John Zorn). Upon arrival, the Farbers find their neighbors in an apparent conversation with two young men in their early twenties. A short while later, the neighbor comes over and introduces the taller of the two as "Paul, the son of a business associate." While Paul (Arno Frisch/Michael Pitt), Georg and the neighbor get the sail boat into the water, Anna stocks the fridge and prepares lunch. The other young man (Frank Giering/Brady Corbet)—later introduced as Peter—knocks at the door, claiming that he came through "a hole in the fence" and that the neighbors sent him to borrow some eggs. Extremely polite and well-spoken but apparently quite clumsy, he drops the eggs and pushes the cell phone into a sink full of water. Peter, who claims to be afraid of the family dog, is joined by Paul, who gushes about the Georg's expensive set of gold clubs. He asks to take a practice swing and leaves the house.

Anna, irritated by Peter and Paul's unwillingness to go back to their hosts, finally asks them to leave. The young men appear overtly astonished, with Paul accusing Peter of misbehaving, a well-rehearsed shtick between friends, it seems. Joined by Georg, the situation quickly escalates until Georg slaps Paul in the face. In retaliation, Peter breaks his kneecap with a golf club. Paul and Peter—who during the film also address each other as Tom and Jerry, or Beavis and Butthead—quickly overpower the family and send Anna out to look for the dog in a game of "warm" and "cold." The body of the dog proves what the Farbers—and the audience—had suspected: Peter has killed the dog with the golf club. In this sequence, and several times during the film, Peter breaks the fourth wall and directly addresses the audience.

When other neighbors come by on a boat to call on the Schobers, Anna, with her family held hostage, has no choice but to play along. Back inside the house, after roughing up the family, Paul and Peter engage in another game. Asked why they are doing this, Paul and Peter mockingly recite the gamut of explanations: divorced parents, sexual problems, etc. Finally, they announce their wager: they bet that the family will be "kaput," as they put it, in less than 12 hours, unless the family wins a series of games. It is no surprise that those "games" are rigged.

At one point, the young Schorschi manages to escape. However, he is unable to escape from the gated grounds and hides in the neighbors' house, where Peter quickly tracks him down. Schorschi tells his parents that Paul and Peter have massacred the entire family. While Paul prepares a sandwich, Peter shoots Schorschi with a shotgun. Paul and Peter leave the grieving parents alone. Anna manages to free herself and runs out to call for help. But the passing car that Anna attempts to hail is driven by the killers. Back inside their blood-spattered living room, Anna is able to grab the shotgun and shoot Peter point blank—the only violence that the audience sees. Paul frantically looks for "the remote control," which he uses to rewind the film back to the point where he can safely take the gun away from Anna.

Paul now shoots the tied and gagged Georg. The two killers take Anna out to the lake in the sail boat. While they discuss "matter and antimatter universes" and whether what you see in the movies is "as real as reality," they throw Anna overboard even though "she had another hour left." It is early morning when Peter and Paul arrive at another house. This time it is Paul who politely waits until asked in. He states that Anna sent him and that the Schobers would like to borrow some eggs. His mocking face in close-up, the Zorn music from the beginning of the film sets in and the credits begin to roll.

Lumière et compagnie/*Lumière and Company* (1995, 1 minute)

For this project, 40 directors were asked to shoot a film with one of the original cameras the Lumière brothers used in 1895. The directors were only allowed to film one reel, lasting under a minute. For his contribution, Haneke created a video of the evening news edited down to the allotted time frame. He then played the video on a TV and filmed it using the Lumière camera.

Das Schloß nach Franz Kafka/*The Castle* (1996, TV, 123 minutes)

K. (Ulrich Mühe) arrives at a remote village. Everything and everybody seems to depend on the castle. He learns that he has been hired as

"Landvermesser," land surveyor, but that he is not allowed near the castle. His two helpers, Artur (Frank Giering) and Jeremias (Felix Eitner), seemingly twins "similar as two snakes," appear without the necessary surveying equipment. A messenger named Barnabas (André Eisermann) is his only means of communication with the powerful Castellan, Klamm. At an inn that is reserved for castle hands, where Klamm is dining behind closed doors, K. meets the barmaid Frieda (Susanne Lothar), who introduces herself as Klamm's mistress. K. and Frieda make love on the floor. K. declares that he intends to marry Frieda who then has to leave her employment due to their affair.

K. attempts to meet with Klamm end in frustration. Furthermore, the Council Chairman (Nikolaus Paryla), to whom K. has to report, tells K. that there is no need for a surveyor at all. The search through a gigantic pile of documents for an earlier order concerning the demand for a surveyor leads nowhere. K. shows a letter written by Klamm, but the Council Chairman points out that it has not been written on letterhead and is thus not official. Urged by Frieda, K. reluctantly takes on an interim job as school janitor. K. refuses to be interrogated by Momus (Paulus Manker), one of Klamm's secretaries. Barnabas arrives with a letter by Klamm, praising K.'s and his assistants' work.

K., Frieda, and the assistants now sleep in the classroom. To their embarrassment, they wake up surrounded by the children. The teacher (Johannes Silberschneider), angry that K. broke into the shed for firewood, fires K. who refuses to leave and, in turn, fires his assistants. K. is friendly to a boy whose mother is from the castle. At Barnabas' house, Olga (Dörte Lyssewski), one of Barnabas' sisters, tells him that she was forced into prostitution because her younger sister Amalia (Inga Busch) refused to give herself to a secretary, resulting in her family becoming ostracized.

Barnabas arrives with news: K. has been allowed to speak to Erlanger (Hans Diehl), one of Klamm's senior secretaries. Arriving at the inn, K. is forced to wait for the sleeping Erlanger to wake up. He sees Frieda, who seems to now live with Jeremias and who accuses him of having a relationship with Barnabas' sisters, a false accusation that K. seems to be too tired to deny. Frieda sends K. away, telling him that he is manipulative and has only his career in mind. Looking for Erlanger, he enters the wrong room. A jovial secretary (Norbert Schwientek) attempts to explain the balance of power, but K. is too exhausted to listen. Erlanger calls for K., telling him on the way out that Frieda is needed at the bar because Klamm is very sensitive to change and that it would be to K.'s advantage if he could convince Frieda to return to her former post.

K. is woken up by Frieda's replacement, Pipa. The girl tells K. that Frieda conspired to get her old job back and insinuates that Frieda never was Klamm's mistress. K. tells Pipa that she overestimates the importance of this job. Pipa suggests that K. should move in with her and her girlfriends until spring. Suddenly, the door opens and Gerstäcker (Wolfram Berger), one of the farmers, arrives and tells K. that he has a place and a job for K. He drags the reluctant K. outside. While K. and Gerstäcker wade through the snow, the voice-over informs us that K. encountered Gerstäcker's mother in his hut. The narration ends mid-sentence and the film ends abruptly. A white title appears: "At this point, Franz Kafka's fragment ends."

Code inconnu: Récit incomplet de divers voyages/*Code Unknown* (2000, 118 minutes)

Written and directed by Michael Haneke. Cinematography by Jürgen Jürges. The full title translates to: "*Code unknown: incomplete tale of several journeys.*" Like *72 Fragmente*, the film consists of loose fragments (in this case 39, plus a prologue and an epilogue) without conventional transitions and interrupted by a short, black frame of about 1 second. There are no sequences in the traditional sense. The scenes are shot in one continuous take, with four notable exceptions: twice, the viewer sees photos that Georges took, and twice, excerpts from films in which Anne appears are inserted.

After the credits but before the film's title, a brief prologue is shown. In a medium long shot, a young girl is gesturing silently with a white wall for background. Other children, who appear to be deaf-mute, are watching her performance, guessing to no avail what emotion she is expressing. The title appears. The following scene lasts over 9 minutes and is shot in one continuous take, framing the action mostly in a medium long to long shot. Here, the viewer is filled in on the back story. The scene begins abruptly with Anne Laurent (Juliette Binoche) leaving her apartment, when she is suddenly being hailed by Jean (Alexandre Hamidi), her boyfriend's younger brother who was waiting outside the door of her apartment building for an hour because the door code he had was outdated. Asked by Jean when his brother would be back, Anne tells him that she does not know. It appears that Jean ran away from home not wanting to take over the family farm and is now looking for a place to stay. Anne, who is late for an important appointment, is visibly not thrilled about the idea of him staying with her, but gives him the key to her apartment, telling him in clear terms that this will be a temporary solution. Upset, Jean walks back and thoughtlessly disposes of a paper bag by dropping it into the lap of a beggar, Maria (Luminita Gheorghiu). Jean is accosted by Amadou (Ona Lu Yenke) who asks that Jean apologize to the beggar. Jean refuses and the situation escalates into a scuffle. Called by a store owner, two policemen arrive. Anne, who witnessed the arrival of the police but not Jean's behavior, sides with Jean. Amadou—first calm, then increasingly irate about the situation—gets into an argument with the police, who take his passport and arrest him. The long take ends as abruptly as it began, with the struggling Amadou being led away.

While snapshots of atrocities from the war in Bosnia appear, we hear a letter by Georges to Anne referring to past relationship problems, wishing her good luck for her play.

Amadou's father (Djibril Kouyaté), an African immigrant and cab driver, receives a phone call informing him about his son's arrest. This is not the first time that this has happened. His fast driving irritates the passenger, who is never shown and whose voice we hear from off-camera, to the point where Amadou's father deposits the man summarily at a taxi stand.

The next scene opens with a medium long shot of a dark, rundown room. A voice, obviously that of the camera operator, gives instructions to Anne to come in front of the camera. Anne is told matter-of-factly that she will die and that there is no way out. She becomes irritated while the camera zooms in on her, until we see her face in close-up. Finally Anne breaks down and begins to beg for her life.

The Farmer (Sepp Bierbichler), Jean's and Georges' father, sits alone at his kitchen table eating a simple meal. Jean joins him and they eat in silence. The father leaves the table and stands alone in the dark.

The pattern established here in the first part of *Code inconnu* is repeated throughout. Slowly, the fragments allow the viewer to understand some of the characters.

While Anne is ironing in her apartment, she hears horrible screams and hits the mute button on the TV. It seems that a child is being abused next door. Anne continues ironing after the noise dies down and finally turns the volume back on. Later, she receives a note asking for help. While Anne and Georges (Thierry Neuvic) are shopping, Anne mentions the note and that she suspects that the elderly neighbor wrote it. Anne wants advice from Georges as to what to do. Georges refuses, impatiently telling Anne that this is her problem. Anne counters by asking Georges what he would do if she were pregnant, adding abruptly that she might have aborted his child but refusing to discuss it further. She asks him: "Have you ever made somebody happy?" Suddenly, Georges and Anne kiss passionately. Later, Anne attends a funeral that is obviously that of the abused girl next door.

A conversation at Amadou's place reveals some new information. The father has left the family and gone back to Africa. While Amadou's older sister seems to be convinced that he left the family to start a new life with a much younger woman, Amadou tries to reassure his younger, deaf-mute sister that he will be back, telling her that he has family and friends in Africa. The little girl doesn't even know where Africa is. Again, the mother speaks in her native language, while the older daughter answers her in strongly accented but fluent French.

Maria, who has been deported to Romania, proudly inspects a large house that her family is building, while her daughter fills her in on the local gossip. Later, Maria is pressured by her family to return to Western Europe.

Anne and Georges are having dinner, chatting with friends about their work. When Amadou and a young woman walk past their table, the camera follows them. Amadou is annoyed about the waiter's arrogant snub, but the young woman tells him to let it go. Anne walks by and the camera follows her back to her table, where a friend questions the meaning of Georges' work. Anne points out Amadou to Georges as "the kid who harassed Jean."

Apparently alerted by a neighbor, Anne and Georges visit Georges' father who has killed all his cows after Jean left him one day. He complains about the young generation's refusal to work hard, accusing Georges of setting a bad example. When Anne tries to comfort Georges' father who is fond of her, he abruptly leaves, mumbling an excuse.

Among the fragments, two sequences stand out. One is a harrowing, last second rescue of a little boy who almost falls from a rooftop and which turns out to be a film in which Anne starred, and which she is dubbing in a studio. This sequence is shot and edited like a typical Hollywood film. The second shows Anne taking the metro home when a young Arab tough (Walide Afkir) harasses her. None of the passengers makes a move. Only an older Arab man (Maurice Bénichou) stands up to defend her. Finally, the young man gets off, spitting at Anne who breaks out in tears.

The film ends with Maria back in Paris. She finds her usual place in the street occupied by a gypsy girl who is part of an organized gang.

The closing epilogue returns to the school for the deaf mute, where we see a lively drum performance.

LA PIANISTE/THE PIANO TEACHER (2001)

This film—written and directed by Michael Haneke—is based on the 1983 novel *Die Klavierspielerin* by the Austrian writer Elfriede Jelinek. Even though it is set and filmed on location in Vienna, all characters speak French. Haneke's original script has been published (Haneke 2001). The cinematography is by Christian Berger (aspect ratio 1:1.85).

Erika Kohut (Isabelle Huppert), in her late thirties and a piano teacher at a prestigious Viennese music academy, still lives with her overprotective and jealous Mother (Annie Girardot) who berates her daughter for not having the career for which she hoped. With the father committed to an asylum, Erika is the only person in her mother's life; they even sleep in a double bed. At a piano recital that a rich patron (Udo Samel) and his wife (Cornelia Köndgen) have organized, Kohut meets their nephew, the cocky and charming Walter Klemmer (Benoît Magimel), a young man in his twenties. He is instantly smitten with Erika and performing Schubert at the *soirée*, plays especially for her.

A second mother–daughter dyad is introduced with Anna Schober (Anna Sigalevitch), a shy and insecure girl of about 16 years, and her mother (Susanne Lothar), who seems to be determined to make a concert pianist out of her. Next, we see a local porn shop, where Kohut rents a cabin, chooses a video and sniffs a sperm-soaked tissue. Later in the film, she locks herself in the bathroom and cuts her genital area with a razorblade. She also goes to the local drive-in cinema to observe couples having sex in their cars and gets caught.

Walter Klemmer applies to be admitted into Kohut's master class. While her colleagues are taken by his talent, Kohut resists accepting him. During their first lesson, Klemmer declares that he is obsessed by her, but Kohut spurns him. Still, she secretly follows him to his ice hockey practice to spy on him.

During a rehearsal for an important recital, Anna Schober loses her nerve, but Klemmer puts her at ease, a scene that Kohut watches from afar. Kohut then retires to the cloak room, breaks a glass, and puts it in Anna's coat. The young girl lacerates her hand. Erika Kohut feigns nausea and goes to the restroom, followed by Klemmer. Instead of the sex act that he envisions, Erika attempts to establish her mastery over him: she will send her demands by letter, the first of which she hands to him during their next lesson. The two go home and—over the objections of Erika's mother—barricade themselves in her room. The letter contains a carefully scripted scenario for Erika's masochistic subjection. Disgusted, Klemmer leaves. Later in bed, Erika lies on top of her mother and, submitting her to a punishing abjection, tries to kiss her on the mouth.

At the ice hockey ring, Erika attempts to satisfy Klemmer orally, but he can't get an erection and she finally throws up. That same night, Klemmer intrudes into the Kohuts' place, locks the mother in the bedroom, and brutally beats and rapes Erika.

The evening of the recital, Erika looks for Klemmer in the concert hall armed with a kitchen knife. She sees him with a group of his friends. She rams the knife into her upper chest area and leaves the hall.

Le Temps du loup/The Time of the Wolf (2003, 113 minutes)

Written and directed by Michael Haneke; the cinematography is by Jürgen Jürges. Wide shots of the rural landscape—the film is shot in a ratio of 1:2.35—stand in contrast to the medium shots and close-ups of the *huis clos* situation of the shelter. The film appears to be set in France as it is shot in French, but, keeping in mind that *La Pianiste* is set in Vienna with French speaking characters, there are no markers that tie the action to a specific region.

The film opens with a minivan arriving at an isolated cabin in the woods. The Laurent family—Anne (Isabelle Huppert), Georges (Daniel Duval), Eva (Anaïs Demoustier), and Ben (Lucas Biscombe)—discover that their country cabin is already occupied by another family. The man, armed with a shotgun, demands their food and water supplies. While the father suggests an amicable solution, he is shot dead point blank. Anne, Eva and Ben find themselves without clothing, food, or shelter. It appears that an unknown event has destroyed the environment, ensuing in a breakdown of the public order.

Benjamin, traumatized by his father's death and also the death of his pet parakeet, runs away into the night. Trying to look for him, Anne and Eva accidentally burn down the shed where they found shelter. The next morning, Benjamin returns, brought back by a feral boy (Hakim Taleb) around Eva's age. He reluctantly joins them on the search for a railway station where they hope to receive help from the authorities. Eva quickly establishes herself as the mediator between her mother and Benjamin and between them and the boy. The boy, in turn, is more experienced in survival, taking clothes off a dead body for Eva.

A passing train doesn't stop. By following the tracks, they find a station occupied by a small band of fugitives who hope that eventually a train will bring help. The community—a microcosm of society—is controlled by Koslowski (Olivier Gourmet), whose authority is secured by the pistol he carries. He trades the little remaining clean water for valuables or sexual favors and organizes the bartering with the local farmers. Koslowski suspects the boy of theft and expels him from the community, over Eva's desperate pleas. Leaving, the boy admits to Eva that he stole glasses in order to be able to light a fire.

The last hour of the film takes place in and around the train station. A woman tells Anne the myth of the "36 Just Ones" who watch over humankind. If ever one of them should be killed, it would mean the end. Eva writes letters to her dead father and sneaks away to meet with the feral boy who is camping in the woods. A young boy dies of malnutrition and lack of clean water.

The arrival of a large group of travelers changes the balance of power significantly. This group seems to be more democratically organized. Among them, however, is the father's killer. While Anne and Eva try in vain to convince the community of his guilt, a horse is shot and killed. Later, an old man says that he witnessed acts of self-sacrifice, people jumping into fire to bring the world back on track. At night, the young daughter of one of the few kind men in the group (Maurice Bénichou) and barely older than Eva, is raped. Eva covers Benjamin's ears. The girl later kills herself. When she learns that he feral boy has stolen one of the goats, Eva berates him for his selfish action. To evade discovery by a posse, the boy is forced to kill the goat.

One night, Benjamin gets up and walks towards a large fire that the community keeps lit in the hope of signaling its whereabouts. He adds wood and undresses, obviously in order to throw himself into the flames. One of the guards—a man who earlier exhibited brutish and racist qualities—prevents this and tells Benjamin that the intention of the sacrifice is enough.

The films ends with a 5-minute long continuous take from a passenger train moving though a rural landscape. It is not clear whether outside help has arrived or who is operating the train.

CACHÉ/HIDDEN (2005, 113 MINUTES)

Written and directed by Michael Haneke, cinematography is by Christian Berger (aspect ratio 1:1.78). Majid is played by Maurice Bénichou, who already had a role in *Le temps du loup* and who defends Anne in *Code Inconnu* against a young Arab thug played by Walide Afkir. The latter now plays Majid's son.

When the films opens, Anne (Juliette Binoche) and Georges (Daniel Auteuil) Laurent are reviewing a tape that Anne has found in a plastic bag at the front door. The tape shows their house in a quiet part of Paris. Slightly disquieted, they argue that it might have been a prank pulled off by one of their son's friends or by a fan of Georges, who hosts a successful literary talk show on television.

The next tape is filmed at night, showing Georges coming home in his car. This time, the tape is accompanied by a childish drawing of face. While we watch the tape, a brief fragment shows a little boy wiping blood from his mouth. The phone rings and an anonymous male caller asks for Georges, upsetting Anne. Leaving the police station, a cyclist—a young black man riding against the direction of traffic on a one-way street—barely avoids running into Georges, who yells after him. It almost comes to blows, but Anne is able to persuade Georges to walk away. The police is of no help. The next day, their son Pierrot (Lester Makedonsky), a young teenager, tells his father that he has received a postcard signed "from your father." The card shows a drawing similar to the first.

At a dinner party in the Laurent's chic home, their friend Yvon (Denys Podalydès) tells an anecdote about an old lady who claimed that he reminded her of her dog. The dog died the day Yvon was born. The dog was hit by a truck on the spot where Yvon has a scar. When Anne feels the spot, Yvon suddenly barks, breaking the tension built up by his narrative. While they talk about a friend who now has a younger girlfriend named Marianne, the doorbell rings. Georges finds another package on the doorstep. He does not tell his friends about the tapes. This time, the crude drawing shows a cock with its throat cut and the video shows Georges' childhood home, a farm in the countryside.

Georges visits his mother (Annie Girardot). He tells her that he dreamed of Majid, a boy Georges' parents had planned to adopt, but his mother is obviously unwilling to talk about an incident that happened long ago. The same night, Georges dreams about something that happened when he was just 6 years old: Majid, who appears a year or two older than he, has slaughtered a cock, his face covered in blood. He approaches Georges with a hatchet.

The next tape brings some clues as it shows a street, a social housing complex and finally an apartment outside the city limits. Anne is upset that Georges seems to suspect someone but is unwilling to share the person's identity with her. Georges finds Majid (Maurice Benichou), aged beyond his years. Majid seems to be surprised that Georges found him, while Georges accuses Majid of "terrorizing" his family. Noticeably, Georges uses the polite "vous" form with Majid, while Majid addresses George in the familiar "tu." Georges leaves, threatening Majid with legal consequences. Asked by Majid whether he is threatening him, Georges answers, "Yes, I am threatening you!"

Georges calls Anne and tells her that nobody was at the apartment. But by next evening, Anne has received a tape that shows Georges' and Majid's conversation. Georges tells Anne that Majid was orphaned by the massacre that happened on October 17, 1961, when the French police, acting under the orders of chief of police Maurice Papon, summarily executed more than 200 Algerian protesters and threw their bodies into the Seine. His parents wanted to adopt Majid, but Georges, as he puts it, tattled on him ("Je l'ai cafté.").

The next day, Georges is interrogated by his boss (Bernard Le Coq), who has received the same tape. Even though the boss expresses his sympathies, his threat is thinly veiled: Georges must find a way to control the situation. Georges returns to Majid's place, but nobody opens. Anne, in tears, confides in her boss (Daniel Duval) who was also a guest at the dinner party a few nights ago. Coming home, Anne and Georges find out that their son is missing. The police arrest Majid and his son (Walide Afkir), even though there is no trace of Pierrot or the tapes at their place. Early the next morning, Pierrot is dropped off by the mother of a schoolmate at whose house he has spent the night. When Anne confronts him, Pierrot is defensive and accuses Anne of having an affair with her boss. He rejects Anne's attempt to embrace him.

The next day, Georges is editing his latest show. He cuts short a contribution on Rimbaud because it is "too theoretical." When Georges appears at Majid's place, the latter tells him that he wanted him to be present ("Je voulais que tu sois présent."). While Georges watches helplessly, Majid unexpectedly takes out a razor and cuts his throat. Georges leaves and goes to a cinema. At home, he tells Anne to get rid of her friends under a pretense. Georges finally comes clean, telling Anne about Majid's suicide and that, when they were children, he lied to his parents, telling them that Majid had spit blood. When this did not work, he told Majid that he was supposed to kill a cock, and then told his parents that Majid killed the cock to frighten him, essentially framing Majid and preventing his adoption by Georges' parents.

The next day, Georges is accosted by Majid's son in the lobby of the TV station. While the latter stays calm and denies that he sent the tapes, inquiring how it feels to have someone's life on his conscience, Georges becomes more and more irate, insisting that he is not responsible. At home, Georges takes two sleeping pills, telling his wife that he has to sleep off a cold. A short fragment, shot from the point-of-view of Georges as a child, shows Majid being forcefully removed from the farm.

The last shot mirrors the camera set-up of the surveillance tapes and shows the outside of Pierrot's high school. Pierrot is barely recognizable among the many students. Majid's son walks towards Pierrot and they exchange a few words.

Das weiße Band: Eine deutsche Kindergeschichte/The White Ribbon (2009, 144 minutes)

The full title of the film translates to *The White Ribbon: A German Children's Tale*. Shot in digital format, with deep focus photography (ratio 1:1.85) by the Austrian Christian Berger, who worked for Haneke before, beginning with *Benny's Video*, the film has the appearance of old photos (the color was removed digitally in post-production). Static and symmetric compositions of interiors and exteriors dominate the film, but sometimes the steadycam follows walking characters very closely, so that their head and shoulders fill the screen.

Das weiße Band (2009) is set in the year preceding the outbreak of World War I, in an isolated protestant village in the Northeast of Germany. The film opens with a black screen over which the narrator, in the voice of a frail old man (Ernst Jacobi), begins his tale with a caveat: he has not witnessed all the events, nor has he found an explanation for what happened. However, he believes that his tale "might shed light onto some occurrences in this country." A slow fade in reveals a rural setting in a long shot. The narrator—the village's underpaid Schoolteacher (Christian Friedel), as it turns out later—begins his story with recalling the first of several violent incidents. The Doctor (Rainer Bock) is severely hurt when his horse is tripped by a hidden wire and has to be transported to the next town. In his absence, the Midwife of the village (Susanne Lothar), "a woman in her forties," unmarried and living with a son who has Down's syndrome, takes care of the doctor's children, the 14-year-old Anna (Roxane Duran) and the 4-year-old Rudolph (Miljan Chatelain). The narrator draws our attention to Klara (Maria-Victoria Dragus), an uncannily precocious 14 year old, the oldest daughter of the Pastor (Burghart Klaußner), a stern man who rules over his flock and his numerous children with a subtle mix of psychological pressure and brutal punishment. The film's title is derived from the white ribbon that the Pastor's two older children, Klara and Martin (Leonard Proxauf), have to wear on their sleeves as a reminder of purity and chastity. The weal and woe of everybody in the village depends on the landowner, the Baron (Ulrich Tukur), whose cultured wife (Ursina Lardi) is obviously unhappy in this rural community. When the wife of a poor peasant Farmer (Branko Samarovski) dies in an accident that might have been caused by negligence, the Farmer reminds his son Max (Sebastian Hülk), who is demanding justice, that they cannot survive without the Baron's patronage.

During the harvest festival, the highlight of the year, Max vandalizes a field of the Baron's cabbage. Max' sister is immediately dismissed from the Baron's service. That same night, the Baron's son, 9-year-old Siegmund, is kidnapped and severely beaten. Max is the prime suspected but has an alibi. The following Sunday in church, the Baron appeals to the villagers to bring the guilty party to justice. The Baroness moves to Italy with her son and infant twins, dismissing the private tutor and Eva (Leonie Benesch), the twins' nanny, in the middle of the night. The Schoolteacher, a clumsy man in his early thirties who has fallen in love with Eva, only 17 years old, spends a *nuit blanche* with her in the school house.

An additional subplot emerges with the return of the Doctor. He has been physically and psychologically abusing the Midwife for years, and it emerges that her handicapped son might be his. Later in the film, little Rudolph walks in on the Doctor who had obviously just molested his own daughter.

During winter and spring, other incidents occur. The Steward's infant has been left by an open window and catches a severe cold. A barn belonging to the Baron is set on fire. The next morning, the poor farmer is found hanged in the barn. The Midwife's son is brutally tortured. Erna (Janina Fautz), the Steward's daughter, tells the Schoolteacher that she foresaw the incidents in her dreams. The police, alerted by the Schoolteacher, interrogates Erna but cannot force her to confess. Klara, after being psychologically tormented by her father in front of other candidates for confirmation, kills her father's beloved parakeet by ramming scissors down its throat. She displays the dead bird on her father's desk.

The Baroness, just returned, tells her husband that she will leave him for another man and move back to Italy with the children. Their fight is interrupted by the Steward (Josef Bierbichler), who brings the news that the heir to the Austrian throne has been killed in Sarajevo. The Schoolteacher hopes that the impeding war is reason enough to move up his wedding with Eva, which Eva's father (Detlev Buck) had postponed for another year.

The outbreak of the war overshadows two other events. The Doctor, the Midwife, and all their children leave the town without a trace. The same day, the Teacher—strongly suspecting that the village children committed the various acts of violence—shares his findings with the Pastor. The latter is incensed and forbids that those accusations be made public.

Over the final images—a festive mass honoring the fresh recruits at which the children sing the chorale cantata by Johann Sebastian Bach, "*Ein' feste Burg ist unser Gott*" (A mighty fortress is our God)—the narrator informs us that, after serving in the war, he opened a tailor's shop and never saw any of the villagers again.

NOTES

Introduction

[1] I return to this point in detail later. To add a personal example of this shift onto the viewer, the dark secret at the heart of *Caché*—the massacre of unarmed protesters by French police under the command of Maurice Papon, the Parisian Prefect of Police in the sixties—was not known to me, as it was probably not known to many viewers. After watching the film, I felt the need to research what had happened, discovering the connection to German Fascism in the form of Papon, a known Nazi-collaborator.

[2] The very possibility of "mixing genres," proves, in the words of Derrida, the "essential purity of their identity" in the first place (Derrida 1980: 204). These loaded terms from the mouth of the essential anti-essentialist, of course, are marked as highly self-reflexive—not ironic—for, after all, we can only mix what we *already* perceive as pure.

[3] In 1992, Michael Haneke described the trilogy as "reports on the progression of the emotional glaciation [*Vergletscherung der Gefühle*] of my country" (1992: 89).

[4] The website of the "Motion Picture Association of America, Inc.," whose board rates films in the United States, specifies: "There may be depictions of violence in a PG-13 movie, but generally not both realistic and extreme or persistent violence." The films by Haneke that were released theatrically in the United States (*La Pianiste* and all the following films) received an R-rating: "Children under 17 are not allowed to attend R-rated motion pictures unaccompanied by a parent or adult guardian" (http://www.mpaa.org/FlmRat_Ratings.asp).

[5] Camhi (2004) quotes Haneke: "I wrote the script for 'Time of the Wolf' 12 years ago, [...] But after Sept. 11, I decided that I had to do it right away. [...]."

[6] Wolfram Knorr, "Trilogie der Vereisung," *Kultur* 3, October 1994, quoted after Peucker (2000: 176).

[7] In an interview with a web-based German journal Haneke criticizes "the trivialization through aestheticization" of violence in mainstream film (Köhler 1997). In another interview, the director certainly doesn't mince

words when it comes to his contempt: "Speaking about cinema, the mainstream cinema tries to feed you the idea that there are solutions, but that's bullshit. You can make a lot of money with these lies" (Foundas 2002). He also does not believe that an audience necessarily wants to see through these lies: "People don't like to be confronted with reality. They like to be confronted with a consumable reality. Even the most brutal violence is shown in a way that you can consume it so that you are thrilled, not touched" (Calhoun 2007). Asked about the relevance of *Funny Games* 10 years after the first one was released, Haneke states: "In fact I think it is more relevant than ever because the pornography of violence in the media has increased" (Brady 2009). The most reflected statement about television can be found in an interview with *Cineaste*: "I am most concerned with television as the key symbol primarily of the media representation of violence, and more generally of a greater crisis, which I see as our collective loss of reality and social disorientation. Alienation is a very complex problem, but television is certainly implicated in it. We don't of course anymore perceive reality, but instead the representation of reality in television. Our experiential horizon is very limited. What we know of the world is little more than the mediated world, the image. We have no reality, but a derivative of reality, which is extremely dangerous, most certainly from a political standpoint but also in a larger sense to our ability to have a palpable sense of the truth of everyday experience" (Sharrett 2003: 30).

8 Stephen Prince mentions especially films by Akira Kurosawa as model for Peckinpah (1998: 51–58). A comparison between the cinema of Haneke and that of Peckinpah would not be so farfetched. Prince determines the reactions by characters in Peckinpah to violence as "didactic tableaux" (167, see also 172). This, more static concept seems to be related to Haneke's moving shifts. Prince also compares Peckinpah's cinema to Artaud's "Theater of Cruelty." Here, however, it seems to me that Prince misunderstands Artaud as a Brechtian. I discuss Artaud and Haneke in the following chapter.

9 That this claim is made in almost identical form does not prove that it is really true. See Calhoun (2007), where Haneke is quoted: "The idea of the original was to address the American viewer of violent films a little bit, but unfortunately and because of the German-speaking cast, the original film worked only on the arthouse circuit." In Wray (2007), Haneke states: "'Funny Games' was always made with American audiences in mind, since its subject is Hollywood's attitude toward violence. And nothing has changed about that attitude since the first version of my film was released—just the opposite, in fact." The Guardian quotes Haneke (Jeffries 2008) as follows: "The original was in German, and English-speaking audiences don't often see subtitled films. When I first envisioned *Funny Games* in the mid-1990s, it was my intention to have an American audience watch the movie. It is a reaction to a certain American cinema, its violence, its naivety, the way American cinema toys with human beings. In many American films, violence is made consumable. But because I made *Funny Games* in German

with actors not familiar to US audiences, it didn't get through to the people who most needed to see it." In an interview with *The Filmmaker Magazine* (2008), Haneke states, "when I did the first *Funny Games* it was intended to be for a public of violence consumers in the English-speaking world, [but] because [it was in] the German language the film stayed always in the art-houses and so didn't reach the public that it would need to have." See also, for example, an interview with the certainly very bourgeois weekly special *Le Figaro Madame*, where Haneke makes the same point (Quin 2008).

[10] For example, Schager (2008). *The Strangers* varies the genre formula only insofar as the killers succeed and vow to continue their sadistic games. Interestingly, most web-sites dedicated to horror/slasher films understood that *Funny Games* is not a typical "home invasion thriller," but a filmic reflection on the genre. See, for example, MrDisgusting (2008) or Benamor (2008). The discussion board dedicated to *Funny Games U.S.* on the Internet Movie Database (imdb.com) also gives this impression.

[11] An admittedly unscientific survey of the comments on message boards on the Internet Movie Database shows that the audience of Haneke's films clearly possesses a superior knowledge of grammar and spelling and mostly argues on the basis of a clear thesis, while fans of so-called "torture porn" (e.g., the *Hostel* and *Saw* series) tend to express like and dislike without much critical insight. However, some of the especially unsophisticated posts admiring "torture porn" might be acts of posing and provocation. Also, several interrelated blogs developed around *Code Inconnu* in the spring of 2006 (http://www.girishshambu.com/blog/). Judging by their style and critical acumen, most posts were written by educated people, probably graduate students.

[12] The posters are featured on the Internet Movie Database. The ad for *Code Inconnu*, for example, tellingly depicts Juliette Binoche in a still-shot from the film-within-the film. Here, she is apparently screaming while swimming in a pool, looking a lot more glamorous than in the film itself. The poster for *La Pianiste* shows Isabelle Huppert in the passionate embrace of a man on the floor of a restroom. The casting of the well-known actors Naomi Watts and Tim Roth for *Funny Games US* was without doubt an attempt to duplicate this strategy, especially since Naomi Watts has been widely dubbed "the Queen of Remake," because of her starring roles in several high-profile remakes.

[13] Horwath (1991: 14–16) and Lane (2009: 60). Wheatley (2009: 15), mostly relying on Horwath (1991: 14–16), gives a similar overview as Wray (2007). The *Torino Film Festival* (1997) introduces Michael Haneke as follows on their website: "Michael Haneke was born in Munich on March 23, 1942, the son of Austrian actress Beatrix von Degenschild and the director and actor Fritz Haneke, from Dusseldorf. Michael spent his youth in Wiener Neustadt (Lower Austria), and graduated from the local high school in 1962. When his plan to study acting at the Reinhardt-Seminar of Vienna fell through, as

did his plan to become a pianist, Michael enrolled in Psychology and Philosophy at the University of Vienna. He tried his hand at writing (a short story intitled [sic!] *Persephone*) and, besides studying, he worked as a movie and literary critic." (http://www.torinofilmfest.org/?action=detail&id=1153).

[14] In a special issue of *Screen* (2007), dedicated to *Caché*, Mark Cousins seems to follow a similar line of argument. Cousins mentions the film's appeal to the "ideas-aware elite metropolitan groupings" (224). He then correctly describes *Caché*'s program: "The film structures our experience in a generically gripping way but then the structure melts away at the moment when it should most cohere, requiring us to look back along its length (the structure's length and the film's) to work out where we went wrong" (226). However, Cousins then suggests that *Caché* does not really exceed other films that defy a simple interpretation due to built-in paradoxes and thus inspire "social conversation," such as *Dallas, Twin Peaks, Lost* and *The Crying Game* (224). In the end, Cousins' short reflections appear to be stalled by his normative assumptions, that is, a refusal to accept that he sets the milieu of the "metropolitan elite" as a point of origin and the final measure of the film.

[15] As a last example of the futility of such a speculative reading, I refer to an interesting critical short-circuit that is typical for a lot of Haneke's less cautious critics. Pacze Moj (2008) begins by arguing that Haneke's critique of society is typical for the 1968 generation with its disdain for the establishment: "Haneke [. . .] is continuing to explore ideological fascinations born and firmly-rooted in the very specific time and place of his youth." Moj comes to the conclusion that Haneke falls prey to the same delusions as the German terrorists of the seventies and that Haneke's cinema is "an ideologically anachronistic cinema, a great cinematic flashback to Western Europe in the late 1960s by means of a transplanted, displaced West German urban guerilla."

[16] In July 2009, the web-based *Slate* and *Salon* posted discussions concerning the controversial joke on the topic of date-rape in *Observe and Report* by Jody Hill (2009), but the outrage elicited by this scene seemed to be more perfunctory. Haneke, on the other hand, seems to inspire especially vile dismissals, particularly on blogs dedicated to cinema, and even extreme visceral reactions. One viewer confesses on Roger Ebert's website that she threw up after seeing *Funny Games U.S.*

[17] The scene opens with the family lying on the bed, exhausted from their destructive labor, staring at the TV. When the scene begins, Rush is in mid-sentence: "in your arms / When the world outside's too much to take / That all ends when I'm with you." The camera cuts back and forth between the performance on TV and the bed. While Rush can be heard singing "We're heading for something," Evi drinks the dissolved sleeping pills, protesting meekly: "s so bitter." A little bit later, when Rush is singing "'Cause I am your lady / And you are my man," Evi nestles into her mother lap and says her children's prayer, her last words, "Lieber Gott mach mich fromm,

daß ich in den Himmel komm (Dear God, make me good / so I can go to heaven)," while the lyrics are heard: "Whenever you reach for me / I'm gonna do all that I can."

FRAME I

1. Carol Clover looks at the psychosexual implications of the final girl in detail in her fine study *Men, Women, and Chain Saws: Gender in the Modern Horror Film* (1992: esp. 35–40 and 48–53). Concerning the "final girl" in *Funny Games* see also Brinkema 2007: 154.
2. While I was trying to find an adequate term for the styling of the family's house in *Funny Games U.S.*, Robert von Dassanowsky kindly directed my attention to the "Ralph Lauren Home" website, especially their so-called "American Summer collection," which, with a very up-scale-look, already nostalgically emulates a bygone era of protestant, old money America. It is this expensive interior style that the middle class wants to achieve and that, in turn, Pottery Barn makes accessible to a non-upper-middle-class pocketbook. On the web, I found the "Pottery-Barn-look," described very often as "sophisticated-yet-casual," together with tips on how to emulate that look. See here, among many thousand Google hits: http://mommysavers.com/frugal-decorating/pottery-barn-look-for-less.htm, a post from a web site dedicated to "Money Saving Tips for Frugal Moms."
3. Benjamin (1998: 165)—the original is as follows: "Das Zeitmaß der Symbolerfahrung ist das mystische Nu, in welchem das Symbol den Sinn in sein verborgenes und, wenn man so sagen darf, waldiges Innere aufnimmt" (Benjamin 1991: 342).
4. Deleuze and Guattari (1994: 60); in the French edition: Deleuze and Guattari, *Que-ce que la philosophie?*, Paris: Editions de Minuit (1991: 59). The parallels of Deleuze's thought with the thought of Blanchot and Foucault, who interprets Blanchot's notion in an article (1987), can only be signaled here.
5. Even though there are, by now, quite a few books that provide, or claim to provide, an introduction to Deleuze—see here my review of two of them (Speck 2001)—it seems that, due to Deleuze's moving concepts, one would need an introduction to every single aspect of Deleuzian thought that acquires subtly different shapes in relation to the element of thought under discussion.
6. Haneke's favorite films are listed as: "1. *Au hasard Balthazar* (Bresson), 2. *Lancelot du Lac* (Bresson), 3. *Mirror* (Tarkovsky), 4. *Salò* (Pasolini), 5. *The Exterminating Angel* (Buñuel), 6. *The Gold Rush* (Chaplin), 7. *Psycho* (Hitchcock), 8. *A Woman under the Influence* (Cassavetes), 9. *Germany Year Zero* (Rossellini), 10. *L'eclisse* (Antonioni)" (*Sight & Sound* 2002).
7. I return to this important aspect of historical films in the last chapter where I discuss Haneke's last film, *Das weiße Band* and Haneke strategies to avoid any form of a universal history.

[8] An interesting project in narration is the TV-series *24* that began in 2001. The basic premise is that the action takes place in real time, suggesting an invisible camera that follows each of the characters for 24 hours.

[9] Although *The Fold* is primarily a book on the privileged role of the fold for Baroque thinking, it can be considered a culminating work that shares a philosophical and political impetus with Deleuze's books on the cinema. For an excellent introduction, an exemplary reading of *Le pli* and its place in Deleuze's oeuvre, see Conley (1997).

[10] There is always the danger of inadvertently making children into symbols of innocence. The touching scene in das *Das weiße Band*, where Gustav, the Pastor's younger son, asks his stern father, whether he can nurse an injured bird is clearly centered on Gustav's perspective. The intention is to show a true perspective—the love for the authority of those who "grew up in captivity," as the pastor says. But the disarming charm of the little boy might distract from such a reading, instead centering on a conflict between symbols of repression and innocence. I return to this point in the last chapter.

[11] Artaud (1976: 230). Capitals in the original: Artaud, *Œuvres complètes: Tome IV*, 44. All translations from Artaud's *The Theatre of Cruelty* amended. In the following, the page numbers refer to the original, followed by the page numbers of the English edition. The painting is "Lot and His Daughters" by Lucas van Leyden.

[12] It would therefore be a complete misunderstanding of Artaud to look for scenes of cruelty in this cinema of cruelty or to look for a metaphysical message. Here, a study on horror films by Will H. Rockett, *Devouring Whirlwind: Terror and Transcendence in the Cinema of Cruelty*, can stand as an especially simplistic misappropriation of Artaud. Apparently not having read Bazin's essays on the cinema of cruelty, Rockett (1988) paints Artaud as a sadistic *über*-director who shocks the audience into submission (see here esp. Rockett's discussion of Artaud: 57–77). His rendition of a Cinema of Cruelty would only work for the genre of torture-porn: "For these films try one, test one, push one through terror of the supernatural or supranatural to emotional and mental limits in which one is reduced to the most primitive of human spiritual levels, fearful wonder and astonishment at the inexplicable. To achieve this, these films work upon the most primitive level of human consciousness, for they require their audience to construct a coherent universe and a narrative meaning from a chaos of a series of shots, uttered in the synaesthetic language of the film. This savage, powerful nonverbal language of shocks and the collision of images appear almost tailor made for provoking terror. The audience instinctively seeks to establish limits upon what is indeterminate, and to classify it; when balked, they are left uncertain and in terror. The terror is underscored by the physical and psychological savagery that the demonic can exact upon humanity, and which is portrayed on the screen. While the transcendent cause of such savagery remains indeterminate and terrifying, its horrible effects are quite

concrete and clear, so as to lend credence to the terrible reality of that cause" (1988: 88–89).

[13] The quote is: "A cliché is a sensory-motor image of the thing" (Deleuze 1989: 20).

Frame II

[1] The weak point in the early Rossellini is exactly his symbolism, that is, his unfortunate tendency to equate moral perversion with sexual perversion. *Roma, città aperta/Rome, Open City* (1945), a film that is situated between comedy and tragedy, is especially homophobe.

[2] Michael Haneke claims in his article "Schrecken und Utopie der Form— Süchtig nach Wahrhaftigkeit: Eine Kinoerzählung über Robert Bressons 'Au Hasard Balthazar'," "daß Bresson der Erfinder des 'schmutzigen' Bildes im Kunstfilmbereich ist" (1995). The article has been translated into English as "Terror and Utopia of Form—Addicted to Truth: A Film Story about Robert Bresson's *Au hasard Balthazar*" (Haneke 1998: 551–559).

[3] Adam Bingham finds an interesting comparison: "The opening scenes set up the tone and theme in a wordless, synecdochic way reminiscent in effect of Jean-Pierre Melville's *Le Samourai* (*The Samurai*, 1967)" (2004).

[4] For a detailed comparison between book and film see Lothar Ruttner's Master's thesis that is available for download on the web (Ruttner 2002).

[5] Bachmann (1972: 156), translation modified from Bachmann (1989: 141). The published English translation is very inadequate and does not give a good impression of Bachmann's prose.

[6] According to Haneke, he completely rewrote the script for *Wer war Edgar Allan?* that the author had provided. Therefore, the script is credited to "Hans Brosciner," a pseudonym for Peter Rosei and Michael Haneke (Haneke 1995: 14–15).

[7] Rainer Werner Fassbinder uses a very similar fake point-of-view shot in *The Marriage of Maria Braun/Die Ehe der Maria Braun* (1978), a film that Haneke has seen (see here the following chapter). A medium long shot shows Maria watching passengers at a busy train station, then a countershot shows what she is seeing. The camera begins to pan 180 degrees, only to reveal Maria walking away.

[8] Already in *Wer war Edgar Allan?* we see a cinema showing Wim Wenders' *Der amerikanische Freund/The American Friend*, pointing to the mysterious American. At one point in *Fraulein*, the audience is watching the famous fire scene from *Johnny Guitar* by Nicholas Ray (1954) with Joan Crawford as Vienna, Sterling Hayden as Johnny 'Guitar' Logan and Mercedes McCambridge as Emma Small. This film has been praised for its subversive "gender-bending" and use of composition. However, I could not see the

point of Walt Disney's *Snow White and the Seven Dwarfs* (David Hand 1937) that is screened in Johanna's cinema. A few years later, in *Benny's Video*, we see Benny watching *The Toxic Avenger* (Michael Herz and Lloyd Kaufman 1984), a famous horror film spoof that was criticized at the time for breaking a taboo in showing violence against a child, just as *Funny Games* will be criticized a few years afterwards.

9   Larcher 2005: 29. The chapter is a reprint (Larcher 1996). Indeed, a more recent collection of essays in German—Christian Wessely, Gerhard Larcher, and Franz Grabner, eds., *Michael Haneke und seine Filme: Eine Pathologie der Konsumgesellschaft*. Marburg: Schüren, 2005. —reprints all chapters (except one) from Franz Grabner, Gerhard Larcher, Christian Wessely, eds., *Utopie und Fragment. Michael Hanekes Filmwerk*, Thaur: Kulturverlag, 1996, without mentioning, only switching around the order of editors and adding a few newer essays—a rather dubious editorial practice at best.

10 Schacht uses an untranslatable pun, "Wett*kampf*," playing on a faux-etymology by emphasizing the word "Kampf," German for "combat" and "struggle" and the word "Wette," meaning "bet" that, of course, plays an important role in the film (2005: 184).

11 In a review of *Funny Games U.S.*, Thomas Assheuer revisits some of arguments from his earlier review. He finishes the article with a speculation about the negative reception of this film in the US: "A country that has experienced real terror and started a war itself, will not be willing to face the horror of the imaginary" (2008: 46).

12 An interesting film for a comparison would be *La cérémonie* by Claude Chabrol (1995). The title, "The Ceremony," refers to the family's ceremonial watching of opera on television but also evokes the ritual before a capital punishment is enforced. This thriller, a take on Jean Genet's famous play *Les Bonnes/The Maids* (1947), is about an affluent and well-cultured family, Lelievre ("The Jackrabbit"), who hires an analphabetic maid. The maid's friend, Jeanne, is played by Isabelle Huppert. As in *Caché*, the family's father is named Georges (Jean-Pierre Cassel). It seems that the crime committed by the family, punishable by death, consists of their sense of entitlement. Parallels like these raise the question of actors as intertexts. In an insightful article, Birgit Birchall compares Isabelle Huppert's roles of the mentally unstable woman in *La dentellière/The Lacemaker* (Claude Goretta 1977), her break-through role, with the one she plays in *La Pianiste* almost 25 years later. Birchall argues that Goretta's close-ups frame the character as the object of the male gaze, while Haneke, by showing the actress often from behind and watching something, assigns to her directorial powers (2005: 13). Birchall does not raise the issue of intertextuality.

13 In an interview from May 21, 2009 (Cineuropa 2009), Haneke is quoted: "I'd been working on the project for over 10 years. My main aim was to look at a group of children who are inculcated with values transformed into an

absolute and how they internalize them. If we raise a principle or ideal, be it political or religious, to the status of an absolute, it becomes inhuman and leads to terrorism."

14. The interview can be found on the web site of Les Films du Losange: http://www.filmsdulosange.fr/videos_pages/ruban_ext6.html
15. "[Ich glaube] dass ich die seltsamen Ereignisse, die sich in unserem Dorf zugetragen haben, erzählen muss, weil sie möglicherweise auf manche Vorgänge in diesem Land ein erhellendes Licht werfen können . . ." (Haneke 2008: 2).

FRAME III

1. I would like to thank Todd Berliner, University of North Carolina Wilmington, who commented on an earlier version of this chapter.
2. The urge to psychologize Michael Haneke who abhors psychology is hard to resist. After all, his international career began right after his posthumous dispute with Fassbinder's German trilogy in *Fraulein* with his own "glaciation of feelings" trilogy. And only now, more than 20 years after Fassbinder's death, does Haneke emerge from Fassbinder's shadow as the "most prolific German-speaking director."
3. See Gleber (1990), Friedman (1990), and also the chapter on *Komödianten* in Schulte Sasse (1996: 176–202).
4. Apart from the above-mentioned *Scream*, there are countless examples: *The Avengers*, The *Mission Impossible*-series, *Palmetto* by Schlöndorff, etc.
5. One character in *Scream*, for example, shares the name Loomis with the Doctor in *Halloween*, which in turn is a homage to Hitchcock's *Psycho*. I do not dare to speculate how many teenagers actually recognize the killer's mask as deriving from Edward Munch's painting "Scream."
6. Douglas Sirk, who, under the name Detleff Sierck made films for the Nazis. Sirk's famous film within a film, *Imitation of Life*, admittedly influenced Fassbinder strongly. *Veronika Voss* can be read as an examination of the heritage of the Nazi-melodramas by the German film industry in the 1950s. *Lola* can be read as dealing with the upcoming alliance between capital and politics, an obvious intertext to von Sternberg's *The Blue Angel* and the kitschy sing-along films of the 1950s. See here also Reimer (1996).
7. I make a similar argument, which I summarize here briefly for the benefit of the English-speaking reader, in Speck 1999.
8. In the TV-film *Lemminge Teil 2—Verletzungen/Lemmings Part 2—Injuries* (1979), a character is watching a news story on the 1978 mass-suicide in Jonestown, Guyana, of over 900 people, members of a cult led by Jim Jones. However, the two-part film centers on suicides and murder-suicides and the clip therefore has a thematic function.
9. In the background of the station-restaurant, a well-known propaganda message is still partially visible: "Räder müssen rollen für den . . ."—wheels

must roll for . . . —the word "Sieg" (victory) is scratched away. The thumping sound of the steam train is heard overloud on the soundtrack. The palimpsest of the "Endsieg," the final victory, constitutes a transposition of this message from its initial purpose—inspiring the railway workers and excusing delays of passenger trains—to a commentary. The historical hindsight provides the paradigmatic substitution: now, wheels must turn for the economic miracle. But the writing on the wall, combined with the noise of the train, remind us of a repressed truth: the very same trains that just a few weeks before rolled for the "Final Solution" now roll for the new Germany.

10 . . . und über uns der Himmel is available on a region-free DVD in Germany. Hans' walk last about 4 minutes in the film. Haneke condenses the footage to about 45 seconds, showing the rebuilding and Hans with the Trümmerfrauen, and uses the soundtrack for the parallel montage of Mike running to see Jean at the wrestling venue while Johanna is screening the film.

11 Like probably every German family, mine shares several "Black Market" stories. Another example would be the scene in *Maria Braun* where children explode firecrackers and a man instinctively drops to the ground for cover. My American students needed an explanation, while I had heard a similar story involving my grandfather and his friend.

12 "[A] remembrance is in very large measure a reconstruction of the past achieved with data borrowed from the present, a reconstruction prepared, furthermore, by reconstructions of earlier periods wherein past images had already been altered" (Halbwachs 1980: 69).

13 The German weekly, *Die* Zeit, published an insightful review of *Das Wunder von Bern*, calling it "unabashedly neo-conservative" (Diedrichsen 2003).

14 Again, a specific cultural knowledge is needed to understand and place these recordings. The sad litany of the missing, the secret fear that the Germans would have to atone for the war, the almost mythical figure of Adenauer, exert an emotional power.

15 Deleuze (1986: 114). Since Deleuze introduces the virtual only later, in his book on the *Time Image*, I have to translate the notion of the choice into terms of actual/virtual.

16 Other examples can be found in Fassbinder's oeuvre for the topic of choice: *Fontane Effie Briest* from 1975, just to mention one, concentrates on Instetten's choice—should he or must he kill the former lover of his wife?

Frame IV

1 Le Cain (2003) underlines his position in a response to a letter to the editors that perfectly sums up his position: "He [Haneke] is not simplistically preaching a message, but creating cinematic constructs that cause us, the viewers, to think and to analyse along with him. Therefore if the film should fail on a formal level—as, it seems to me, *Funny Games* does—there is the

possibility of ideological distortion, something less gifted and courageous directors, content with mere didacticism, do not risk."

2. The penchant for frame-in-frame composition is something that Haneke shares with Rainer Werner Fassbinder; the tightly framed shots through doors and windows in *Benny's Video* or, for example *La Pianiste* (2001), bear a strong resemblance to Fassbinder's famous *Angst essen Seele auf* (*Ali: Fear Eats the Soul*, 1974). While the cinematography for *Benny's Video* (1992), *71 Fragmente einer Chronologie des Zufalls* (1994), *La Pianiste*, and *Caché* (2005) was done by Christian Berger, Haneke chose to work with the cinematographer Jürgen Jürges who shot *Angst essen Seele auf* for *Funny Games* (1997), as well as *Code inconnu: Récit incomplet de divers voyages* (2000) and *Le temps du loup* (*The Time of the Wolf*, 2003). For the American remake of *Funny Games*, *Funny Games U.S.* (2008), Haneke worked with Darius Khondji who could be called a veritable specialist of threatening interiors. He is responsible for the cinematography of *The Interpreter* (2005), *Panic Room* (2002), and *Se7en* (1995), among others. Khondji is also a favorite cinematographer of Jean-Pierre Jeunet: *Alien: Resurrection* (1997), *La Cité des enfants perdus* (1995) and *Delicatessen* (1991).

3. In narratological terms, this is clearly a metalepsis in the sense of Genette (2004), insofar as this move between narrated world (*histoire*) and the world of narration (*discours*) is aimed at exploring the implicit rules of representation itself (see the introductory chapter).

4. Michael Hardt points out in his excellent introduction to Deleuze that the concept of actualization "relies heavily on the primary French meaning of *actuel* as 'contemporary'" (Hardt 1993: 16).

5. Of course, Haneke is not the first director to play with those generic frames. In *Lola rennt/Run Lola Run* (1998), Tom Tykwer contrasts Lola's world, shot with film stock in saturated colors with her father's soap opera-universe, filmed with a hand-held video camera. See here my forthcoming article "Overcoming Metaphysics in Three Easy Steps: Tom Tykwer's *Lola rennt*," in: *Humorous Strategies in Post-Unification German Literature and Film*. Barbara Mabee and Jill Twark, eds., Cambridge Scholars Publishing.

6. However, the shadow of the surveillance camera is clearly visible in the second tape, when the lights of a passing car briefly illuminate the scene. That Georges rewinds this tape, showing the shadow again, could indicate that Haneke included this silhouette on purpose, again an indication for a metalepsis.

7. Martine Beugnet therefore misses the point, when she states: "As the actual and the virtual become enmeshed, it is not, in the more poetic Deleuzian fashion, the past that comes to haunt the present but, rather, almost simultaneously presents that overlap in an uncanny fashion" (Beugnet 2007: 230). Mathias Frey seems to argue along similar lines when he confounds the virtual with virtual reality: "This conflation of the actual and the virtual (Deleuze) and the role of information providers and transmitters

(Baudrillard) in the loss of this distinction is clearly one of the central problematics that Haneke seeks to address in the film" (Frey 2002: 6).

8 The difference between the two films can not be stressed too much: Tasma's film, produced by the French TV channel Canal+, is a gripping film, using consequently all available cinematic means to give the rendering of the events the strongest emotional impact possible, also introducing several protagonists with whom the viewer can identify. The fierce intensity of the climactic massacre is certainly worthy of the beach assault in *Saving Private Ryan* (Spielberg 1998).

FRAME V

1 "I provide a construct and nothing more—its interpretation and its integration into a value and belief system is always the work of the recipient" (Haneke 2000: 171).

2 Falcon (2001: 46). For a convincing reading of Haneke as modernist see also Peucker (2000, 2007). As further proof of my thesis I would like to point to the interesting fact that critics on a regular basis vehemently attack one film in Haneke's oeuvre that they perceive as bad, because it does not deliver the modernist critique they expect: "Without considerable reflection and inner struggle, serious social analysis, and compassion for human difficulty, one ends up with a mirror that merely reflects back at the spectator a vision of the world that is far too familiar, far too unmediated" (Walsh 2006); "*Funny Games* (1997) stands as the one truly bad film on Haneke's otherwise consistently excellent filmography. [...] *Funny Games* puts a naive faith in the confrontational power of the spectacle of sadistic violence, which Tarantino had already definitively tamed and thus undermined in his first two films" (Le Cain 2003); "The conspicuously humourless Haneke started working with stars only *in Code Unknown*, one film ago, and hasn't yet found a credible way to reconcile his determinedly dark-side view of humanity with his new-found need to attract the mass arthouse audience" (Rayns 2001: 54). What I suggest is a reading that takes seeming "exceptions" seriously and sees how they make sense in the entire oeuvre.

3 Badiou 2006 and Felman 1995. For an in-depth analysis of Badiou's concept of pedagogy in relation to art and philosophy, see Bartlett (2006).

4 To put bluntly, what I have mentioned above in the introduction, Haneke formulates his concepts in images. I would therefore strongly disagree with Frey, who, referring amongst others to Baudrillard, Foucault, and Deleuze, claims in his "Supermodernity, Capital, and Narcissus": "Haneke and these thinkers share an important common perspective in their respective endeavors, seeking to revive moribund fields with a respective cinematic/theoretical shock therapy" (2002).

⁵ I exclude here the films Michael Haneke made for television. However, my arguments can certainly be extended for his adaptation of Kafka's *The Castle, Das Schloß* (1997), where Haneke also points to the madness and lack of meaning the protagonist encounters in the castle with his use of fragmentation and black screen. For an analysis of this film, see Knauß (2005). I will not address the music in Haneke's films, which could also be seen as taking another perspective (see Wood 2002; Wheatley 2006b).

⁶ See also Deleuze (1989: 248). For a detailed reading of Deleuze and Godard's pedagogy, see Landy (2001).

⁷ Deleuze points out in "Three Questions on 'Six Fois Deux'" that the just images, or "just ideas," as he calls them, have to be understood in the form of questions (see 1978: esp. 38–40).

⁸ As a tongue-in-cheek reference in *Caché*, Haneke puts posters in the son's bedroom, amongst others, of *The Matrix Reloaded* (2003), *The Chronicles of Riddick* (2004), *In Hell* (2003), and *Van Helsing* (2004), all action-films whose plot revolves around the violent destruction of an evil, sometimes literally inhuman adversary.

⁹ See here esp. Baudrillard (1995). An interesting and very personal perspective on the event of war and its mise-en-scène can be found in Jakovljevic (1999).

¹⁰ In an otherwise insightful exploration of Isabelle Huppert's image, Bridget Birchall concludes "that her status as subject, as manifest in *La Pianiste*, remains frustratingly problematic" (2005: 6). I would argue that *La Pianiste* only makes sense from the perspective of the traumatized character of the piano teacher. Jean Wyatt seems to be the only critic who remarked on the necessary shift in perspective (2005: 466).

¹¹ This should be understood as a pedagogy: Badiou (2006) uses Lacan's Borromean knot to explain the vocation of the philosophical institution.

¹² The film apparently divided the jury in Cannes (Anon. "Special Cannes"; see also Cieutat 2005).

FRAME VI

¹ The attempted exclusion of violence actually includes it, Naqvi claims, following René Girard's theses and Jörg Metelmann's study. Naqvi repeats and reevaluates this claim on several occasions (2004: 182, 2007a: 64, 2007b: 243). For the sake of brevity, I cannot engage Naqvi's arguments nor discuss Girard or Metelmann's take on Girard. In her book-length study of victimhood, Naqvi comes to the conclusion that Haneke embraces "rather conservative politics" (2007a: 72). My argumentation here attempts to prove the contrary.

² Whence the proclivity for self-sacrifice in the films of Nazi-Germany's top director, Veit Harlan, which brought his wife, the actress Kristina Söderbaum, the nickname "*die Reichswasserleiche*," the Reich's water-logged corpse: *Die*

Goldene Stadt/ The Golden City (1942), *Immensee* (1943), *Opfergang/ The Great Sacrifice* (1944), films that are still considered apolitical, and, obviously, the infamous *Jud Süß/Jew Süss* (1940), and *Kolberg* (1945), the ultimate *Durchhaltefilm*, the film that was supposed to convince the German population to never surrender.

3. I can not review the discussion surrounding Agamben's immensely influential analysis here. However, it seems that Agamben's critics—just as Haneke's critics—are struck by the compulsory nature of his analysis; see here a collection of essays which—with a few notable exceptions—attempt to find flaws in the minutiae of Agamben's interpretations instead of a fruitful discussion (Norris 2005). For an introduction to Agamben's concepts see the very insightful review essay by Hussein and Ptacek (2000).

4. See here Deleuze and Guattari (1987: esp. 351–423). Agamben (1998: 18) and Hardt and Negri (2000) are strongly influenced by this idea. "Empire" is the state-machine that has only an interior. Consequently, there are no wars in the common sense but only police-actions. However, Hardt and Negri claim that Agamben's interpretation of the *homo sacer* is still too "anthropological" (421).

5. Marc Augé (1995: 78–79) defines nonspace as follows: "If a place can be defined as relational, historical and concerned with identity, then a space which cannot be defined as relational, or historical or concerned with identity will be a non-place." Frey (2003) also mentions Augé, however, Jameson's and Deleuze's concepts of postmodernity seems to be more useful here than Augé's "supermodernity" (see esp. Augé 1995: 29 and 78).

6. Intercourse in *Der siebente Kontinent* seems to take place in a race against the clock, with the well-timed orgasm achieved shortly before the alarm goes off.

7. Foucault (1978: 142, see also 135–145). See also Foucault's concise seminar description in Foucault (1997: 73–79). Agamben (esp. 1998 and 2005) expands Foucault's notion, since biopolitics is always inscribed in the founding act of sovereignty. Hence Agamben's provocative notion that the paradigmatic site of biopolitics is the camp and not the city (1998: 181).

8. In the same film, a character is apparently untroubled by watching a news story on the 1978 mass-suicide in Jonestown, Guyana, of over 900 cult-members.

9. Significantly, he goes to the movies. The film shifts here into an allegoric mode as Ezra and Sillars (2007: 217) explain in a clever reading (quoted above in the second chapter).

10. It is telling that there is an element of sadistic pleasure in all anecdotal versions of this double-bind situation. The best known is probably that of the general of an occupying army who orders a barber, under threat of punishment by death, to shave those men, and only those, who do not shave themselves. The paradoxical element is obviously the barber himself—as soon as he gives himself a shave, he acts against orders.

Frame VII

[1] *The New York Times* (Catsoulis 2008) compares *Funny Games US* to Peckinpah and *The Strangers* (Bryan Bertino 2008).

[2] Haneke cites these films (*Sight & Sound* 2002): 1. *Au hasard Balthazar* (Bresson); 2. *Lancelot du Lac* (Bresson); 3. *Mirror* (Tarkovsky); 4. *Salò* (Pasolini); 5. *The Exterminating Angel* (Buñuel); 6. *The Gold Rush* (Chaplin); 7. *Psycho* (Hitchcock); 8. *A Woman under the Influence* (Cassavetes); 9. *Germany Year Zero* (Rossellini); and 10. *L'eclisse* (Antonioni).

[3] Domarchi (1959: 5) and Domarchi in Hillier (1985: 62). Jim Hillier, in his admirable English edition of some of the key articles of the *Cahiers du cinema* of this period, reminds us that Luc Moullet already uttered a similar dictum (1985: 69, see also 148).

[4] This certainly holds true for the West-German filmmakers of Haneke's generation. As Robert von Dassanowsky explains in his comprehensive history of Austrian cinema, the rising popularity of television and especially the lack of state subsidies made it impossible for Austrian cinema to develop an equivalent to the critical and aesthetical success of the German New Wave, apart from experimental and non-commercial film (2005: 178 and 194–197). See here also the introduction to a collection on New Austrian Film (von Dassanowsky and Speck 2010).

Frame VIII

[1] "Since the traumata scenes in *Caché* resurface in Georges's guilt-ridden memory and haunted nightmares, they remain unreliable witnesses which question memory's relationship to history" (Saxton 2008: 108).

Frame IX

[1] Bachmann (1972: 233): "Sie schlief ein, schon am Schlafrand getroffen von einem Traum und griff sich an den Kopf und an ihr Herz, weil sie nicht wusste, woher das viele Blut kam. Sie dachte trotzdem noch, es ist nichts, es ist nichts, es kann mir doch gar nichts mehr geschehen, es kann mir etwas geschehen, aber es muss mir nichts geschehen."

BIBLIOGRAPHY

Agamben, Giorgio. *State of Exception*, Chicago, IL: University of Chicago Press, 2005.
—*Homo Sacer. Sovereign Power and Bare Life*, Stanford, CA: Stanford University Press, 1998.
Althusser, Louis. *Lenin and Philosophy, and Other Essays*, New York: Monthly Review Press, 1972.
Altman, Rick. *Film/Genre*, London: BFI, 1999.
Anon. "Special Cannes," *Positif: Revue Mensuelle de Cinéma* 437/438 (juillet/août 1997): 94–95.
Artaud, Antonin. *Selected Writings*, Berkeley: University of California Press, 1988.
—*Œuvres complètes: Tome IV, Le Théâtre et son double*, Paris: Gallimard, 1964.
Arthur, Paul. "Endgame," *Film Comment* 41:6 (November 2005): 24–28.
Assheuer, Thomas. *Nahaufname. Michael Haneke. Gespräche mit Thomas Assheuer*, Berlin: Alexander Verlag, 2008.
—"Der Unerbittliche," *Die Zeit* Nr.23 (26. Mai 2009): 58.
Augé, Marc. *Non-Places Introduction to an Anthropology of Supermodernity*, London: Verso, 1995.
Austria Presse Agentur. "Michael Haneke: Das Spiel mit der Angst", *Kurier*, 24.05.2009, http://www.kurier.at/kultur/321162.php (accessed June 27, 2009).
—"Michael Hanekes 'Matura'-Feier," *Der Standard*, (28 Mai 2009), http://derstandard.at/?url=/?id=1242316922163 (accessed June 27, 2009).
Bachmann, Ingeborg. *Three Paths to the Lake: Stories*, New York: Holmes & Meier, 1989.
—*Simultan; neue Erzählungen*, München: Piper, 1972.
Badiou, Alain. "What is a Philosophical Institution? Or: Address, Transmission, Inscription," *Cosmos and History: The Journal of Natural and Social Philosophy* 2.1/2 (2006): 9–14.
—*Deleuze: The Clamor of Being*, Minneapolis: University of Minnesota Press, 2000.
Baranger, Madeleine, Willy Baranger, and Jorge M. Mom. "The Infantile Psychic Trauma from Us to Freud: Pure Trauma, Retroactivity, and Reconstruction," *The International Journal of Psychoanalysis* 69 (1988): 113–28.
Bartlett, A. J. "Conditional Notes on a New Republic," *Cosmos and History: The Journal of Natural and Social Philosophy* 2.1/2 (2006): 39–67.

Bataille, Georges. *The Accursed Share: An Essay on General Economy. Volume 1: Consumption*, New York: Zone Books, 1988.
Baudrillard, Jean. *The Gulf War Did Not Take Place*, Bloomington, IN: Indiana University Press, 1995.
Bazin, André. *The Cinema of Cruelty: From Buñuel to Hitchcock*, New York: Seaver Books, 1982.
—"Ontologie de l'image photographique," in *Qu'est-ce que le cinéma? Vol. 1. Ontologie et langage*, 11–19, Paris: Éditions du Cerf, 1958 ["The Ontology of the Photographic Image," in *What is Cinema?* selected and translated by Hugh Gray, 9–16, Berkeley: University of California Press, 1967.].
Benamor, Dan. "The Strangers—Copycat Horror With Bad Ending," slasher-films (June 6, 2008), http://slasher-films.suite101.com/article.cfm/unsatisfying_ending_the_strangers (accessed June 16, 2009).
Beney, Christophe. "*Funny Games U.S.*" *Cahiers du cinema* 633 (avril 2008): 60.
Benjamin, Walter. "On the Concept of History," in *Selected Writings*, vol. 4, eds Howard Eiland and Michael W. Jennings, trans. Edmund Jephcott et al., Cambridge, MA: Harvard University Press, 2003, 390–392.
—*Gesammelte Schriften, Band I-1*, eds Rolf Tiedemann and Hermann Schweppenhäuser, Frankfurt am Main: Suhrkamp, 1991.
—*The Origin of German Tragic Drama*, London: Verso, 1998.
Beugnet, Martine. "Blind spot," *Screen* 48 (2007): 227–231.
Bingham, Adam. "Life, or something like it: Michael Haneke's Der siebente Kontinent (The Seventh Continent, 1989)," *Kinoeye* 4:1 (March 8, 2004), http://www.kinoeye.org/04/01/bingham01_no2.php (accessed October 15, 2007).
—"Long Night's Journey into Day," *Kinoeye* 4:1 (March 8, 2004), http://www.kinoeye.org/04/01/bingham01.php (accessed October 15, 2007).
Birchall, Bridget. "From Nude to Metteuse-en-scène: Isabelle Huppert, Image, and Desire in La Dentellière (Goretta, 1977) and La Pianiste (Haneke, 2001)," *Studies in French Cinema* 5.1 (2005): 5–15.
Booth, Wayne C. *The Rhetoric of Fiction [2nd ed.]*. Chicago: University of Chicago Press, 1983.
Bordwell, David. *The Way Hollywood Tells It: Story and Style in Modern Movies*, Berkeley, University of California Press: 2006.
—*Narration in the Fiction Film*, Madison: The University of Wisconsin Press, 1985.
—"The Art Cinema as a Mode of Film Practice," *Film Criticism* 4/1 (Fall 1979): 56–63.
Boxofficemojo. "Funny Games," (n.d.), http://www.boxofficemojo.com/movies/?id=funnygames.htm (accessed June 16, 2009).
Bradshaw, Peter. "The White Ribbon—Cannes film festival," *The Guardian*, Friday 22 May, 2009, http://www.guardian.co.uk/film/2009/may/21/cannes-white-ribbon-review (accessed July 25, 2009).

Brady, Martin. "Michael Haneke Interview," *Little White Lies Truth & Movies* http://www.littlewhitelies.co.uk/interviews/michael-haneke-interview/ (accessed June 16, 2009).

Branigan, Edward. *Point of View in the Cinema: A Theory of Narration and Subjectivity in Classical Film*, Berlin: Mouton, 1984.

Brinkema, Eugenie. "'Not to scream before or about, but to scream at death': Haneke's Horrible *Funny Games*," in *Caligari's Heirs: The German Cinema of Fear after 1945*, ed. Steffen Hantke, 145–159, Lanham, MD: Scarecrow Press, 2007.

Brophy, Philip. "Bring the Noise," *Film Comment* 42/5 (September 2006): 16.

Calhoun, Dave. "Michael Haneke: Interview," *Time Out London*, October 2007 http://www.timeout.com/film/features/show-feature/3658/michael-haneke-interview.html (accessed June 16, 2009).

Camhi, Leslie. "The Disaster On the Doorstep," *The New York Times* (June 20, 2004), http://www.nytimes.com/2004/06/20/movies/film-this-week-the-disaster-on-the-doorstep.html?scp=1&sq=The+Disaster+On+the+Doorstep&st=nyt&pagewanted=print (accessed March 11, 2009).

Catsoulis, Jeannette. "A Slow Crescendo of Intimidation," *The New York Times* (May 30, 2008), http://movies.nytimes.com/2008/05/30/movies/30stra.html (accessed October 5, 2008).

Chion, Michel. *The Voice in Cinema*. New York: Columbia University Press, 1999.

Cieutat, Michel. "Funny Games," in *50 Films qui ont fait scandale*, ed. and intro. Gérard Camy, 203–206, Condé-sur-Noireau, France: Corlet, 2002.

Cieutat, Michel and Philippe Rouyer. "Entretien avec Michael Haneke: On ne montre pas la réalité, juste son image manipulée," *Positif: Revue Mensuelle de Cinéma* 536 (October 2005): 21–25.

Cineuropa. "Michael Haneke, Director: 'An ideal raised to the status of an absolute becomes inhuman,'" *Cineuropa* (May 21, 2009), http://www.cineuropa.org/interview.aspx?lang=en&documentID=108748 (accessed August 30, 2009).

Clover, Carol J. *Men, Women, and Chain Saws: Gender in the Modern Horror Film*, Princeton, NJ: Princeton University Press, 1992.

Combs, Richard. "Living in Never-Never Land," *Film Comment* 38:2 (March/April 2002): 26–29.

Conley, Tom. "From Multiplicities to Folds: On Style and Form in Deleuze," *South Atlantic Quarterly* 96:3 (Summer 1997): 629–646.

Cousins, Mark. "After the end: word of mouth and Caché," *Screen* 48 (2007): 223–226.

Daney, Serge. "Le travelling de Kapo," *Trafic* 4 (Fall 1992): 5–19.

Dargis, Manohla. "Cannes review 2001: Old masters," *Film Comment* 37/4 (July 2001): 62–65.

Dassanowsky, Robert von. *Austrian Cinema: A History*, Jefferson, NC/London: McFarland, 2005.

—"'Wherever You May Run, You Cannot Escape Him': Leni Riefenstahl's Self-Reflection and Romantic Transcendence of Nazism in *Tiefland*," *Camera Obscura* 35 (May 1995): 106–129.
Dassanowsky, Robert von and Oliver C. Speck, eds. *New Austrian Film*, Berghahn, NY: 2010 (forthcoming).
Dayan, Daniel. "The Tutor Code of Classical Cinema," in *Movies and Methods I*, ed. Bill Nichols, 483–451, Berkeley: University of California Press, 1976.
Debord, Guy. *The Society of the Spectacle*. http://www.bopsecrets.org/SI/debord/index.htm (Last accessed March 8, 2009).
Deleuze, Gilles. *Essays Critical and Clinical*, Minneapolis: University of Minnesota Press, 1997.
—*Francis Bacon: The Logic of Sensation*, London: Continuum, 2003.
—"Three Questions on Six Times Two," in *Negotiations 1972–1990*, ed. Martin Joughin, 37–45, New York: Columbia University Press, 1995 [also: "Three Questions on 'Six Fois Deux'," *Afterimage* 7 (Summer 1978): 113–119; "Trois questions sur Six fois deux," *Cahiers du Cinéma* 271 (1976): 5–12.
—*Difference and Repetition*, New York: Columbia University Press, 1994.
—*The Fold: Leibniz and the Baroque*, Minneapolis: University of Minnesota Press, 1993.
—"What is a dispositif?" in *Michel Foucault, Philosopher: Essays Translated from the French and German*, ed. Timothy J. Armstrong, 159–168, New York: Routledge, 1992.
—*The Logic of Sense. European perspectives*, New York: Columbia University Press, 1990.
—*Cinema 2: The Time Image*, Minneapolis: University of Minnesota, 1989.
—*Bergsonism*, New York: Zone Books, 1988.
—*Foucault*, Minneapolis: University of Minnesota Press, 1988.
—*Cinema 1: The Movement-Image*, Minneapolis: University of Minnesota Press, 1986.
—"Postscript to the Societies of Control," *The Watson Institute* [1986], http://www.watsoninstitute.org/infopeace/vy2k/deleuze-societies.cfm (accessed April 15, 2009).
—*Nietzsche and Philosophy. European Perspectives*, New York: Columbia University Press, 1983.
Deleuze, Gilles and Félix Guattari. *What is Philosophy?* New York: Columbia University Press, 1994.
—*A Thousand Plateaus: Capitalism and Schizophrenia*, Minneapolis: University of Minnesota Press, 1987.
Derrida, Jacques. *Given Time: 1. Counterfeit Money*, Chicago, IL: University of Chicago Press, 1992.
Domarchi Jean, Jacques Doniol-Valcroze, Jean-Luc Godard, Pierre Kast, Jacques Rivette, Eric Rohmer. "Hiroshima, notre amour," *Cahiers du cinéma* 97 (juillet 1959): 1–18.

Dupont, Joan. "CANNES FESTIVAL: The Return of Godard," *International Herald Tribune*, Thursday May 17, 2001, http://www.iht.com/articles/2001/05/17/cannes_ed3_.php (accessed February 13, 2009).

Durkheim, Eìmile. *Suicide: A Study in Sociology*, Glencoe, IL: Free Press, 1951.

Eagleton, Terry. *Sweet Violence: The Idea of the Tragic*, Oxford: Blackwell, 2003.

Ebert, Roger. "Cage relishes operatic role in tragic `Leaving Las Vegas,'" *Chicago Sun Times* (November 5, 1995). Web April 15, 2009, http://roger-ebert.suntimes.com/apps/pbcs.dll/article?AID=/19951105/PEOPLE/111010327.

Evans, Dylan. *An Introductory Dictionary of Lacanian Psychoanalysis*, New York: Routledge, 1996.

Evren, Sureyyya. "The Man Who Could Walk through In-Between Positions," in *Sarai Reader 2006 (Turbulence)*, 440–449, http://www.sarai.net/publications/readers/06-turbulence (accessed July 26, 2009).

Ezra, Elizabeth and Jane Sillars. "Hidden in plain sight: bringing terror home," *Screen* 48 (2007): 215–221.

Falcon, Richard. "The Discreet Harm of the Bourgeoisie," *Sight and Sound* 8:5 (May 1998): 10–12.

Falcon, Richard. Review of *Code Unknown*. *Sight & Sound* (May 2001): 46.

Felman, Shoshana. "Education and Crisis, or the Vicissitudes of Teaching," in *Trauma: Explorations in Memory*, ed. Cathy Caruth, 13–60. Baltimore, MD: Johns Hopkins University Press, 1995.

Filmmaker. "The Director Interviews: Michael Haneke, Funny Games U.S.," *Filmmaker Magazine: The Magazine for Independent Film*, Friday (March 14, 2008), http://www.filmmakermagazine.com/directorinterviews/2008/03/michael-haneke-funny-games-us.php (accessed February 28, 2009).

Florida, Richard L. *The Rise of the Creative Class: And How It's Transforming Work, Leisure, Community and Everyday Life*, New York, NY: Basic Books, 2002.

Flos, Birgit. "Ortsbeschreibungen," in: *Der siebente Kontinent. Michael Haneke und seine Filme*, ed. Alexander Horwath, 164–169. Vienna and Zürich: Europaverlag, 1991.

Fludernik, Monika. "Scene Shift, Metalepsis, and the Metaleptic Mode," *Style* 37/4 (Winter 2003), 382–400.

Foucault, Michel. *Society Must Be Defended: Lectures at the Collège De France, 1975–76*, ed. and trans. Mauro Bertani, Alessandro Fontana, François Ewald, and David Macey, New York: Picador, 2003.

—"Governmentality," in *Essential Works, Volume III: Power*, ed. James D. Faubion, 201–222. New York: New Press, 2000.

—"The Birth of Biopolitics," in *Essential Works, vol. I: Ethics—Subjectivity and Truth*, ed. Paul Rabinow, 73–79. New York: New Press, 1997.

—*The History of Sexuality—Vol. 1: An Introduction*, New York: Vintage, 1990.

—and Maurice Blanchot. *Foucault, Blanchot: Maurice Blanchot, the Thought from Outside*, New York: Zone Books, 1987.

Foundas, Scott. "TV Makes You Smarter: The small-screen pleasures (and pain) of Michael Haneke's other career," *The Village Voice*, Tuesday (September 25, 2007), http://www.villagevoice.com/2007-09-25/film/tv-makes-you-smarter/ (accessed July 25, 2009).

—"Interview: Michael Haneke: The Bearded Prophet of 'Code Inconnu' and 'The Piano Teacher'," *indieWIRE* (March 29, 2002), http://www.indiewire.com/article/interview_michael_haneke_the_bearded_prophet_of_code_inconnu_and_the_piano1/ (accessed June 16, 2009).

Frey, Mattias. "Supermodernity, Capital, and Narcissus: The French Connection to Michael Haneke's Benny's Video," *Cinetext: Film & Philosophy* (September 2002), http://cinetext.philo.at/magazine/frey/bennys_video.pdf (accessed October 1, 2007).

—"Michael Haneke," *Senses of Cinema: An Online Journal Devoted To The Serious And Eclectic Discussion Of Cinema* (August 2003), http://archive.sensesofcinema.com/contents/directors/03/haneke.html (accessed May 31, 2009).

Friday, Jonathan. "André Bazin's Ontology of Photographic and Film Imagery," *The Journal of Aesthetics and Art Criticism* 63:4 (Fall 2005): 339–350.

Friedman, Regine Mihal. "Ecce Ingenium Teutonicum: Paracelsus (1943)," in *The Films of G.W. Pabst: An Extraterritorial Cinema*, 184–196, ed. Eric Rentschler, New Brunswick and London: Rutgers UP, 1990.

Gemünden, Gerd. "Re-Fusing Brecht: The Cultural Politics of Fassbinder's German Hollywood," *New German Critique* 63 (Fall 1994): 55–75.

Genette, Gérard. *Métalepse: De la figure à la fiction*, Paris: Editions du Seuil, 2004.

—*Narrative Discourse: An Essay in Method*, Ithaca, NY: Cornell UP, 1980.

Gibson, Brian. "Bearing witness: the Dardenne brothers' and Michael Haneke's implication of the viewe," *CineAction* 70 (December 2006): 24–38.

Gilroy, Paul. "Shooting crabs in a barrel," *Screen* 48 (2007): 233–235.

Girard, René. *Violence and the Sacred*, Baltimore: Johns Hopkins University Press, 1977.

Gleber, Anke. "Masochism and Wartime Melodrama: *Komödianten* (1941)," in *The Films of G.W. Pabst: An Extraterritorial Cinema*, 175–183, ed. Eric Rentschler, New Brunswick and London: Rutgers UP, 1990.

Grabner, Franz, Gerhard Larcher, and Christian Wessely, eds. *Utopie und Fragment: Michael Hanekes Filmwerk*, Thaur: Kulturverlag, 1996.

Grabner, Franz. "'Der Name der Erbsünde ist Verdrängung': Ein Gespräch mit Michael Haneke," in *Michael Haneke und seine Filme*, eds Christian Wessely, Gerhard Larcher, and Franz Grabner, 33–46. Magdeburg: Schüren Verlag, 2005.

Grissemann, Stefan. "In zwei, drei feinen Linien die Badewannenwand entlang," in *Haneke/Jelinek: die Klavierspielerin: Drehbuch, Gespräche, Essays*, ed. Stefan Grissemann, 11–31. Wien: Sonderzahl, 2001.

—"Ballett des Untergangs," in *Der siebente Kontinent: Michael Haneke und seine Filme*, ed. Alexander Horwath, 131–134. Wien, Zürich: Europaverlag, 1991.

Grissemann, Stefan and Michael Omasta. "Herr Haneke, wo bleibt das Positive? Ein Gespräch mit dem Regisseur," in *Der siebente Kontinent: Michael Haneke und seine Filme*, ed. Alexander Horwath, 191–214. Wien, Zürich: Europaverlag, 1991.

Grossvogel, D. I. "Haneke: The Coercing of Vision," *Film Quarterly* 60/4 (2007): 36–43.

Grundmann, Roy. "Michael Haneke's Subversive Games," *The Chronicle of Higher Education* 54:25 (February 29, 2008), B14, http://chronicle.com/cgi-bin/printable.cgi?article=http://chronicle.com/weekly/v54/i25/25b01401.htm (accessed March 11, 2009).

—"Auteur de Force: Michael Haneke's 'Cinema of Glaciation,'" *Cineaste* 32.2 (Spring 2007): 6–14.

Halbwachs, Maurice. *The Collective Memory*, New York: Harper & Row, 1980.

Haneke, Michael. "Die Klavierspielerin. Das Drehbuch," in *Haneke/Jelinek: die Klavierspielerin: Drehbuch, Gespräche, Essays*, ed. Stefan Grissemann, 33–31-114. Wien: Sonderzahl, 2001.

—"Beyond Mainstream Film: An Interview with Michael Haneke," in *After Postmodernism: Austrian Literature and Film in Transition*, ed. Willy Riemer, 159–170. Riverside, CA: Ariadne Press, 2000a.

—"*71 Fragments of a Chronology of Chance*: Notes to the Film," in *After Postmodernism: Austrian Literature and Film in Transition*, ed. Willy Riemer, 171–175. Riverside, CA: Ariadne Press, 2000b.

—"Terror and Utopia of Form—Addicted to Truth: A Film Story about Robert Bresson's Au hasard Balthazar," *Robert Bresson [Cinémathèque Ontario monographs, no. 2.]*, ed. James Quandt, 551–559. Toronto: Cinematheque Ontario, 1998.

—"Schrecken und Utopie der Form—Süchtig nach Wahrhaftigkeit: Eine Kinoerzählung über Robert Bressons 'Au Hasard Balthazar'," *Frankfurter Allgemeine Zeitung*, 07.01.1995, Nr. 6: B2.

—"Film als Katharsis," *Austria (in)felix: zum österreichischem Film der 80er Jahre*, ed. Francesco Bono, 89, Graz: Blimp, 1992.

—"Interview. Literatur folgt einer anderen Struktur als Film," in *Fern-Sicht auf Bücher: Materialienband zu Verfilmungen österreichischer Literatur : Filmografie, 1945–1994* [Zirkular, 37], eds Diethardt, Ulrike, Evelyne Polt-Heinzl, and Christine Schmidjell, 11–22. Wien: Dokumentationsstelle für Neuere Österreichische Literatur, 1995.

Hardt, Michael. "The Global Society of Control," *Discourse* 20:3 (1998 Fall): 139–152.

—*Gilles Deleuze An Apprenticeship in Philosophy*, Minneapolis: University of Minnesota Press, 1993.

Hardt, Michael and Antonio Negri, *Empire*, Cambridge, MA: Harvard University Press, 2000.

Hart, Gail K. "Michael Haneke's *Funny Games* and Schiller's Coercive Classicism," *Modern Austrian Literature*, 39:2 (2006): 63–75.

Hillier, Jim. *Cahiers Du Cinéma, the 1950s: Neo-Realism, Hollywood, New Wave*, Cambridge, MA: Harvard University Press, 1985.

Hoberman, J. "Michael Haneke's Funny Games: One-Trick Phony," *Village Voice* (March 11, 2008), http://www.villagevoice.com/2008-03-11/film/one-trick-phony/ (accessed June 16, 2009).

Horwath, Alexander, ed. *Der siebente Kontinent: Michael Haneke und seine Filme*, Vienna and Zürich: Europaverlag, 1991.

—"Die ungeheuerliche Kränkung die das Leben ist," in *Der siebente Kontinent: Michael Haneke und seine Filme*, ed. Alexander Horwath, 11–39. Vienna and Zürich: Europaverlag, 1991.

Hussein, Nasser and Melissa Ptacek. "Thresholds: Sovereignty and the Sacred," *Law & Society Review* 34:2 (2000): 495–515.

Jacobowitz, Florence. "Michael Haneke's Caché (Hidden)," *Cineaction* 68 (January/February/March 2006): 62–64.

Jakovljevic, Branislav. "Theatre of War in the Former Yugoslavia: Event, Script, Actors," *The Drama Review* 43.3 (1999): 5–13.

James, Nick. "Darkness Falls," *Sight and Sound* 13:10 (October 2003): 16–18.

Jeffries, Stuart. "Master manipulator," *The Guardian*, Monday (March 31, 2008), http://film.guardian.co.uk/interview/interviewpages/0,%20,%202269560,%2000.html (accessed June 16, 2009).

Khanna, Ranjana. "From Rue Morgue to Rue des Iris," *Screen* 48 (2007): 237–244.

Kilb, Andreas. "Fragmente der Gewalt: Bildfetisch und Apparatur in Bennys [sic!] Video." in *Michael Haneke und seine Filme: Eine Pathologie der Konsumgesellschaft*, eds Christian Wessely, Gerhard Larcher, and Franz Grabner, 67–77, Marburg: Schüren, 2005.

—"Die Wahrheit ist ein scharfer Gegenstand—Das kämpfende Kino des Michael Haneke: Zum sechzigsten Geburtstag des österreichischen Filmregisseurs," *Frankfurter Allgemeine Zeitung* (March 23, 2002), Nr. 70: 48.

Kirchmann, Kay. "Blicke auf Trümmer. Anmerkungen zur Filmischen Wahrnehmungsorganisation der Ruinenlandschaften nach 1945," in *Die zerstörte Stadt: Mediale Repräsentationen urbaner Räume von Troja bis SimCity*, eds Andreas Böhn and Christine Mielke, 273–287, Bielefeld: Transcript Verlag, 2007.

Knauß, Stefanie. "Vom Fremdsein, der Befremdlichkeit und der Einsamkeit: DAS SCHLOSS von Michael Haneke," in *Michael Haneke und seine Filme*, eds Christian Wessely, Gerhard Larcher, and Franz Grabner, 261–282. Magdeburg: Schüren Verlag, 2005.

Köhler, Margret. "Die Lüge des Genre-Kinos: Ein Gespräch mit Michael Haneke," *kinofenster.de*, November 1997, http://www.kinofenster.de/filme-undthemen/archivmonatsausgaben/kf9711/die_luege_des_genre_kinos/ (accessed June 16, 2009).

Kuttenberg, Eva. "Allegory in Michael Haneke's *The Seventh Continent*," in *New Austrian Film*, eds Robert von Dassanowsky and Oliver C. Speck, 289–314 [forthcoming, the page numbers are only approximate]. New York: Berghahn, 2010.

Lacan, Jacques. *Écrits: A Selection*, trans. Alan Sheridan, London: Tavistock, 1977.

Landy, Marcia. "Just an Image: Godard, Cinema, and Philosophy," *Critical Quarterly* 43.3 (October 2001): 9–31.

Lane, Anthony. "Happy Haneke: Michael Haneke and his movies," *The New Yorker* (October 5, 2009): 60–67.

Lane, Anthony. "The Current Cinema: Recurring Nightmare," *The New Yorker* (March 17, 2008): 92–93.

Laplanche, J. and J. B. Pontalis. *The Language of Psycho-Analysis*, New York: W. W. Norton, 1967.

Larcher, Gerhard. "Theologie und Ästhetik. Fundamentaltheologische Prolegomena und filmische Konkretionen zum Werk Hanekes," in *Michael Haneke und seine Filme: Eine Pathologie der Konsumgesellschaft*, eds Wessely, Christian, Gerhard Larcher, and Franz Grabner, 13–31, Marburg: Schüren, 2005. [also in Larcher, Gerhard, "Theologie und Ästhetik. Fundamentaltheologische Prolegomena und filmische Konkretionen zum Werk Hanekes," in *Utopie und Fragment. Michael Hanekes Filmwerk*, eds Franz Grabner, Gerhard Larcher, and Christian Wessely, 19–36, Thaur: Kulturverlag, 1996.

Le Cain, Maximilian. "Do the Right Thing: The Films of Michael Haneke," *Senses of Cinema* 26 (May–June 2003), http://esvc001106.wic016u.serverweb.com/contents/03/26/haneke.html (accessed December 6, 2007).

Lemercier, Fabien. "Michael Haneke: An ideal raised to the status of an absolute becomes inhuman," *cineuropa* (May 21, 2009), http://cineuropa.org/interview.aspx?lang=en&documentID=108748 (accessed June 27, 2009).

Loshitzky, Yosefa. "Holocaust Others: Spielberg's Schindler's List versus Lanzman's Shoah," *Spielberg's Holocaust: Critical Perspectives on Schindler's List*, ed. Yosefa Loshitzky, 104–118. Bloomington, IN: Indiana University Press, 1997.

Lyotard, Jean-François. *The Differend: Phrases in Dispute*, Minneapolis: University of Minnesota Press, 1988.

MacCabe, Colin and Sally Shafto. *Godard: A Portrait of the Artist at 70*, New York: Farrar, Strauss, and Giroux, 2004.

Masson, Alain. "*Funny Games*: Une allégorie fallacieuse," *Positif: Revue Mensuelle de Cinéma* 443 (janvier 1998): 39–40.

Mecchia, Giuseppina. "The Children Are Still Watching Us, Caché/Hidden in the Folds of Time," *Studies in French Cinema* 7:2 (2007): 131–141.

Meindl, Harald. "Zum Erhabenen in der Kinotrilogie Michael Hanekes," in *Utopie und Fragment. Michael Hanekes Filmwerk*, eds Franz Grabner, Gerhard Larcher, and Christian Wessely, 55–79, Thaur: Kulturverlag, 1996.

Metelmann, Jörg. *Zur Kritik der Kino-Gewalt: die Filme von Michael Haneke*, München: Fink, 2003.

Moeller, Hans Bernhard. "Fassbinders und Zwerenz' im deutschen Aufstieg verlorene 'Ehe der Maria Braun': Interpretation, vergleichende Kritik und neuer filmisch-literarischer Adaptionskontext," in *Film und Literatur: Literarische Texte und der neue deutsche Film*, 105–123, eds Sigrid Bauschinger, Susan Cocalis and Henry A. Lea, Bern: Francke, 1984.

Moj, Pacze. "Michael Haneke U.S.," *Critical Culture*, Vol. IV, No. 145, 2008 http://criticalculture.blogspot.com/search?q=Haneke (accessed June 16, 2009).

Morgan, Daniel. "Rethinking Bazin: Ontology and Realist Aesthetics," *Critical Inquiry* 32 (Spring 2006): 443–480.

MrDisgusting. "Scott Speedman Talks 'Funny Games' vs 'Strangers'," bloody-disgusting.com (Wednesday, May 28, 2008), http://www.bloody-disgusting.com/news/12412 (accessed June 16, 2009).

Nadar, Thomas R. "The Question of Cultural Identity: The Figure of the Outsider in Michael Haneke's Adaptations of Joseph Roth's *Die Rebellion*," in *After Postmodernism: Austrian Literature and Film in Transition*, ed. Willy Riemer, 199–208. Riverside, CA: Ariadne Press, 2000.

Naqvi, Fatima. *The Literary and Cultural Rhetoric of Victimhood. Western Europe, 1970–2005*, New York: Palgrave MacMillan, 2007a.

—"The politics of contempt and the ecology of images: Michael Haneke's Code inconnu," in *The Cosmopolitan Screen: German Cinema and the Global Imaginary, 1945 to the Present*, eds Stephan K. Schindler and Lutz P. Koepnick, 235–252. Ann Arbor: University of Michigan Press, 2007b.

—"Opfer: Zur strukturellen Gewalt in den Filmen Michael Hanekes," in *Ich kannte den Mörder, wußte nur nicht wer er war: Zum Kriminalroman der Gegenwart*, eds Friedbert Aspetsberger and Daniela Strigl, 171–188. Innsbruck, Austria: Studienverlag, 2004.

Neale, Stephen. *Genre*. London: British Film Institute, 1980.

Nietzsche, Friedrich Wilhelm and Daniel Breazeale, eds. *Philosophy and Truth: Selections from Nietzsche's Notebooks of the Early 1870's*, Atlantic Highlands, NJ: Humanities Press, 1990.

Norris, Andrew. *Politics, Metaphysics, and Death: Essays on Giorgio Agamben's Homo Sacer*, Durham: Duke University Press, 2005.

Ossenagg, Karl. "Der wahre Horror liegt im Blick," in *Michael Haneke und seine Filme: Eine Pathologie der Konsumgesellschaft*, eds Christian Wessely, Gerhard Larcher, and Franz Grabner, 115–144, Marburg: Schüren, 2005.

Palm, Michael. "Quartett zu Fünft," in *Der siebente Kontinent: Michael Haneke und seine Filme*, ed. Alexander Horwath, 176–180, Wien, Zürich: Europaverlag, 1991.

Peucker, Brigitte. *The Material Image: Art and the Real in Film*, Stanford, CA: Stanford University Press, 2007.

—"Fragmentation and the Real: Michael Haneke's Family Trilogy," in *After Postmodernism: Austrian Literature and Film in Transition*, ed. Willy Riemer, 176–188, Riverside, CA: Ariadne Press, 2000.

Pfandl, Andrea. "Filmtexturen. Literaturtheoretische Annäherungen an Hanekes Fernsehwerk," in *Utopie und Fragment. Michael Hanekes Filmwerk*, eds Franz Grabner, Gerhard Larcher, and Christian Wessely, 187–205, Thaur: Kulturverlag, 1996.

Philip, Claus. " 'Zusammenhalten, was längst auseinandergegangen ist' oder 'Die Zeit vergeht. Es ist ein Irrsinn'," in *Der siebente Kontinent: Michael Haneke und seine Filme*, ed. Alexander Horwath, 170–175. Wien, Zürich: Europaverlag, 1991.

Pillip, Frank. "Michael Haneke's Film *Funny Games* and the Hollywood Tradition of Self-Referentiality," *Modern Austrian Literature* 32:4 (1999): 353–363.

Price, Brian. "Pain and the Limits of Representation," *Framework: The Journal of Cinema and Media* 47.2 (2006): 22–29.

Prince, Stephen. *Savage Cinema: Sam Peckinpah and the Rise of Ultraviolent Movies*, Austin: University of Texas Press, 1998.

Quin, Élisabeth. "Michael Haneke—'je veux décrire la glaciation'," *Le Figaro Madame, Samedi* (avril 19, 2008), 118–119.

Rayns, Tony. Review of *The Piano Teacher*. *Sight & Sound* (November 2001): 54.

Rebhandl, Bernd. "Kleine Mythologie des Schwarzfilms," in *Michael Haneke und seine Filme: Eine Pathologie der Konsumgesellschaft*, eds Christian Wessely, Gerhard Larcher, and Franz Grabner, 79–86, Marburg: Schüren, 2005.

Reimer, Robert C. "Comparison of Douglas Sirk's *All That Heaven Allows* and R. W. Fassbinder's *Ali: Fear Eats the Soul*: Or, How Hollywood's New England Dropouts Became Germany's Marginalized Other," *Literature Film Quarterly* 24:3 (1996): 281–287.

Riemer, Willy. "Michael Haneke, The piano teacher (Die Klavierspielerin): repertoires of power and desire," in *Elfriede Jelinek: Writing Woman, Nation, and Identity : A Critical Anthology*, eds Matthias Konzett and Margarete Lamb-Faffelberger, 270–284. Madison, NJ: Fairleigh Dickinson University Press, 2007.

—"Michael Haneke, Funny Games: Violence and the Media," in *Vision and Visionaries in Contemporary Austrian Literature and Film*, eds Margarete Lamb-Faffelberger and Pamela S. Saur, 93–102, New York, NY: Peter Lang, 2004.

—"Iterative Texts: Haneke/Rosei, Wer war Edgar Allan?" in *After Postmodernism: Austrian Literature and Film in Transition*, ed. Willy Riemer, 189–198, Riverside, CA: Ariadne Press, 2000.

Rivette, Jacques. "De l'abjection," *Cahiers du cinéma* 120 (juin 1961): 54–55.

Rodrick, Stephen. "Judd Apatow's Family Values." *The New York Times Magazine* (May 27, 2007), http://www.nytimes.com/2007/05/27/magazine/27apatow-t.html?scp=2&sq=judd%20apatow&st=cse (accessed March 8, 2009).

Roth, Joseph. *Rebellion*, trans. Michael Hofmann, New York: St. Martin's Press, 1999.

—*Die Rebellion und Die Legende vom heiligen Trinker*, München: Deutscher Taschenbuch Verlag, 1962.

Ruttner, Lothar. Kritische Analyse der Verfilmung von Ingeborg Bachmanns Erzählung "Drei Wege zum See," *Diplomarbeit zur Erlangung des Magistergrades der Philosophie aus der Studienrichtung Deutsche Philologie, eingereicht an der Geistes- und Kulturwissenschaftlichen Fakultät der Universität Wien*, Wien, 2002, http://edocs.ub.uni-frankfurt.de/volltexte/2009/12057/pdf/Ruttner_DA_DreiWege.pdf (accessed June 16, 2009).

Ryan, Marie-Laure. *Possible Worlds, Artificial Intelligence, and Narrative Theory*. Bloomington, IN: Indiana University Press, 1991.

Saxton, Libby. "Close encounters with distant suffering: Michael Haneke's disarming visions," in *Five Directors: Auteurism from Assayas to Ozon*, ed. Kate Ince, 84–111. Manchester: Manchester University Press, 2008.

—"Secrets and Revelations: Off-screen Space in Michael Haneke's *Caché* (2005)," *Studies in French Cinema* 7:1 (2007): 5–17.

Schacht, Benjamin. "Rituale, Regeln und Paradoxien in Michael Hanekes Gsellschafts-Spielen," in *Michael Haneke und seine Filme: Eine Pathologie der Konsumgesellschaft*, eds Christian Wessely, Gerhard Larcher, and Franz Grabner, 172–192, Marburg: Schüren, 2005.

Schager, Nick. "The Strangers," *Slant Magazine* (May 18, 2008), http://www.slantmagazine.com/film/film_review.asp?ID=3672 (accessed June 16, 2009).

Schlemmer, Gottfried. "Tote zu Lebzeiten," in *Der siebente Kontinent: Michael Haneke und seine Filme*, ed. Alexander Horwath, 126–130, Wien, Zürich: Europaverlag, 1991.

Seeßlen, Georg. "Strukturen der Vereisung," in *Michael Haneke und seine Filme: Eine Pathologie der Konsumgesellschaft*, eds Christian Wessely, Gerhard Larcher, and Franz Grabner, 47–65. Magdeburg: Schüren Verlag, 2005.

Sharrett, Christopher. "The World That Is Known: An Interview with Michael Haneke," *Cineaste: America's Leading Magazine on the Art and Politics of the Cinema* 28:3 (2003 Summer): 28–31.

Shklovskii, Viktor. *Theory of Prose*, Elmwood Park, IL: Dalkey Archive Press, 1990.

Sight & Sound. "Sight & Sound Top Ten Poll 2002. How the directors and critics voted: Michael Haneke, Austria," *BFI*, 2002, http://www.bfi.org.uk/sightandsound/topten/poll/voter.php?forename=Michael&surname=Haneke (accessed June 16, 2009).

Silverman, Kaja. *The Acoustic Mirror: The Female Voice in Psychoanalysis and Cinema and Literature*, Bloomington, IN: Indiana University Press, 1990.

Silverman, Max. "The empire looks back," *Screen* 48 (2007): 245–249.

Smith, David. "Introduction: 'A Life of Pure Immanence': Deleuze's 'Critique et Clinique' Project," in *Gilles Deleuze, Essays Critical and Clinical*, ed. David Smith, xi–liii. Minneapolis: University of Minnesota Press, 1997.

Smith, Douglas. "'A world that accords with our desires'?: Realism, Desire and Death in André Bazin's Film Criticism," *Studies in French Cinema* 4/2 (2004): 93–102.

Solibakke, Karl Ivan. "Musical discourse in Elfriede Jelinek's Die Klavierspielerin (The piano teacher)," in *Elfriede Jelinek: Writing Woman, Nation, and Identity: A Critical Anthology*, eds Matthias Konzett and Margarete Lamb-Faffelberger, 250–269. Madison, NJ: Fairleigh Dickinson University Press, 2007.

Sorfa, David. "Uneasy domesticity in the films of Michael Haneke," *Studies in European Cinema* 3:2 (2006): 93–104.

Speck, Oliver C. "Mastering the Major Discourse," *Ephemera: Critical Dialogues on Organization*, vol. 1 (2) 2001: 182–189, http://www.ephemeraweb.org/journal/1-2/1-2speck.pdf (accessed January 17, 2009).

Szalai, Jennifer. "Habits of seeing: The unsettling films of Michael Haneke," *Harper's Magazine*, vol. 315, issue 1890, November 2007: 68–75.

Valentine, Debra A. "Prepared statement of Debra A. Valentine, General Counsel for the U.S. Federal Trade Commission on 'Pyramid Schemes' presented at the International Monetary Fund's seminar on current legal issues affecting central banks, Washington, DC, May 13, 1998," http://www.ftc.gov/speeches/other/dvimf16.shtm (accessed October 15, 2007).

Van Natta Jr., Dan and Abby Goodnough. "2 Cambridge Worlds Collide in an Unlikely Meeting," *The New York Times* (July 26, 2009) http://www.nytimes.com/2009/07/27/us/27gates.html?hp=&pagewanted=all (accessed July 27, 2009).

Vogel, Amo., "Of Nonexisting Continents. The Cinema of Michael Haneke," *Film Comment* 32.4 (July 1996): 73–75.

Walker, Alexander. "The Piano Teacher," *The Evening Standard* (8 November 2001): 29.

Walsh, David. "Michael Haneke's *Caché*: The Artist Has Not Done the Most Difficult Work." *World Socialist Web Site* (April 21, 2006), http://www.wsws.org/articles/2006/apr2006/cach-a21.shtml (accessed December 2006).

Wessely, Christian, Gerhard Larcher, and Franz Grabner, eds. *Michael Haneke und seine Filme: Eine Pathologie der Konsumgesellschaft*, Marburg: Schüren, 2005.

Wheatley, Christine. "Unseen/Obscene: The (Non) Framing of the Sexual Act in Michael Haneke's La Pianiste, in *New Austrian Film*, eds Robert von Dassanowsky and Oliver C. Speck, 335–356 [forthcoming, the page numbers are only approximate]. New York: Berghahn, 2010.

—*Michael Haneke's Cinema: The Ethic of the Image*, New York: Berghahn Books, 2009.

—"The Masochistic Fantasy Made Flesh: Michael Haneke's *La Pianiste* as Melodrama," *Studies in French Cinema Journal* 6.2 (2006a): 117–127.

—"Secrets, Lies & Videotape," *Sight and Sound* 16:2 (February 2006b): 32–36.

—"The Spectator as Moral Agent: Kantian Ethics and the Films of Michael Haneke," in *From Plato's Cave to the Multiplex: Contemporary Philosophy and Film*, eds by Barbara Gabriella Renzi and Stephen Rainey, 63–73. Newcastle, UK: Cambridge Scholars Press, 2006c.

Wollen, Peter. "Godard and Counter Cinema: Vent d'Est," in *Readings and Writings: Semiotic Counter-Strategies*, ed. Peter Wollen, 79–91. London: NLB, 1982.

Wood, Robin. "In Search of the Code Inconnu," *CineAction* 62 (October 2003): 41–49.

—"'Do I Disgust You?' or, Tirez pas sur La Pianiste," *CineAction* 59 (2002): 54–61.

Wray, John. "Minister of Fear," *The New York Times Magazine* (September 23, 2007), http://www.nytimes.com/2007/09/23/magazine/23haneke-t.html?scp=1&sq=Haneke&st=cse (accessed March 11, 2009).

Wrye, Harriet. "Perversion annihilates creativity and love: A passion for destruction in The Piano Teacher (2001)," *International Journal of Psychoanalysis* 86 (2005): 1205–1212.

Wurmitzer, Gabriele. "'What-goes-without-saying': Michael Haneke's Confrontation with Myths in Funny Games," in *New Austrian Film*, eds Robert von Dassanowsky and Oliver C. Speck, 316–334 [forthcoming, the page numbers are only approximate]. New York: Berghahn, 2010.

Wyatt, Jean. "Jouissance and Desire in Michael Haneke's The Piano Teacher," *American Imago: Psychoanalysis and The Human Sciences* 62:4 (2005 Winter): 453–482.

Yacowar, Maurice. "Caché and the Private/Public Secret," *Queen's Quarterly* 113:2 (2006 Summer): 225–233.

Žižek, Slavoj. "The Act and its Vicissitudes," *The Symptom* 6 (2005), http://www.lacan.com/symptom6_articles/zizek.html (accessed April 15, 2009).

—*Organs Without Bodies: Deleuze and Consequences*, New York: Routledge, 2004.

—*Did Somebody Say Totalitarianism? Five Interventions in the (Mis)Use of a Notion*, London/New York: Verso, 2001a.

—*The Fright of Real Tears Krzysztof Kieślowski between Theory and Post-Theory*, London: BFI Pub, 2001b.

—*The Ticklish Subject: The Absent Centre of Political Ontology*, London: Verso, 1999.

INDEX

71 Fragmente einer Chronologie des Zufalls 3, 6, 55, 65, 76, 83, 88, 96, 144, 148–50, 152, 154, 156, 160, 165–6, 170, 172, 188, 190, 207, 210, 236
71 Fragments of a Chronology of Chance see *71 Fragmente einer Chronologie des Zufalls*
9/11 8–10, 24, 40, 95, 167

Abu Ghraib 32, 166–7
Adenauer, Konrad 104, 118, 126, 235
affect 9, 24–6, 48, 54, 69, 80, 81, 84, 99, 143, 162, 173
Agamben, Giorgio 161, 164–5, 168, 239
Albers, Hans 74, 106, 107, 113–15
Alien (*film title) 30, 212, 236
All That Heaven Allows 108
allegory 34–6, 43, 63, 70, 76–9, 84, 97–8, 157, 175, 195
Allen, Woody 33, 71, 202
Althusser, Louis 11, bib. 241
Amadou 19, 92–3, 171, 216–17
Amistad 182, 185
Angelopoulos, Theo 146
Angst essen Seele auf 108, 211, 236
Ann, Anna, Anne 1, 3, 5, 19, 34, 39, 42, 48, 70–1, 88, 90, 92–5, 97–8, 109, 127, 136–7, 145, 147, 156–7, 182, 187, 201–2, 205–7, 211–13, 215–22, 224
année dernière à Marienbad, L' 50, 51
Annie Hall 71, 202
Antiheimatfilm 75
Antonioni, Michelangelo 61–2, 137, 179, 230, 240
Apatow, Judd 25, 36, 37, 61

aporia 13, 130, 140
Arendt, Hannah 164
Arnold 75
Artaud, Antonin 28, 52–6, 185, 227, 231
Au hasard Balthazar 230, 232, 240
Augé, Marc 239, 241
Auschwitz 12
Auteuil, Daniel 6, 17, 55, 178, 221
auteur 5–6, 12–14, 18, 22–3, 30–1, 36, 45, 52, 59, 69, 109, 123, 128, 146–7, 160–1, 178, 182

Bachmann, Ingeborg 6, 16, 64–6, 125, 197, 233, 240
Badiou, Alain 49, 124–5, 148, 237, 238
Balibar, Etienne 170
Baron Münchhausen 74–5, 106–7, 113, 115, 120–1, 124, 203–4
Bataille, Georges 152
battement d'ailes du papillon, Le 178, 188
Baudrillard, Jean 148, 237
Bay, Michael 196
Bazin, André 28, 45, 52–4, 182–4, 188, 195, 231, bib. 242, 246, 250, 253
Benjamin, Walter 35, 62, 77–8, 86, 143, 164, 194–5, 219–20, 230, 242, 252
Benny 16, 25, 48–9, 82, 83, 97–8, 125, 131, 133–7, 143–5, 149–50, 154, 157–8, 164, 172, 174, 207–8, 233
Benny's Video 6, 9–10, 16–17, 34–5, 48, 65, 82–3, 94, 98, 121–2, 125, 129–31, 133–7, 139, 143, 148–50, 152, 154, 156, 164, 166, 169, 172, 174, 207, 223, 233, 236

Bergman, Ingmar 31, 80
Bertolucci, Bernardo 66
Bildungsbürgertum 15–16
Binoche, Juliette 6, 17, 19, 94, 178, 180, 215, 221, 228
biopolitics/biopower 28, 74, 84, 102, 161, 168, 239
Blanchot, Maurice 38, 230, bib. 246
Bonnes, les/The Maids 233
Booth, Wayne 14
Bordwell, David 3, 49–51, 196
Brecht, Berthold 62, 110, 124, 132, 140, 227
Bresson, Robert 23, 59, 62, 179, 230, 232, 240
Brosciner, Hans 202, 232, 240

Caché 4, 6, 10, 14, 16, 21, 22, 26, 28–30, 34–9, 46, 48, 69, 93–8, 121–2, 126–7, 129, 137–8, 140–1, 144–5, 153–4, 156, 158, 160, 171, 173, 175, 178, 182, 186–7, 189–90, 194, 207, 221, 226, 229, 233, 236, 238, 240
Cage, Nicholas 163
cahiers du cinéma, Les 32
Carpenter, John 108
Cassavetes, John 230, 240
Castle, the see Schloß, Das
Catch Me If You Can 61
Chabrol, Claude 93, 178, 233
children 10, 18, 38, 40, 44, 47–8, 55, 59, 60–1, 65, 68–70, 78, 91, 92, 99–101, 127, 167, 172–4, 185–6 191, 193–4, 200, 214–15, 222–6, 229, 231, 233, 235
Chion, Michel 135, 136
Chronicles of Riddick, The 238
cinema of cruelty 28, 52–3, 55, 57, 147, 182, 185–6, 231
cliché 24, 48, 56–7, 69, 84, 155, 232
close-up 1, 5, 11, 14, 20, 23, 31, 34, 37, 42, 54, 63, 70–1, 73, 76, 79–80, 83, 109, 112, 118–20, 130, 133, 136, 147, 150–1, 166, 169, 172, 185–6, 195, 204, 204–6, 213, 216, 219, 233
Code inconnu: Récit incomplet de divers voyages 1, 3, 6, 7, 16, 19, 34–5, 37, 41–2, 65, 73, 92, 94, 121–2, 126–7, 130, 133, 136–7, 147, 156–8, 171, 174, 178, 182, 187, 188, 211, 215–16, 221, 228, 236
Code unknown see Code inconnu
Crash 81, 156, 170, 188, 200, 201
Craven, Wes 108
Creative Class 15
Creature of the Black Lagoon, The 75
crime de Monsieur Lange, Le 37
Cultural Logic of Late Capitalism, the 117, 165

Daney, Serge 181–9
Dardenne, Jean-Pierre and Luc 21
Dark Knight, the 8
Debord, Guy 130–1, 133, 144–5
Deleuze, Gilles, Deleuzian 13, 14, 23, 26, 38–41, 43–4, 47, 49, 50–2, 54, 56–7, 62, 80, 84, 104, 124–7, 130, 132–3, 140–4, 148–9, 155, 161, 165, 170, 195, 230–2, 235–9
dénouement 123, 163, 179
dernier combat, Le 178
Derrida, Jacques 5, 148, 151, 226, bib. 244
Difference and Repetition 143
differend, le 173
discours 122, 236
discourse 33–5, 38, 45, 93, 120, 139
dispositif 81, 99, 104, 121, 127
Drei Wege zum See 6, 16, 63–5, 69, 187, 197
Durkheim, Emile 169

Eagleton, Terry 163
Ebert, Roger 163, 229
eclisse, L' 62, 230, 240
Ehe der Maria Braun, die 103–6, 109, 111–12, 116–20, 122, 126–7, 232, 235
Eisenstein, Sergei 46, 150
Empire 66, 71, 239
Erika 87–90, 145, 218–19, 232
Essays Critical and Clinical 148
Eva/Evi 25, 27, 44, 69, 71, 76–8, 81, 91, 99, 112, 136–7, 151–2, 174, 199, 200–1, 205–7, 219–20, 224, 225, 229

Index

exchange 5, 24, 100, 118–20, 130–1, 147, 149–53, 158–9, 163, 165–6, 169, 202, 223
Exterminating Angel, the 230, 240

Fanon, Frantz 94
fascism 62, 86, 99, 101, 113, 143, 163, 173, 176, 192–3
Fassbinder, Rainer Werner 7, 15, 74, 103–15, 117–20, 122–3, 125–7, 168, 192, 201, 211, 233–6
Faustrecht der Freiheit 127
fetish 18–19, 111–12, 115, 139, 184
Figgis, Mike 163
Film/Genre 107
final girl 230
flashback 122
For Ever Mozart 154
form/content 4, 8, 9, 14, 22, 62
Foucault 28, 38, 100, 148, 161, 164, 168, 170, 237, 239
frame 2–5, 7–8, 10, 12, 13, 19–21, 23, 25, 28, 30, 33, 36–41, 43, 48, 50, 52, 54, 55, 57–60, 66, 70, 72, 75, 78–9, 82–4, 86–7, 90, 93–4, 96, 99–100, 106, 109–11, 113, 115, 120–2, 125, 129, 133–42, 145, 149, 153–5, 166, 174, 176, 178–9, 182, 185–6, 190–6, 201, 204, 205, 213, 215, 233, 236
frame of reference 2–5, 7, 10, 12, 19, 20, 23, 25, 28, 30, 33, 36–7, 39, 43, 50, 52, 57, 75, 79, 82, 94, 96, 99, 122, 129, 135–7, 140, 174, 182, 193
framing 4, 10, 23, 68, 75, 84, 91, 95, 104, 110, 112, 120–1, 136, 215, 223
Fraulein 6, 7, 60–3, 74–5, 103–7, 109, 111, 113, 116–18, 120–2, 127, 129, 160, 173, 192, 202–3, 232, 234
Funny Games 6, 9–10, 14–15, 17, 21, 23, 31–3, 35, 46, 60, 85–7, 94, 98, 109, 122, 129, 132, 136, 139, 147–8, 157–8, 160, 166–7, 172–4, 179, 211, 212, 227–30, 233, 235–7, 240
Funny Games U.S. 14–15, 33, 85–6, 98, 211–12, 228–30, 233, 236

Genet, Jean 233
Genette, Gérard 33, 34, 122, 236

genre 2–5, 11, 15, 22–3, 30–1, 35, 37, 40, 42, 45, 50, 57, 63, 66, 68, 71, 74–5, 90, 93, 100, 105, 107–11, 114–16, 122–3, 139, 150, 161–3, 178–9, 226, 228, 231
Georg /George/Georges 3, 5, 16, 22, 26, 38, 39, 42, 48, 65–6, 69–71, 77, 81, 92–9, 109, 122, 127, 140, 142, 144–5, 147, 150, 153–4, 156, 158, 171, 173, 175–6, 186–8, 190, 194, 201–2, 205, 204–7, 212, 213, 215–17, 219, 221–3, 233, 236, 240
Germany Year Zero 61, 230, 240
glaciation of feelings 6, 46, 65, 69, 83, 127, 130, 132, 148, 165, 166, 170, 210, 226, 234
God 12, 71, 97, 139, 192, 209, 225, 230
Godard, Jean-Luc 12, 31, 44–5, 47, 61, 66, 149–50, 154, 167, 180–1, 184–6, 238
Goebbels, Joseph 74
Goethe, Johann Wolfgang von 63, 70, 201
Greenaway, Peter 146
Guantanamo Bay 167
Guattari, Felix 39, 56, 165, 230, 239
Gustav 193, 231

Halbwachs, Maurice 116, 235
Halloween 108, 111, 234
Händler der vier Jahreszeiten 127
Harry Potter 30
Heidegger, Martin 5
Heimatfilm 74–5
Herzog, Werner 74, 168
Hidden see *Caché*
Hiroshima, mon amour 50, 180–1, 186
histoire 34–5, 236
historicism 143–4, 153
Hitchcock, Alfred 108–9, 172, 230, 234, 240
Hitler, Adolf 70, 99, 111–12, 168
Hollywood 3, 11, 21, 34–5, 37, 40, 42–5, 47, 50, 52–3, 61, 70, 82, 107, 110, 115, 120, 123, 125, 127, 128, 132, 136, 138–9, 146–7, 153, 160, 167, 169, 173, 179, 182, 185, 195–6, 217, 227

Holocaust 12, 155, 168, 186
homo sacer 164, 166, 176, 239
hors cadre 31, 135, 140, 149
hors champs 135–6
Hostel 13, 86, 228
Huppert, Isabelle 6, 17, 55, 87, 91, 218–19, 228, 233, 238, 242

In einem Jahr mit 13 Monden 127
In Hell 238
intermediality 104, 116, 121, 123, 127–8
intertextuality 41, 47, 66, 70, 74–5, 89, 96, 103–4, 111, 115, 120, 127, 137–8, 168, 179, 203, 233, 234

Jackson, Michael 190
Jameson, Frederic 117, 165, 239
Jean 19, 92–3, 156, 158, 215–16, 235
Jelinek, Elfriede 6, 88–9, 125, 218
jetée, La 178
Johnny Guitar 232

Kafka, Franz 73–4, 162, 209, 213, 215, 238
Kapò 181–2, 185, 188
Kaufman, Charlie 33
Khondji, Darius 212, 236
Kierkegaard, Søren 126
Klara 193, 209, 224
Klavierspielerin, Die see *Pianiste, La*
Klemmer 89, 218–19
Kohut 88–9, 218
Kristeva, Julia 111, 181
Kubrick, Stanley 21, 24, 31, 109, 167
Kurosawa, Akira 227

Lacan, Jacques 87–8, 152, 156, 171, 188, 193, 238
Lancelot du Lac 230, 240
Last House on the Left, the 32
Leaving Las Vegas 163
Lemminge 16, 68–70, 75, 109, 160, 170, 173, 199–200, 234
Lili Marleen 109
Liverpool 6
Lola 104
Lola rennt 23, 188, 234, 236
Lost Highway 23

Lubitsch, Ernst 34
Lumière et compagnie 211
Lynch, David 23
Lyotard, Jean-François 173–4

Majid 10, 22, 38, 48, 95–7, 140–2, 144–5, 153–4, 160, 171, 173, 175–6, 186–8, 194, 221–3
Malevil 178
Maria 19–20, 92, 171, 211, 216–17
Matrix Reloaded 238
Mauss, Marcel 151
Melville, Jean-Pierre 108, 232
metalepsis 33–5, 122, 236
middle class 16–20, 28, 32, 63, 70, 77, 87, 92, 94, 95, 98, 103, 158, 161, 162, 171, 200, 230
Minority Report 31
Mirror 230, 240
mise en abyme 31, 33, 35, 39, 45, 67, 86, 122, 135
money 9, 19, 33, 48, 84, 90, 118, 120, 130–1, 133, 147–51, 166, 169, 172, 199, 206, 207, 211, 227, 230
Moravia, Alberto 66
Morel, Pierre 8
Morricone, Enrico 66

National-Socialist 105, 193
Natural Born Killers 11, 21, 23, 132
Negri, Antonio 170, 239
Nietzsche, Friedrich 14, 41, 43, 47, 49, 51, 147
nihilism 40, 69, 117, 140, 145
Notre musique 154
Novecento 66
nuit américaine, La 34
Nuit noire, 17 octobre 1961 144, 186–7, 189

Observe and Report 229
ontology/ontological metalepsis 29, 30, 34–5, 37–8, 43, 82, 94, 121–3, 137–41, 161, 167, 170, 182, 183, 187, 189

Pascal, Blaise 126
passage à l'acte 161, 171–2, 176
Peckinpah, Sam 14, 23, 109, 191, 227, 240

Index

perspective 4–5, 13, 23, 26, 38, 43, 44, 47–9, 52–7, 60–1, 63, 69, 78, 80, 85, 87–8, 97, 99, 104, 116–17, 120, 122–5, 130, 136, 141, 145, 147, 149, 150, 153, 155–9, 165, 167, 169, 175, 184–6, 188–9, 191–3, 196, 231, 237, 238
Pianiste, La 6, 16, 25, 46, 85, 87–8, 90, 94, 125, 145, 156–7, 173, 175, 178, 207, 218, 219, 226, 228, 233, 236, 238
Piano Player, The see *Pianiste, La*
Pierrot 94, 96–7, 221–3
Poe, Edgar Allan 67
point-of-view 20, 34, 42, 65, 67, 87, 113, 130, 133, 136–9, 142–3, 167, 176, 223, 232
postmodern 2, 12, 17, 19–20, 38–9, 51, 79, 83, 86, 94, 104, 108, 110, 115, 117, 129–31, 145, 146–8, 165, 170–1, 196, 239
potlatch 17, 131, 151–3
Pottery Barn 230
Predator 30
Preminger, Otto 179
Psycho 108, 230, 234, 240
Pum 73, 209–10
Purple Rose of Cairo, The 33
pyramid scheme 48, 82, 143–4, 207–8

Ralph Lauren 230
Ray, Nicholas 232
Reagan, Ronald 75
realism 21, 40, 42, 45, 50–1, 54, 105, 107, 182–6, 195
Rebellion, Die 6, 71, 73, 103, 125, 208
Resnais, Alain 50, 180–1, 186
Rimbaud, Arthur 96, 222
Rivette, Jacques 181–2
Rope 172
Rosei, Peter 66–7, 202, 232
Rossellini, Roberto 61, 179, 230, 232, 240
Roth, Joseph 6, 66, 71, 73, 103
Roth, Tim 212, 228
Rush, Jennifer 25, 78, 229

Salò 230, 240
samourai, Le 108, 228

Saving Private Ryan 228, 237
Saw 228
Schiller, Friedrich 132
Schindler's List 11–12, 35, 61, 167, 182, 185
Schloß, das 6, 73–4, 125, 213–14, 238
Schwarzwaldmädel 74
Scorsese, Martin 171, 179
Scream 107–8, 110–11, 115, 234
Seventh Continent, The see *siebente Kontinent, Der*
shift 2–5, 7, 10, 12, 21, 23, 26, 28, 30, 33–4, 37, 41, 43–4, 52, 54, 57, 62, 75, 78, 82, 86–7, 94, 96, 104, 106, 110, 115, 120, 129, 132, 138, 139, 147, 149, 155, 156–7, 161, 185, 187, 226, 227, 238–9
Shining, The 31, 61, 109
Shklovskii, Victor 30
siebente Kontinent, der 6, 16, 18, 24, 44, 54–5, 61, 76–9, 94, 99, 121–2, 131, 136, 144, 148–52, 160, 164–6, 169–70, 172, 174, 188, 204, 239
Sight & Sound 40, 61, 179, 230, 240
Sigrid 68–70, 200, 201–2
Sigurd 68–70, 200
simulacrum 129
Sirk, Douglas 108, 234
society of control 161, 170, 172
Spielberg, Steven 8, 11, 31, 40, 61, 167, 182, 185–6, 195–6, 237
Star Wars 30
Stella 70, 201
Stone, Oliver 11, 21, 23
Strangers, the 15, 31–2, 228, 240
Straw Dogs 109
Stroheim, Erich von 52–4
Stunde Null 104
suicide 10, 22, 55, 58, 65, 69–70, 71, 96–7, 108, 144–5, 148–9, 151–2, 154, 160–4, 165, 169, 171–3, 175–6, 181, 198, 200–2, 206–7, 222, 234, 239
suture 4, 138–40

Taken 8
Tarantino, Quentin 23, 237
Tarkovsky, Andrei 179, 230, 240
Tasma, Alain 144, 186, 237

Taxi Driver 171
television/TV 4–7, 11, 15–16, 18, 20, 25, 31, 39, 56, 60, 63, 66, 68–9, 71, 73–8, 83, 87, 91, 94–5, 103, 106, 109–11, 120–3, 125–6, 129–31, 133–4, 143, 145–6, 147, 154, 156, 159, 160, 162, 170–1, 175, 183, 186–7, 189, 190, 197, 201, 203, 205, 206–7, 208, 209, 210–11, 213, 216, 221, 223, 227, 229, 231, 233, 234, 237–8, 240
temps du loup, Le 6, 10, 25, 40, 83, 90–1, 93, 147, 154, 156, 157, 160, 166, 172, 174, 178, 211, 219, 221, 236
theater of cruelty 52–4, 87, 227, 231
Three Paths to the Lake
  see *Drei Pfade zum See*
time image 13–14, 49, 57, 125, 235
Time of the Wolf, The see *temps du loup, Le*
To Be or Not to Be 34
torture porn 228
Toxic Avenger, The 233
trauma 5, 94, 144, 146–9, 153–9, 173, 175, 181, 188, 219, 238, 240
Trotta 65–6, 198
Truffaut, François 34, 52, 182
Trümmerfilm 105–6, 114, 116
Tykwer, Tom 23, 188, 236

Ufa 74, 109
... *und über uns der Himmel* 106, 113–15, 235

Van Helsing 238
Variation oder "Daß es Utopien gibt weiß ich selber!" 70–1, 126, 199, 201
Verdrängung 112
Vergletscherung der Gefühle *see* glaciation of feelings
Veronika Voss 109, 234
Verschiebung 112
video 8, 16, 23, 30, 32, 34, 48, 82–3, 88, 94–7, 121, 123, 125, 129, 131, 133–41, 143, 148, 149–50, 156–7, 163, 170, 175, 176, 186–7, 207–8, 213, 218, 236
Vienna 16, 18, 25, 68, 88, 147, 198–200, 204, 218, 219, 228, 229, 232, 221
viewer 1–4, 7, 9–12, 16–19, 21, 24, 28, 29, 30, 32–9, 41–4, 48–50, 52, 55–7, 59–60, 62–3, 69–70, 73–5, 78–9, 81–3, 86–7, 91, 93, 96–7, 101, 103, 108, 119, 123, 125, 135, 137–8, 140, 148–50, 152, 154–9, 161, 167, 172, 177, 179–80, 182–3, 185–6, 190, 192–3, 196, 200, 206, 215–16, 226, 227, 229, 235, 237
violence 3, 5, 8, 9, 10–14, 21, 23–4, 26, 28, 35–6, 40, 48, 54, 57, 58–9, 63, 65, 68, 85–7, 90, 93–6, 100–1, 109–10, 132, 145, 146–7, 158, 160–3, 166, 168, 173–5, 177, 179, 181–2, 186–7, 191, 193, 213, 225, 226, 227, 228, 233, 237, 238
virtual/virtuality (Deleuze) 13–14, 28, 60, 65, 83, 97, 104, 123–7, 129–32, 141–5, 177, 235, 236

Walsh, Raoul 237
War of the Worlds 8–9, 40
Watts, Naomi 212, 228
weiße Band, Das 20, 99–102, 103, 148, 160, 191–5, 207, 223–5, 230, 231
Welles, Orson 68, 180, 184
Wenders, Wim 74, 85, 127, 168, 232
Wer war Edgar Allan? 31, 63, 66, 67, 69, 125, 202
White Ribbon, the *see* weiße Band, das
Who was Edgar Allan? see *Wer war Edgar Allan?*
Wirtschaftswunder 103
Woman under the Influence, a 230, 240
Wortmann, Söhnke 117
Wunder von Bern, Das 117

Žižek, Slavoj 18, 20, 23, 49, 139, 168, 171
Zorn, John 212–13